MW00905885

Winnipeg Beach

WINNIPEG
Beach

Leisure and Courtship in a Resort Town, 1900–1967

DALE BARBOUR

University of Manitoba Press

© Dale Barbour 2011

University of Manitoba Press
Winnipeg, Manitoba
Canada R3T 2M5
uofmpress.ca

Printed in Canada on chlorine-free, 100% post-consumer recycled paper.

All rights reserved. No part of this publication may be reproduced or transmitted in any form or by any means, or stored in a database and retrieval system, without the prior written permission of the University of Manitoba Press, or, in the case of photocopying or any other reprographic copying, a licence from Access Copyright (Canadian Copyright Licensing Agency) 6 Adelaide Street East, Suite 901, Toronto, Ontario M5C 1H6, www.accesscopyright.ca.

Cover and interior design: Karen Armstrong Graphic Design

Cover image: Archives of Manitoba, Peter McAdam Collection 69.
Digital Colourization by Sandy Pawlitsky, Pixel Genie.

Map: Weldon Hiebert

Library and Archives Canada Cataloguing in Publication

Barbour, Dale, 1970–
         Winnipeg Beach : leisure and courtship in a resort town, 1900–1967 / Dale Barbour.

Includes bibliographical references and index.
ISBN 978-0-88755-722-4 (pbk.)–ISBN 978-0-88755-403-2 (e-book)

         1. Winnipeg Beach (Man.)–History–20th century. 2. Resorts– Manitoba–Winnipeg Beach–History–20th century. 3. Courtship–Manitoba– Winnipeg Beach–History–20th century. 4. Leisure–Manitoba–Winnipeg Beach– History–20th century. 5. Tourism–Social aspects–Manitoba–Winnipeg Beach. I. Title.

FC3399.W56B37 2011   971.27'4   C2010-906078-4

The University of Manitoba Press gratefully acknowledges the financial support for its publication program provided by the Government of Canada through the Canada Book Fund, the Canada Council for the Arts, the Manitoba Department of Culture, Heritage and Tourism, the Manitoba Arts Council, and the Manitoba Book Publishing Tax Credit.

FSC
Mixed Sources
Cert no. SW-COC-001271
© 1996 FSC

Contents

For My Parents

Acknowledgements

I could not have done this without help.

My greatest debt is to the department of history at the University of Manitoba where the project began as a master's thesis. Gerry Friesen was invaluable as an advisor; providing a mixture of suggestions, advice, corrections, patience, and a dollop of "get on with it" when required. He exemplifies everything a student could imagine or ask of a scholar. I cannot imagine having done this work under anyone else. Adele Perry and David Churchill were both my teachers and members of my thesis committee and contributed to this book in both capacities. I would also like to thank University of Winnipeg professor John Lehr, the third member of my thesis committee, for his suggestions and his own contribution to the historiography of Winnipeg Beach. In various ways the instruction I received from Mark Gabbert, Greg Smith, Timothy Anna, and others at the University of Manitoba all made a contribution to this work. The University of Manitoba was also my place of employment while I was working on my master's degree and I'd like to thank the department of public affairs for allowing me to live the double life of student and employee. Particular thanks go to Pat Goss in the department for being a great co-worker and sounding board for various Winnipeg Beach stories over the years. I also feel I would be remiss if I did not give a nod to the Creative Communications program at Red River College. Thank you, Irene Mann, for teaching me that words can sing.

The finishing touches on this book have been completed while I have been studying at the University of Toronto. I appreciate the tangible support of the university and the scholarly atmosphere of the department of history. Special thanks go to Steve Penfold for his help and advice on the final draft of this book and to Alison Norman and Julia Rady-Shaw for their input.

I will have more to say about the people who were interviewed in this book within the Note on Sources. However, I would like to acknowledge here that this book is as much their work as it is mine. If people had not been willing to share their memories, this book would not exist. The staff at the University of Manitoba Archives, the Archives of Manitoba, and the Canadian Pacific Archives helped me find many of the sources within this book. Once again, this book would not exist without their help.

While not quoted within the text, Fred Kelly shared his memories of Winnipeg Beach's Main Street and boardwalk, helping to clarify the location of rides and businesses. I would also like to thank Rob McInnes for sharing postcards of Winnipeg Beach and filling me in on the ins and outs of the turn-of-the-century postcard industry.

The team at the University of Manitoba Press has been exceedingly generous in taking this project on. I would like to thank David Carr and Cheryl Miki, for their help and support. Two anonymous readers lent their time and effort to reviewing this work and I appreciate their contribution to the final product. Laura Cardiff provided valuable copy-editing skills to shave the rough edges from my writing. What errors remain are my own. Finally, Glenn Bergen has been the front-man on this project and I would like to thank him for guiding it from thesis to publication.

Of course, none of this would exist if my parents John and Flo Barbour hadn't taken our family on trips to Winnipeg Beach, and other parks across Manitoba, when we were growing up, ensuring that Winnipeg Beach was part of my own history. Everything I do rests on the foundation of support they gave me growing up and continue to give me.

A Note on Sources

For my research on the history of Winnipeg Beach I have depended on a great many sources, from fictional retellings of life at the beach, to news reports and photographs, and, most importantly, to interviews with people for whom this particular beach community was a place important to their lives.

Gabrielle Roy, Bess Kaplan, and Harold Dundas provide literary accounts of Winnipeg Beach. All three give vivid descriptions of the Winnipeg Beach experience. But these descriptions are, as with the oral accounts, reconstructions of the Winnipeg Beach experience. These writers published their stories years after the periods they are describing. Given that, the literary sources are more interesting for how they use Winnipeg Beach than they are for their historical accuracy. Roy uses it to consider the encounter between culture and nature, and to allow her protagonist to approach the lake and encounter something bigger than herself. Kaplan's character considers questions of sexual maturity, or notions of men and women being together at the beach, while Dundas uses the trip to Winnipeg Beach as a literal and metaphorical transition of youth into sexual maturity.

Winnipeg's newspapers, including the *Winnipeg Free Press* (called the *Manitoba Free Press* until 1931), the *Tribune,* and the *Telegram*, had plenty to say about Winnipeg Beach throughout the twentieth century. Advertisements tell us how Winnipeg Beach was being constructed and marketed, and their placement—they moved from the travel section to the entertainment section—tells us something of how the area was imagined. Classifieds give a glimpse of how the beach functioned on the ground and reveal a stark gender divide in who could work at the beach. Until the 1960s job openings were advertised according to gender, not by task, and most of the Winnipeg Beach jobs were listed as "female job openings." "Sunshine letters"—letters from kids looking for pen pals—tell us how children experienced the beach; these letters also tell us that children in the 1920s often nipped into the dance hall in the evening with their families, something people in the 1940s and 1950s would not have considered doing. The Winnipeg Beach column from the first decades of the twentieth century provided a middle-class social calendar of the beach, suggesting how it was supposed to operate.

But for as much as newspapers give us a window into the past, they are not unmediated or unbiased sources. In fact, the *Free Press* cleaves closely to the dominant discourses of the day throughout the Winnipeg Beach story. As Manitoba writer Jim Blanchard notes in his book *Winnipeg 1912*, the prevailing message in the first years of the twentieth century was that Winnipeg was a growing city of the British Empire; its proponents suggested that the city had every reason to believe it would become one of the great cities of the empire. Winnipeg Beach was part of this project, and newspapers such as the *Free Press* and *Telegram* routinely helped the Canadian Pacific Railway (CPR) promote it as a world-class resort for a world-class city. In contrast, the *Free Press* was quick to critique the resort in the 1950s, and it did its part to stir the moral panic of the period by focusing on sex and fighting at the beach. In the 1960s it actively participated in the recasting of Winnipeg Beach as a "family resort" by running news stories detailing the transition and columns promoting it. In that sense, the *Free Press* was not spectator but rather active partner in the making and remaking of Winnipeg Beach.

There are a number of pictures in this book that help tell the Winnipeg Beach story. Handle them with care. They include pictures that were taken by private citizens and postcards, which may have been shot by local citizens out to make a quick buck or professional photographers shooting for a studio. But in either case they were intended to promote the experience of being at the beach. They show a pristine beach, children playing in the water, catching a train or a crowded boardwalk; creating a set of iconic images of what the beach was supposed to be. For people in the first part of the twentieth century, the images and postcards provided a recipe to follow as they tried to create their own beach experiences. We can look to them to see how the beach was presented, read through them to see what else they have to tell us, and question what is not in the imagery.

Finally, the greatest sources in this book are from people who lived, worked or played at Winnipeg Beach. This book would not exist had people not been willing to sit down and talk about what Winnipeg Beach meant to them. I interviewed eighteen people throughout the winter of 2007–2008. I have tapped a selection of interviews from "The History of Winnipeg Beach" oral history project, which was sponsored by The Boundary Creek District Development, Inc., in 1991. I owe the interviewers, D. Harrison and D. Carpenter, my thanks for their work. Listening to their interviews there were several moments when I hoped they would ask a follow-up question to clarify a comment a subject had just made, and they never disappointed me. I have also used interviews from the Gay and Lesbian Historical Project, which were conducted in Winnipeg and Selkirk in 1991 by David Theodore. University of Saskatchewan historian Valerie Korinek has made extensive use of these interviews to map the desire of gay and lesbian people through-out twentieth-century Winnipeg; I am grateful that she shared with me her unpublished paper, "'Winnipeg—One Gay City!': Reconstructing a Gay and Lesbian Geography of Winnipeg."

Oral interviews come with a number of caveats. We are relying on peo-ple's memories, and memories are often a highlight reel or a blooper reel of life's events. My interview subjects remember Winnipeg Beach most vividly as full of life, the boardwalk crowded and the sun shining. Even during its heyday the boardwalk had down times and rain did fall on occasion. Some of the interview subjects do recall these moments, while all of them know intellectually that they existed. But such moments carry no resonance. The interview subjects are also doing more than simply recalling facts and figures: they are looking back—over seventy years, in some cases—to recall their youth. I would go even further to say they are recalling "youth." As one interview subject, "Jessica," noted (and not bitterly): "Why did I stop going to the beach? Well, I got older and I got married and that was it." Winnipeg Beach was not just a moment in time; for many people, it was a moment in their lives. Little wonder that it evokes such nostalgia.

Winnipeg Beach

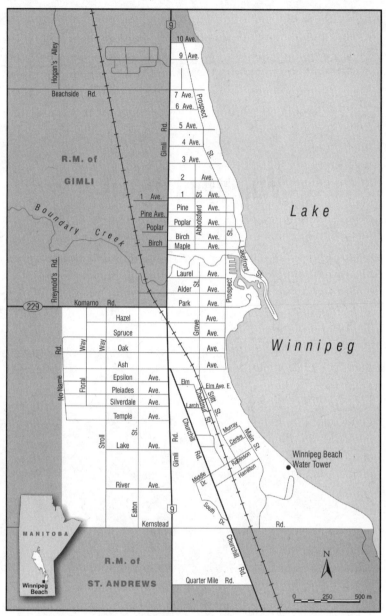

Town of Winnipeg Beach

Introduction

There was a time when going to Winnipeg Beach was the thing to do. The "Moonlight special" train would whisk people to the dance hall and boardwalk at the lake-side resort for an evening of entertainment and then bring them safely home again. During its peak in the 1920s, the resort hosted 40,000 people on busy weekends. The health benefits and breezes of the lake shore were the ultimate escape for Winnipeg's ethnically diverse population. Cabins were filled with vacationers, the beach swarmed with people, and crowds filled the amusement area; Winnipeggers were pushed along in a loop that took them past the rides and games of chance on the boardwalk and the restaurants and arcades of Winnipeg Beach's Main Street. While the beach had an appeal for all ages, it was young men and women looking to share a good time that gave the resort its energy and sometimes naughty reputation. At a time when the rules for how men and women were supposed to behave were clearly drawn, Winnipeg Beach was a place where rules and boundaries could be challenged. This book tries to capture that experience. It tracks the lifespan of Winnipeg Beach as a tourist destination, from its creation by the Canadian Pacific Railway (CPR) in 1901 to the demolition of its dance hall, roller coaster, and boardwalk in 1967.

Winnipeg Beach was a familiar name to Manitobans in the first half of the twentieth century. Just an hour north of Winnipeg—about seventy minutes by train—it was the largest and most dynamic of a string of resort locations that sprang up along the south end of the lake. Grand Beach, founded by the Canadian National Railway (CNR) a few years later on the east side of Lake Winnipeg, was its primary competition. Slightly further north, on the east side of the lake, Victoria Beach would vie for the loyalty of Winnipeg's upper class. This local story looks at what Winnipeggers and other Manitobans did for fun in the first half of the twentieth century. It also considers how they navigated the divisions in their own community. One of the distinctive attributes of Winnipeg Beach was that it provided a place for Winnipeg's Jewish community to play at a time when other resorts were busy keeping them out.

But Winnipeg Beach was more than just a regional pleasure spot. It drew on a carnival tradition that dated back thousands of years and joined an international trend in recreation that brought the carnival into the industrial age. The carnival has its roots in religious festivals where the participants imagine that the world, if only briefly, is turned upside down. It represents a time and a place where the rules of everyday life might be overturned.[1] During the carnival, pre-industrial Europeans "binged in seasonal rites with unrestrained indulgence in food, drink, sex and aggression."[2] For the industrial crowds at the beginning of the twentieth century, the commercial amusement areas came to play a similar role and met a need for those longing for a release from the "rules" of urban/industrial life.[3] Such boisterous affairs were tolerated because they "released tensions and restored and affirmed community in societies that very much needed such reinforcements."[4] Studying Winnipeg Beach helps us see both the limits and the potential of these commercialized carnivals.

Seaside resorts had already been drawing crowds intent on appreciating the natural beauty of the water or seeking a little fun outside the city. But the fairs and exhibitions of the nineteenth century showed how they could be something more.[5] Chicago's 1893 Columbian Exhibition exemplified the new trend. It featured two distinct entertainment areas; the official and carefully crafted "White City," where the architectural and intellectual dreams of the United States were portrayed, and a midway, where commercial entrepreneurs were given free rein to create an entertainment area that became a temporary amusement park.[6] Entrepreneurs at places such as Coney Island and England's Blackpool quickly picked up on the success of the commercial midway and created permanent amusement areas along the shoreline. The mix of natural setting and commercial amusements proved popular, and by 1900 attendance at Coney Island could hit 500,000 on a Saturday. The success provided a framework that entrepreneurs across the continent would follow.[7]

A day at Winnipeg Beach in 1910. The posture of this well-dressed crowd suggests they were taking in an event on Lake Winnipeg.

In Toronto a string of seaside parks and amusement areas—Kew Garden, Victoria Park, and Scarboro Park—rose and fell on the city's eastern Lake Ontario shoreline between 1878 and 1925.[8] On Toronto Island, Hanlan's Point held sway from the end of the nineteenth century into the 1930s. A short distance to the west, Sunnyside Amusement Park had its high tide in the 1920s and 1930s and lasted into the 1950s. Torontonians looking to get further out of the city could also head to Wasaga Beach on Georgian Bay, where cabins and an amusement area rubbed shoulders. In the West, Saskatchewan had its Manitou Beach and Regina Beach, and while Stanley Park never became an amusement park area, even its role within Vancouver was hotly debated, with working-class citizens envisioning a play space while the upper class preferred a preserved setting for the contemplation of nature.[9]

That debate between the contemplation of nature and play was at the heart of the new amusement areas. Coney Island, North America's largest amusement area, has been described as the pivot point between the Victorian period of the nineteenth century and the modern period of the twentieth.[10] During the nineteenth century, a genteel middle class focused on creating settings where nature might be observed and admired and "the Victorian virtues of 'character'—moral integrity, self-control, sober earnestness, industriousness" promoted amongst the population.[11] New York's Central Park is the most famous of these Victorian era–inspired parks, but Toronto's High Park or Winnipeg's Assiniboine Park are cut from the same cloth. The amusement parks at Coney Island represented something new; while the pristine seashore had drawn people in the nineteenth century, now it was the boisterous energy created by the amusement area and the crowd itself that became the attraction.[12] Here we can see the beginning of a true mass culture in North America, one that drew together a heterogeneous population. Rather than the civic elite, it was the commercial values of entrepreneurs determined to attract a mass audience that set the agenda for Coney Island.[13] Fun was commodified, tweaked, and sold to the masses in a tug-of-war between giving the people what they wanted and telling them what they were supposed to want.

This process was at work in Winnipeg Beach. The initial years of the resort were in keeping with the vision of Winnipeg's own, primarily British, middle class. That vision of order and control shows itself in countless Winnipeg Beach postcards and pictures of crowds of well-dressed Winnipeggers standing on the beach and staring out towards the lake. Reports in the first years of the twentieth century focused on Winnipeg's middle class enjoying themselves at the lake. But from a pristine shoreline the seeds of something more quickly began to appear with the addition of water chutes and other activities. Winnipeg Beach developed an extensive entertainment area along its boardwalk, one that increasingly drew Manitoba's working-class citizens.[14] It must have seemed like everyone was invited. Matching the experience at other amusement areas, the boardwalk was a place where it appeared Winnipeg's heterogeneous mix of citizens came together as one people.[15] It would be romantic to think of the beach as a cultural melting pot where new immigrants to Canada joined established residents and merged into a new Canadian identity. There is some truth to that, but the process was far more complicated.

Winnipeg Beach offered ethnic groups a chance to maintain the boundaries around their communities and to transcend them. From the beginning the beach was an ideal site to hold a picnic. So while some citizens were gathering on the beach to contemplate a pristine lake, others were gathering together in a festive atmosphere within the park setting. Distinct ethnic, church, and workplace groups could reserve their own train and head to the beach for the day. The picnics offered workplace groups a chance to bolster working-class identity and ethnic groups the opportunity to strengthen the web of relationships that held their own communities together.[16] As Winnipeg Beach's entertainment facilities grew, tourist cabins sprang up to allow ethnic communities to bunk with one another. Some only served British patrons, but Jewish patrons could gather at others, such as the Torchinskys' White Rabbit Lodge, where kosher rules for eating were followed. Given that other resorts denied them entry, Jewish people staying in Winnipeg Beach often found their neighbours were Jewish as well. The Torchinskys' daughter, Doris Margolis, said it felt like "we were like in our own environment. We only had Jewish people in the cottage, only had contact with Jewish people in the neighbourhood."[17]

Members of Winnipeg's cultural mosaic did mingle at the resort, creating, as local resident Mildred Kelly recalled, a "colourful" mix of languages and customs.[18] The boardwalk and amusements areas functioned as a boundary zone where new immigrants could rub shoulders with one another and with Winnipeg's established British elite.[19] The liberal use of British flags, which were scattered throughout the resort in the early years of the twentieth century, was a constant reminder of who were considered the established Canadians. But people lodging in the cabins and tourist cabins of the resort would have met neighbours of different ethnicities or turned to local Ukrainian and Icelandic residents for their food and supplies during the summer.

American writers have looked at amusement areas such as Atlantic City or Coney Island and seen the relationship between whites and African Americans as being the critical dynamic in understanding how the parks operated. Amusement areas helped the ethnic communities that flooded into the United States at the turn of the twentieth century come to think of themselves as "Americans." African Americans, whether through their exclusion from segregated amusement areas or through their inclusion as part of the entertainment, "provided a heterogeneous white audience with a unifying point of reference and visible and constant reminders of its privileged status."[20] At Atlantic City the racial dynamic stood out clearly on the boardwalk, where African American workers shuttled white Americans up and down the length of the beach in rolling carts. It was always clear to the patrons of that resort who was pushing the cart and who was riding in it.[21]

A holiday crowd on the boardwalk at Winnipeg Beach.

Going to the beach offered white Americans the opportunity to confirm their own sense of privilege even as they were rolled down the boardwalk. Critical to this argument is the view that exclusion was essential to creating a community in the United States.[22]

There are elements of this racial dynamic in Toronto, which had a more homogeneous British population at the turn of the century.[23] One of the nineteenth-century games on Toronto Island involved releasing a black person and seeing which of his white pursuers could catch him first.[24] The game was, hopefully, exceptional, but a common form of entertainment on the island involved white people painting themselves up as black minstrels for the entertainment of a white audience. This dynamic certainly would have helped the white patrons of the park imagine themselves, regardless of their own ethnicity, to be part of a broader white community in contrast to a black community. Similarly, when Torontonians were quizzed about their recollections of the ethnic makeup of the crowd at Maple Leaf Gardens, they remember it as "very Scotch, Irish, English," and a place where "you didn't see any black people." The assumption is that questions about ethnicity were really questions about race, and most specifically about black people, and that everyone else was white.[25]

The same dynamic was not at work in Winnipeg Beach, where black-face, if it happened, was not the entertainment of choice.[26] The labour at the resort was provided by a dynamic mix of ethnic groups that matched the cosmopolitan diversity of ethnic groups in Winnipeg—the most ethnically diverse city in Canada at the beginning of the twentieth century.[27] And when people were quizzed about the ethnic dynamics of the resort, they immediately turned to the relations among a wide range of ethnic groups.[28] People did not go to Winnipeg Beach to construct themselves as white Canadians against black Canadians.

But that does not mean that the process of constructing oneself as white through the exclusion of racial others did not take place at Winnipeg Beach. It did. But it was Winnipeg Beach's place within a colonial society that likely played the dominant role in this process of identity formation. The literature surrounding Winnipeg Beach is filled with statements linking Aboriginal people with nature. Thus whether they were British, Jewish, Polish, or Ukrainian, the European subjects who may have imagined themselves becoming "as dark skinned as a native" when they went to the beach were also constructing themselves as Canadian subjects and Aboriginal people as colonial subjects.[29] If we are to consider Winnipeg Beach a boundary zone, we should also consider how Aboriginal people were typically considered outside the collective experience, unless they were prepared to give up their Aboriginal identity to gain entry.[30]

A look at who went to Winnipeg Beach reveals something else about the amusement park patrons in the first half of the twentieth century: the majority of them were adults. Certainly children are there, but the majority of the people crowding the beach, the boardwalk, and the dance hall are young adults. Winnipeg Beach's amusement area was, first and foremost, a place for men and women to meet, mix, and mingle. And it is in this role that Winnipeg Beach illustrates how gender relations were changing at the turn of the century. Everything from how men and women could share space to how they courted was in a state of flux. Even more than places where people of different ethnicities and classes could mingle, amusement parks were places where men and women met. Indeed, Coney Island earned the title "Sodom by the Sea" based on the assumption that men and women were doing more than simply meeting at the resort.[31] Blackpool, Toronto's waterfront, and Winnipeg Beach all carried a similar reputation. In coming together at recreation areas such as Winnipeg Beach, men and women were sharing space in a way they had not before.

Commercial leisure spaces added a new wrinkle to male/female relations at the beginning of the twentieth century. In the latter half of the nineteenth century, leisure spaces had most often been divided by gender. Men might drink with other men in public saloons, and they developed a shared public culture through their presence in the workplace.[32] Generally lacking access to a commercial venue for their socializing, women got together with other women closer to home. Historians such as Kathy Peiss have referred to this divided culture of recreation activities as a *homosocial culture*, a phrase that refers to the social mixing of people of one gender and not, it should be noted, to sexual orientation.[33] At Winnipeg Beach, men gathering with fellow men to drink at the hotels was one example of homosocial leisure. The Empress Hotel, Winnipeg Beach's signature place to stay in the early decades of the twentieth century, was famed for its lavish bar, but few if any women would have gathered around it. Those women who did would have faced suspicions that they were prostitutes.[34]

How men and women courted reflected this gendered division. Calling was the preferred approach to courting. This approach was so named because a man would call upon the family's household, where he would be invited in to settle in the parlour, ideally, to talk with his love interest or perhaps watch her play the piano.[35] It was expected that other family members would be close at hand to ensure propriety. Of course not everything happened in the parlour. Calling was also part of the social networking that went on within protected groups, most often bounded by ethnicity, religion, or employment. This sort of courtship can be seen in the early years of Winnipeg Beach, in particular up until World War I, within the cabins of its tourism infrastructure and through the large picnics that used to take place at the resort. Courtship would have taken place in Winnipeg's ethnic communities, within the web of relationships.

But, in what some writers have termed a "sexual revolution" (an ironic term given how tightly regulated female sexual behaviour was in this period), courtship went public in the first decades of the twentieth century, with men and women seeking to go on dates in commercial entertainment areas.[36] Another way to describe this change would be to say that courtship moved from the private sphere to the public sphere. In terms of ethnicity, courtship moved from within the web of relationships to the boundary zone, opening up opportunities for people of different ethnicities to meet. This dating approach began at the turn of the century, but it was not until the 1920s that the notion of dating in public had firmly replaced the idea of accepting a caller at home. The shift had economic roots in the growth of

Winnipeg Beach's Leisure zone as it appeared at mid-century: The boardwalk was book-ended by the Dance Palace on the north and the roller coaster on the south.

industrial capitalism at the end of the nineteenth century. Women joined the industrial workforce in increasing numbers, becoming economic actors. And although they faced far more regulation than their male counterparts, they did increasingly have the ability to spend their own money or at times to convince a male partner to take them out.[37] That ability helped them shape the emerging leisure industry as entrepreneurs responded to their desire for public entertainment areas. Within these commercial leisure centres, men and women could play together. Winnipeg Beach changed to fit within this circle of post-1900 leisure centres by creating an elaborate amusement area to meet the needs of its patrons.

The flip side, of course, is that commercial leisure also shaped the behaviour of men and women. In becoming linked to commercial leisure, courting—and love for that matter—became commoditized; it was now an experience that could be bought and sold.[38] At Winnipeg Beach, the CPR actively participated in this commoditization by marketing the resort as a location for dating and by developing the public leisure zone. The construction of the leisure zone during World War I marks a shift from calling to dating at Winnipeg Beach. The resort's patrons were also part of the production of this space. These visitors reconceptualized the CPR's evening excursion trains as "Moonlight specials" and imparted a romance to the trips before the CPR had begun to advertise them as a romantic product.[39] Of course the CPR already had some experience with providing a romantic setting: the train was the preferred transportation approach for wealthy newlyweds at the turn of the century.[40]

The notion of women entering the public sphere to work and date arguably represented both a collision with and a transgression of the public sphere's perceived male space.[41] City streets, for example, had been considered terrain fit only for men; convention dictated how and where women could enter unescorted. Certainly at night a woman alone was considered suspect. But women's growing presence in the workforce and in commercial establishments changed that. Women were heading out in public now, in groups, in couples, and alone. The rise of women as social actors and their movement into this heterosocial space—space where men and women were out together—weakened patriarchal control over their leisure time and, it was feared, their sexuality. A discourse was constructed "that linked women's pleasure to immorality and their independence to danger."[42] This discourse operated across multiple levels, showing itself in the archives through the pronouncements of moral reformers, the police, the courts, and newspapers that exaggerated the threats to women in the social disorder of the city.[43] It mediated women's access to recreation, thus ensuring that recreation was best accessed in public, socially acceptable locations. It ensured that while men and women could head out into public to date, they were regulated by a set of rules that governed how they would behave together. The concerns about what men and women were doing when they got together were responsible for tags such as Coney Island's "Sodom by the Sea." But those same concerns also gave men and women freedom at Winnipeg Beach because they could do their courting in public, finding "islands of privacy" in the midst of the crowd around them.[44] Indeed, the environment of these spaces was developed to bolster their role as meeting places for men and women. The beach, in turn, helped shape the behaviour of men and women.[45] At Winnipeg Beach men and women pushed at the boundaries of how they were expected to behave. It was a place where they could. Of course by coding the beach as a place to take a date, the young suitors were also coding it as heterosocial space, a process that ensured men and women were expected to behave as proper heterosexual men and women.[46]

Concentrating on how Winnipeg Beach was used as a centre for court-ing helps us put a framework around its seeming rise and fall. The transition from calling to dating helped launch the resort's golden years at the begin-ning of the twentieth century; the subsequent transition from dating to the more sexually active form of courtship that is linked with the sexual and cultural changes of the 1950s and 1960s marked the end of Winnipeg Beach, at least as a large-scale amusement area. [47] Dating as people understood it in the first half of the twentieth century ended with the arrival of the sexual revolution of the 1960s. The rules that had underpinned dating, as a system of courting, crumbled as people embraced the sexual freedoms of that decade.[48] Winnipeg Beach, which worked so well as a place to take a date in the 1920s, had no particular advantage for men and women looking to get together in the 1950s and 1960s. I should also raise a word of caution here. Sexual rela-tions did change in the decades after World War II, but that does not mean that preceding generations were entirely chaste. As items such as the Kinsey Reports, published in 1948 and 1953, have confirmed, people were never as sexually inhibited in the decades leading up to the 1960s as public convention would have us believe.[49] If Winnipeg Beach illustrates some of the clear rules that men and women were supposed to follow when they dated each other, it also illustrates that there were moments when those rules were broken. We can see public concerns about changing social mores at the beach again in the 1950s when the raucous amusement area was labelled "honky-tonk" and suspect.

Throughout its lifespan, Winnipeg Beach has drawn on a consistent pub-lic discourse about the value of nature. Statements made at the turn of the twentieth century were neatly repeated when the amusement area was being demolished and the beach cleaned up in the 1960s. The resort's geographic location on the shore of Lake Winnipeg, about eighty kilometres north of Winnipeg, drew upon a discourse that linked nature and health in contrast to the unhealthy, "cultured" environment of the city.[50] This view was repeated often in the early years of Winnipeg Beach, when it was extolled as an oasis for the tired worker and a proper place to install the family for the summer.[51] Within this discourse, the beach itself takes on a special connotation as a boundary point between culture and nature, a place filled with meaning. Theorist John Fiske describes it this way: "The natural is what culture makes of nature. In other words, the natural is a cultural product, and nature ex-ists only as a conceptual opposition to culture." [52] The beach puts people at the threshold of transcending the cultural and embracing the natural. At Winnipeg Beach, people flirted with that boundary through skinny-dipping, tanning, or quiet walks along the shoreline. In that sense, "nature" helped draw people to the resort, but it was also an enabler once they arrived, because it created a boundary area within which people could relax just a little and shed some of their city inhibitions.

The beach was one boundary zone, the darkness was another. The boardwalk's bright lights provided a moral security to the area, but there was darkness in this summertime adventure, whether in the areas beyond the boardwalk, the inky darkness of the beach, or the darkness created when male passengers on the Moonlight train extinguished the lights.[53] Darkness, with its implicit link to the night, has traditionally been conceptualized as a moment of transgression: "The night time has been the right time, a fleeting but regular period of modest but cherished freedoms from the constraints and cares of daily life."[54] At Winnipeg Beach people not only sought out darkness for a little freedom, they created it.

For some people, Winnipeg Beach was none of the things described above. Children may have spent a day at the beach in the 1920s and been completely oblivious to the hopes, aspirations, and flirtations of the young men and women who were strolling the boardwalk or dancing in the dance hall. In that sense, Winnipeg Beach was a relational space "that demanded recognition by other users to be realized or actualized."[55] Certainly the young men and women at the resort had no trouble recognizing its role; and for children, being able to recognize the dating and heterosexual play going on around them was a benchmark upon their own road to sexual maturity. We can go further to look at how Winnipeg Beach was divided into several zones: the transportation corridor that brought people to the resort, the amusement area that was the focal point of gender interaction, and the tourism infrastructure that allowed people to maintain the boundaries of proper behaviour.[56] These zones worked together to create the collective experience of being at Winnipeg Beach.

Generally, if we ever think about sexuality and spaces, we tend to think of the people occupying the space as heterosexual men and women.[57] But that is not a given. Indeed, Winnipeg Beach demonstrates how space is not by nature heterosexual, but rather is constructed, challenged, and defended. Accepting that space is "ambiently" heterosexual—its occupants are assumed to be heterosexual—does not mean that they have complete freedom of

Built in 1924, the Dance Palace was renowned as western Canada's largest dance hall.

behaviour within it or that men and women even have the opportunity to be together. Heterosexuality, like homosexuality, is a sexual identity, and one that changes over time and according to place.[58] As we will see with Winnipeg Beach, men and women had to follow rules of engagement if they wanted to be together.

For some, Winnipeg Beach was defined by the train; the resort arose when the train started running and fell when it stopped. The CPR was not a spectator in this process. In fact the distinctive role that the railway played in the development and later decline of Winnipeg Beach makes analyzing the economics of transportation a critical part of this book. The CPR founded the resort to take advantage of the distinctive attributes that the location offered as a natural escape from the chaotic influences of the urban environment. It did this recognizing that rail travel would make the area an economically viable and accessible resort. The CPR's initial plan did little more than service the upper-middle-class demand for an accessible cabin area, an excursion point for those who could afford the trip, and a picnic spot for groups in the city. But as courting moved from private settings to public, the CPR followed suit and adjusted its marketing approach and the offerings at Winnipeg Beach. The tourism infrastructure was expanded during World War I to create a significant public amusement area, which was bolstered by competition from other service-industry providers. The CPR expanded its marketing from merely mentioning the physical destination to promoting the beach as a distinctive heterosexual experience and

The Empress Hotel represented the idea of high society at Winnipeg Beach and was one of the iconic symbols of the resort's heyday.

a place to go on a date. In doing so it expanded the class base of Winnipeg Beach, establishing a price point that would be affordable to working-class patrons, and thereby tapped a truly mass market. However, by the late 1950s and 1960s, when sexual mores were again in a state of flux, the CPR had retreated from an active role at Winnipeg Beach; it played no part in helping Winnipeg Beach transition to a new order of gender relations.

The CPR's business model also ensured that Winnipeg Beach would reflect Winnipeg's ethnic mosaic; indeed it ensured that Winnipeg Beach would become a boundary point where different ethnic groups could meet. The same discourse that portrayed the city as a threat was very much under the control of the dominant British-Canadian elite, and it should come as no surprise that ethnicity played a role. The British-Canadian elite feared that sexual contact with "lesser" races would "mongrelize" their race.[59] And we can see in the abundant flags and trappings at Winnipeg Beach a real effort to stamp it as British Canadian territory. However, when it came to developing the resort, the CPR wanted to ensure that the cabin development filled up quickly and that as many people as possible could reach the resort. Thus CPR cabin lots were leased rather than sold, to avoid speculators who might purchase them and wait for the price to rise. Train tickets discriminated based on ability to purchase rather than the ethnicity of the purchaser. This approach stands out more clearly when considered in contrast to private developers: Sandy Hook, Victoria Beach, and other resort areas around Lake Winnipeg advertised themselves against Winnipeg Beach, pointing out that their property was restricted to ensure that purchasers could avoid the ethnic diversity that existed in Winnipeg Beach.[60] The exclusivity that could be created at resorts such as Victoria Beach no doubt helped draw the upper-middle class away from Winnipeg Beach. But facing discrimination at these other resorts pushed ethnic groups, and the Jewish community is the most obvious example, towards Winnipeg Beach.

I focus primarily on the experiences of people between eighteen and thirty years old, mainly single people who used the resort as a place for courting. This was the group that drove changes at the resort. In some ways it was during the first half of the twentieth century that this demographic group came into its own. The transition to dating in public increasingly changed the segregation between men and women—each engaged in their own ho-mosocial activities—to one in which age distinguished a youth culture from younger and older cohorts.[61] This is a more complicated process than might initially appear. Winnipeg Beach was constructed with the segregation of the sexes in mind; its cabins were envisioned as proper places for husbands to install their families for the summer while they toiled in the urban environment. However, while the development of a public amusement area provided a draw and focal point for the emerging youth culture, the ability of men and women to be together was still mitigated to a great degree. So while youth gathered on the boardwalk, they still, as convention demanded, went their separate ways when they returned to their living quarters in the more distant portions of the summer resort. This sort of gender separation broke down in the 1950s, creating rising moral panic about youth culture.[62] Quite simply, men and women were bunking together. The challenge facing a destination for a specific demographic is that the destination has to continuously reinvent itself to appeal to the next generation of guests.[63] The challenge becomes more complicated when we realize that places such as Winnipeg Beach were an attraction to young people because they were a site for courting. Winnipeg Beach, with the help of the CPR, was able to transition from the calling system to the dating system in the first decades of the twentieth century and vastly expand its clientele. It was not able to make the same transition to meet the expectations of youth culture moving into the 1950s and '60s. It did not even try. Indeed, it exhibited a marked suspicion of that youth culture.

Other age groups did use the resort, and we will see them in this book. However, for the purposes of tracking courting culture, children under ten can be seen as simply beneficiaries of this natural location or spectators viewing the antics of the amorous young adults. Adolescents from ten to fifteen years old were spectators and future recruits to the dating experience who wondered when they too might be able to take part in the activities of the dance hall. Parents entertained themselves at the beach, taking part in the public entertainment areas, but as often finding their own entertainment within the tourism infrastructure. The parents, whether as landlords/landladies or employers, also functioned as moral guardians on the beach, providing the formal rules for Winnipeg Beach's youth market. Elderly people figure in this narrative rarely, and when they do appear they are often notable in their contrast to the dating culture in existence at the resort.

The discussion around men and women, areas where men and women could be together and where they could not, nature and urban space, land and water, ethnic groups, and different classes should make implicit the final category that figures prominently in this book: boundaries. I am interested in the boundaries that existed between men and women throughout the twentieth century: boundaries maintained by tight sets of rules that did not so much define what men and women could do as shape what men and women were supposed to be; boundaries that ensured that so much of men's and women's lives were lived in homosocial confines. When the CPR created Winnipeg Beach as an excursion point at the beginning of the twentieth century, it was trying to capture the boundary point between land and water, a literal and figurative lookout point to the natural "other." Indeed, the first station at Winnipeg Beach was built mere yards from the beach. For purely functional reasons, it was moved back a few years later. But the move also freed space for the growth of another anomalous region—the boardwalk and dance-hall hub of Winnipeg Beach. It was in this locale that men and women pushed against the boundaries of their own genders. Within this locale men and women found safe space. The term *safe space* does not mean a lack of violence or crime; Winnipeg Beach had its share of both. But this was a place where men and women might be themselves and become themselves.[64] Winnipeg Beach held the same appeal for ethnic groups as well, providing a location where they could meet. By acting as a boundary point between so many divides, Winnipeg Beach was in many ways a place where things could be turned upside down—if only briefly and if only in a controlled manner. In that sense, it was a carnival.

A group of women mug for the camera while swimming in Lake Winnipeg in 1915. The costume on the middle swimmer was probably fairly revealing for the time period.

The following chapters concentrate on the spatial construction of Winnipeg Beach, building a picture of the resort through consideration of its regions. The first chapter focuses on the transportation corridor and examines how the train shaped the creation of Winnipeg Beach and how people experienced the resort. To the CPR, Winnipeg Beach was a product and it tailored that product to the prevailing tastes of the day. Infrastructure was developed to meet the needs of people who used the beach as an excursion point and for socializing with one's ethnic, religious, or class peers, and then the resort was recast to be a public amusement area for a demographic looking to do their dating at the resort. The CPR's patrons were part of this recasting process. The late-night Moonlight special became synonymous with the dating experience at Winnipeg Beach. It appears clear, however, that the term *Moonlight* was in use, unofficially, before the CPR adopted the name and the imagery behind it for its advertisements. The train rides provided their own unique opportunities for social encounters. Manitoba writers such as Val Werier and Frances Russell have argued that Winnipeg Beach moved to the rhythm of the train and that it was the transition from train to auto that signalled the end of the beach.[65] There is some truth to this. By the 1920s plenty of people were driving to the beach, but the train offered, more than anything, a way to focus crowds at Winnipeg Beach. It was a role that the train station provided from 1903 to the 1950s, even when the majority of people were reaching the beach by car.

The second chapter focuses on the tourism infrastructure, looking at where people lived and worked when they were at the resort. Winnipeg Beach was both a turn of the century summer commuter town and a resort. The resort was initially marketed to upper-middle-class people as an oasis of calm against the stresses of city life. Men were expected to commute to and from the city on the "Daddy's train" while their families were ensconced at Winnipeg Beach. Until the First World War, these family cabins would have served as a location for courting at the beach, with verandas stepping in for parlours when it came to hosting visiting gentlemen or, more often, social gatherings. But by the 1920s courting had transitioned into dating. The tourism industry adapted by offering the people who came to Winnipeg Beach a place to stay after an evening's entertainment. The focus on creating a public entertainment zone and the CPR's own focus on running a profitable rail line ensured that the resort would be open to everyone, expanding the class base of the beach to focus more specifically on working-class people. This expansion in market also ensured that Winnipeg Beach would draw fully from Winnipeg's diverse ethnic community.

The amusement area, including the boardwalk, beach, and dance hall, compose the third chapter and, in my view, the heart of Winnipeg Beach, in particular in its role as a home for dating culture after about 1915. Here was where all the diverse groups that came to Winnipeg Beach gathered. If Winnipeg Beach was a centre for courting, the boardwalk was its main stage. And there was a sense of performance in the endless circling of the boardwalk, where people strutted like "peacocks."[66] If we accept that heterosexuality is an identity, the amusement area was where people confirmed and bolstered that identity. In one sense, they were confirming the gender roles of the time, a role made clear when other performances—most notably the hyper masculinity of the Dew Drop gang or the transgressive identity of gay people—enter the scene. In another sense, people at Winnipeg Beach were eking out space of their own, finding privacy in public to challenge gender roles or finding room in the dark spaces around the boardwalk to push the boundaries and expectations of what men and women were supposed to be doing in this time.

Chapter One
Getting to the Beach
THE TRANSPORTATION CORRIDOR

Winnipeg Beach began with a boat trip. That a community so closely tied to the railway owes its beginning to a boat trip should not be seen as ironic. Railways have always been about transporting goods and people between destinations. As a method of transportation a train has to have a destination, and Winnipeg Beach had yet to become one.[1] So it was that in 1901 William Whyte, an assistant to the Canadian Pacific Railway (CPR) president; Captain William Robinson, president of the Northwest Navigation Company; and Charles Roland of the CPR, cruised along the western shore of Lake Winnipeg before landing at a "beautiful crescent" of sand and naming it Winnipeg Beach.[2] They might well have been wading ashore and planting their flag in a new world. And in some ways they were.

Like most new worlds, this one was already inhabited. Lake Winnipeg was familiar terrain to pre-Columbian Aboriginal people, and later it played a role as a conduit in the fur trade during Canada's formation.[3] Indeed, historian Gerald Friesen has said the lake "represented the heart of this chunk of the world ... certainly to 1900" both for Aboriginal people and later for fur traders as well. "Once the railway came, however, that was the end of water. The routes here were so uneconomic. The lake is dangerous and the rivers are just too long," Friesen noted.[4] The transcontinental railway ended Lake Winnipeg's role as a trade conduit. But the arrival of the CPR at Winnipeg Beach in 1901 gave the lake a new role. From that point, it would become an object of consumption for people in Winnipeg.

Aboriginal ownership of this territory had been extinguished by Treaty 5 in 1875.[5] But crediting the treaty process with somehow sweeping Aboriginal people onto reserves and out of sight vastly oversimplifies the process of colonization. The movement of Aboriginal people onto reserves within the Lake Winnipeg region was aided by the Lake Winnipeg smallpox epidemic of 1876–77, during which provincial officials quarantined Aboriginal people onto the newly created reserves, fixing them in this new space.[6] Europeans moving into the area were also quick to dismiss the presence of Aboriginal people. When a *Telegram* reporter toured the Winnipeg Beach site in 1901 he waxed eloquent about the "primeval" forests and how the birds were so unused to the presence of people that they were almost tame.[7] And yet, in the very same article, the reporter mentions Aboriginal people fishing in the area, suggesting that it was hardly primeval or unutilized. He was not so much erasing the Aboriginal presence from the land as he was dismissing Aboriginal people's ability to have a presence at all; they simply were part of the land.[8]

The same article did mention settlers in the district. Gimli, fifteen kilometres north of Winnipeg Beach, had been homesteaded in 1875 by Icelandic settlers, and their colony of New Iceland abutted the future home of the resort. By 1900 the Winnipeg Beach area had been settled by Icelandic, Ukrainian, and British immigrants. Donald Urquhart, a Scotchman, had homesteaded 153 acres at SW34-17-4E in 1895.[9] By the time the CPR came calling, he had built himself a small house and developed a farm that comprised most of what would eventually be the resort's business district and golf course. Winnipeg Beach's first mayor, William J. Wood, notes in his recollections of the community's early days that Urquhart "sold it to the company for the fancy sum of $1,000 cash and thought he made a good deal."[10] In some ways he had, because lake-front property is only of value if people want to go to the beach and can reach it.[11] When it took possession of the land, the CPR's goal was to ensure that both essential conditions would be met. Certainly Robinson, a prominent Winnipeg businessman, knew the value of the land and was more than just a boat pilot for the Lake Winnipeg expedition.[12] In the fall of 1910 he sold the eastern half of section 33, which adjoined the CPR's land, to W.J. Robertson for development into the Beach Grove subdivision—thereby turning, one can assume, his own profit from Whyte's trip.[13]

While there was plenty of forest that still needed to be cleared, the CPR was not breaking new ground when it established Winnipeg Beach. At the turn of the century, the concept of a seaside resort was at its peak.[14] Other examples abounded, from Blackpool in Great Britain to Coney Island in New York.[15] Seaside resorts had a long history in Europe, dating back to the traditional practice of "taking the waters."[16] Tradition had received a boost from medicine in the sixteenth and seventeenth centuries, when scientists argued that mineral waters had health benefits, a suggestion that eventually grew to include both salt and fresh water. With the industrial revolution underway, the natural world was extolled as a virtuous place in contrast to the growing urban centres.[17] Trains helped bridge the gap between city and shoreline. In Great Britain, train links from London to Brighton, on the English Channel, made the seaside city the "lungs of the capital" by 1850, and during one week in May trains transported some 73,000 excursionists to the coast.[18] Similarly, railway links transformed Coney Island from an upper-class hideaway to a middle- and working-class playground.[19] More modestly, trolley companies in urban centres used parks and amusement areas as terminal points on their trolley line to add business as residential areas developed and to generate revenue on weekends.[20] In Toronto the trolley provided a link to amusement parks such as Scarboro Beach Park and Sunnyside Amusement Park, which rose and fell along the shore of Lake Ontario in the early twentieth century. Winnipeg's Elm Park, built in 1891 and located where Kingston Row is now, and River Park, on the southeastern end of Osborne Street, were built to provide an end point for the tram line that ran along Osborne.[21]

The CPR already had an interest in the tourist trade. Its transcontinental line had opened markets in Banff, Victoria, and Quebec City to North American and European travellers. Closer to Winnipeg, the transcontinental line had made Kenora and Lake of the Woods available to the city's elite, and in the 1890s Winnipeg's newspapers carried references to "society" holidaying at their lakeside cottages. Hunters and anglers had ferreted out recreation areas across the southern portions of Manitoba's wilderness. Local railway development offered new opportunities to create regional excursion points that would be financially accessible to middle-class patrons.[22]

The CPR also felt the clock was ticking. The rival Canadian Northern Railway (CNR) had a partially completed line to Delta Beach on the southern shore of Lake Manitoba and was running streetcar excursions to Elm Park and other picnic spots within Winnipeg.[23] The CPR had been

Not quite primeval. This is Winnipeg Beach as it looked in 1903.
There's no tourism infrastructure in place yet, although it does appear that
there may be some tents just behind the tree line.

eyeing the southern shore of Lake Winnipeg in 1899 and in 1900 used its Selkirk branch line to send a train-load of excursionists to Selkirk, where they boarded the City of Selkirk steamer and made their way to a beach at the mouth of the Red River.[24] In 1900 investors were already purchasing lots at Whytewold Beach—then known alternatively as Whitewood and Whitewold—and building a launch to make daily trips from Selkirk.[25] Coney Island followed a similar pattern of development, with ferries and steamships making the initial trips before rail lines were laid down.[26] The method of transportation was everything when it came to developing a resort. It took a *Telegram* reporter over sixteen hours to reach Winnipeg Beach by horse and carriage in 1901.[27] A steamship might make the journey in a few hours, but it was limited in how many people it could carry. Rail travel could trim that time to just over an hour, and a single train could carry over 1000 people. It was the crowds mass transit could bring that helped these places become "laboratories of the new mass culture."[28] In 1901 Winnipeg Beach needed a railway link if it was going to thrive, which is why Robinson, a Winnipeg Beach investor, was happy to use his steamship to take the CPR on a tour of the area.

In the fall of 1902, with a rail line already laid down, the CPR brought a select group of Winnipeg notables to Winnipeg Beach in a private railway car. The party included representatives from Molson Bank, Imperial Bank, and the Bank of Commerce, Chief Justice Killam, and media representatives such as J.W. Dafoe of the *Manitoba Free Press* (which became the *Winnipeg Free Press* in 1931), H.M.E. Evans of the *Telegram*, and R.L. Richardson of the *Tribune*: in other words, the people who were needed to fund, promote, and ensure regulatory approval of such a project. The *Free Press* was upbeat, crediting the CPR with "beautifying" the beach and laying down an "excellent" roadbed.[29] Positive press in Winnipeg Beach's early years was rarely a problem, with articles trumpeting it as "likely to become one of the most popular summer resorts in the west."[30] This was Winnipeg in the midst of its turn-of-the-century boom, when entrepreneurs and workers were captivated by a growing economy, rising wages, and increased purchasing power. In the ten-year period following 1901, when Winnipeg Beach was announced, Winnipeg's population soared from 42,340 to 136,035 people, and city boosters claimed the 1911 tally was closer to 166,000 when seasonal workers and those missed by census takers were included. In *Winnipeg 1912*, James Blanchard describes how Winnipeg's British born envisioned a metropolis on the prairies and waxed poetic in their boosterism. They created the theatres, clubs, and churches necessary to live a life as good as any in the British Empire.[31] For Winnipeg's elite, sitting on the edge of a Western frontier as they were, it was more crucial than ever to stabilize their British identity with these markers of success.[32] They felt they deserved a world-class resort to go with their world-class city, and Winnipeg Beach could be made to fit the bill.

The aspirations and social habits of this genteel middle class coloured the early development of Winnipeg Beach, and initially the CPR seems to have viewed it as a place of rest or the contemplation of nature, similar to Kenora and Lake of the Woods.[33] Interviewed in 1901, Whyte was quoted as saying that he believed "Winnipeg Beach will prove a splendid resort for the toilers of the capital, who are badly in need of a place within easy reach, where they can take a day's outing and enjoy the health-giving breeze from Lake Winnipeg."[34] In 1902 CPR officials said they expected to run one train a day to the beach the following spring and were contemplating developing some cottages, a dance pavilion, and a hotel. They also mused about adding special excursion trains, the "picnic trains" that would become a staple of Winnipeg Beach. The expectation was that the picnickers would fill the pavilion, use its dining room for a meal, and return home to the city after their outing. Finally, the CPR thought that perhaps there would be dancing in the pavilion every Saturday.[35]

There was a class-formation aspect to this plan, which involved unions and workplaces using the baseball games and picnics at the beach to create a sense of solidarity.[36] But ethnic and religious groups also used the beach to draw together their own communities.[37] Perhaps most critically, events such as baseball games, picnics, and dancing threw up a boundary around the community, within which men and women could socialize in a safe setting. Winnipeg's upper and middle classes—the tired business people who would use Winnipeg Beach as a summer home—could be expected to, and did, do much of their entertaining within the confines of their own cabins, thereby, again, maintaining a boundary around what they viewed as "their" community. The various groups that used the beach might come together to stare at the lake or take in a regatta, a fact that suggested how public entertainment at the time focused on spectating rather than participating.[38]

Yet, within a few years the evening excursions ran nightly, and by 1906 the track saw up to thirteen trains a day on busy holiday weekends.[39] By 1920, 15,000 people made the trek on thirteen trains to Winnipeg Beach for the July 1 weekend, and by then dances were being held nightly in the pavilion. And the 1920 figure underestimated the number of people on the train. As an official at the time suggested, "for every adult there was one child for whom no ticket was required, bringing the grand total to about 30,000 souls carried to and from the holiday points," or more than one out of every ten people in Winnipeg.[40] That same article noted that at noon on July 1 there were 109 coaches sitting in the Winnipeg Beach yards waiting to take people home. A crowd of 35,000 to 40,000 was possible on long weekends during Winnipeg Beach's peak in the 1920s.[41] In 1925, a *Free Press* article noted that seventeen trains now made the trip to the beach for the July 1 holiday.[42] Little wonder that the Winnipeg Beach line was claimed to be the most profitable stretch of CPR track in Canada during its heyday.[43]

Traffic on the Winnipeg Beach line was considerable. Accidents were rare, but when they did happen they were dramatic. A crash occurred in 1906 when two trains collided head on near Clandeboye. Line-of-sight vision would have prevented the accident; however, there is a sweeping curve near Clandeboye that prevented the trains from seeing each other until it was too late to avoid a collision. Damage to the front end of the trains was severe, but only one man was killed in the incident: Horace Waters, a

Arriving at Winnipeg Beach, Man.

These people would have been looking out on the lake as they walked out of the train station. Their clothing suggests a middle-class crowd, but that may be deceiving; working-class visitors made sure to wear their Sunday best when they came to the resort.

secretary to CPR vice president William Whyte. The disruption, however, was spectacular. A train was sent out to the accident to pick up people from that site. But the wreck left over 3,000 people stranded at Whytewold and Winnipeg Beach until a train outfitted with eighteen coaches finally arrived to pick them up at around 1:00 a.m.; with delays moving past the accident, it did not reach Winnipeg until after 5:00 a.m.[44] Coordination took place with Winnipeg's streetcar operators to ensure that streetcars ran late and could take the passengers home. Assuming that there were 3,000 people at the beach and perhaps another 1,000 or more on the two trains involved, we can say that some 4,000 people were cut off from the city by the accident. Given a population of 90,000 in Winnipeg at the time, this means nearly one out of every twenty people in the city was potentially involved in the accident.

Communication was slow—it took a seven-mile walk from the accident to a CPR telegraph line before details could be sent into the city. And even once that information arrived in Winnipeg, there was no quick way to distribute it. As a *Free Press* news article noted at the time, "The rumour spread throughout the city and owing to exaggerations caused great anxiety among the large number who had relatives among the excursionists and anxious inquiries were made from the newspaper offices."[45] While

WINNIPEG BEACH TRAIN WRECK
Aug. 20/06 A.W.LAY

A 1906 collision on the Winnipeg Beach line killed one CPR official and stranded thousands of people at the beach; it also warranted commemoration in this postcard.

transportation relied on mass movement in this period, communication was personal. Somebody either had to be told news directly, through telephone, for anyone who might have access to one, or in person, or hear a verbal announcement. The only mass-communication tool available was the newspaper, which was slowed by the need for production and distribution. Contrast that with the immediacy allowed by radio, television, or the Internet. The reflections on the accident a year later summed it up this way: "The accident to the holiday train on that occasion caused great anxiety in the city, as there were few residents who had not friends or relatives at the Beach for the day, and the wild rumours that spread when the meagre details of the accident were received made many flock to the CPR depot in search of news which was slow in coming."[46] No wonder a trip to Winnipeg Beach seemed like a journey to somewhere else.

Winnipeg Beach's popularity grew in tandem with Winnipeg's population. But these soaring crowds also reflected a transition in what people expected out of their resort experience. With its growing public leisure zone, Winnipeg Beach became an "industrial saturnalia," an updated version of the carnival of old that provided "a release from the 'rules' of urban/industrial life."[47] This role worked in tandem with that of the natural attractions that had brought the CPR to Winnipeg Beach. But there were several changes at work in the resort's growth. The genteel middle class that had colonized the beach had done much of its entertaining—including socializing between men and women—within closed social groups. Working-class citizens at the turn of the century also did most of their socializing within controlled ethnic groups.[48] The mass crowds that populated the beach did their dating in public, in the expanding leisure zones at Winnipeg Beach and in Winnipeg. The vast numbers that were coming to Winnipeg Beach by the 1920s suggested not only the loss of middle-class exclusivity but a broader change in ethnic and gender relations. Winnipeg Beach became a boundary zone where people of different ethnicities could meet within the public entertainment area and a place where men and women could easily socialize together in public, outside the surveillance of their community.[49]

In their article "Ethnicity, Religion, and Class: Lake Winnipeg Resorts," John C. Lehr, H. John Selwood, and Eileen Badiuk argue that "the role of the railway company in controlling the development of Winnipeg Beach was limited" to laying track, selling lots, building a dance hall, and constructing the Empress Hotel.[50] But as a company, and more importantly as a system of transportation, the CPR did much to shape Winnipeg Beach. The decision in 1902 to terminate its line at the resort, rather than carrying on to Gimli, ensured that a residential population would develop. Cordwood and fish were both hauled to Winnipeg Beach and shipped out on the new rail line during the winter, and it was both business opportunities offered during the winter, and the summer tourist trade, that initially drew people such as mayor Wood to the community.[51] The line would be extended northward after 1909, creating new entry points for the shipment of resources, but Wood and others like him stayed.

The CPR's earliest discussions called for a hotel at Winnipeg Beach, but the company seems to have been in no hurry to build one. In fact it was Edward Windebank, the developer of the Empress Hotel, who approached the CPR for financial help. Windebank had fallen short of cash during construction and offered to mortgage the hotel to the company if it would advance the money necessary to complete the establishment. Windebank would then repurchase the hotel from the CPR.[52] Whyte, who had moved up the ranks to become CPR second vice president, pitched the idea to CPR president Sir Thomas G. Shaughnessy on 9 June 1908: "The need of a good hotel at Winnipeg Beach has been the means of losing traffic to the

Company, because people who wish to spend the week-end, or perhaps longer, at Winnipeg Beach and desire decent accommodation could not get it."[53] Whyte followed up his letter with a telegram dated 16 June explaining to Shaughnessy that time was of the essence.[54] The term "decent accommodation" hints that servicing Winnipeg's upper- and middle-class clientele is at the base of Whyte's concern. Cabin owners, campers, and day trippers could still use Winnipeg Beach, but the Empress was intended to offer upper-class accommodations. It would hopefully meet the needs of people such as a Winnipeg businessman who wrote the *Free Press* to complain in 1907 that a lack of quality accommodation meant that the "better classes" were "entirely debarred from visiting the beach."[55]

Whyte's concerns were not groundless. In 1910 a group of five Winnipeg investors incorporated the Victoria Beach Investment Company and over the next few years went on to make their vision of an exclusive resort for Winnipeg's elite a reality.[56] Windebank did operate the Empress Hotel, opened in 1908, for the CPR, but difficulties in their financial relationship landed them in provincial court in 1915 and in the Supreme Court in 1917.[57] Beach Attractions Limited, a private company that operated the CPR amusements at Winnipeg Beach, took over management of the Empress Hotel in 1915.[58]

Victoria Beach—not Winnipeg Beach—went on to become synonymous with Winnipeg's elite, at least when it came to Lake Winnipeg resorts. At Victoria Beach entry could be controlled, entertainment options limited, and a genteel middle-class vision of a resort maintained. But the Empress Hotel did become the signature hotel at Winnipeg Beach and, along with the boardwalk and railway, one of the symbolic images of the resort's heyday. It came to symbolize the element of class at the beach. Dr. Paul Adams, born in 1920, recalled a period around 1928 or 1929 when he saw "a man walking down from the hotel looking very distinguished, carrying a cane, wearing a straw hat and I had a vision that he was wearing spats.... He looked very distinctive and I had the feeling that this was an indication of what the hotel at Winnipeg Beach was like."[59] This childhood image left Adams with the impression that Winnipeg Beach in its early days was an upper-class location, exactly what Whyte had hoped for.

When the CPR first laid its tracks to Winnipeg Beach, it rolled them out almost directly to the beach and alongside Main Street, or Railway Street, as it was initially known. The original position allowed people to see the lake as they stepped off the train and provided ready access to the pavilion. There was also space left open around the pavilion to provide room for picnics and ensure that people could experience the natural setting that had drawn them to the beach. At the time, an excursion to Winnipeg Beach was quite literally a trip to the beach.[60] People were brought directly to the meeting point of the cultural setting and the natural. As the *Free Press* explained in 1905:

> Many of the children, Winnipeg born and bred, have never seen a lake and the excitement grows intense as the train nears its destination. The "grown-ups" too, with memories perhaps of distant homes near Ontario or the old country lakes, watch eagerly for the first glimpse of water gleaming through the trees and smile in sympathy with the shrill "I see it," of the proud youngster who catches the gleam. Finally the train pulls into the station and the lake bursts into view, sparkling like a great pale sapphire in the sun.[61]

The references to Ontario and the "old country" provide a sense of who these people were supposed to be: for all that Winnipeg Beach was a meeting place for different ethnic groups, the references to Britain and Ontario, and the ubiquitous British flags and Red Ensigns, were a constant reminder that it was Winnipeg's British elite who envisioned themselves as the cultural leaders of the resort.

As the resort developed, drawing the train through the community's heart became a safety risk, so in 1911 the station was moved several blocks back from the lakefront.[62] The new location opened space for a line of amusements and businesses to grow between station and lake. So it was that people waded through additional cultural artifacts to get to the natural. It was this commercial development that greeted seven-year-old Christine in Gabrielle Roy's *The Road Past Altamont*. Set in the 1920s or 1930s, Roy's novel describes Christine and her elderly travelling companion's excitement at catching a glimpse of the lake during the journey. But when they arrive at the Winnipeg Beach train station, the lake is nowhere to be seen:

> Winnipeg Beach disillusioned me to the point of bitter tears. Somewhere in the sky I could see a circus wheel turning, and from all sides came the intermingled cries of street hawkers, the

tinkling of cheap music, and the odour of hot grease. In the distance the little cars of the roller coaster rushed downhill, full of
people from whom came, after a breathless silence, a long hysteri-
cal shriek. Alas, we were still in a town, which had streets, close-
packed shops, and swarming restaurants, but a very much sadder
town than ours; here people walked about half-naked, a towel over
their shoulders, eating fried potatoes from paper cornets or hot
sausages on rolls. I seized the old man's hand, whimpering, "The
lake? Where's the lake?"[63]

Of course for other travellers it was exactly this carnival atmosphere that
drew them to Winnipeg Beach.

After the decision to change station location and the construction of
the Empress Hotel, the rest of Winnipeg Beach fell into place. The resort's
role evolved as it developed. There is no doubt that competition from the
Canadian Northern at Grand Beach helped spur the CPR into developing
further attractions. The boardwalk continued to grow, culminating with the
addition of the roller coaster in 1919 and the construction in 1924 of Western
Canada's largest dance hall, which had a 14,000-square-foot dance floor.
The original dance hall remained into the 1960s, and was used as picnic
pavilion and for a range of other activities, including badminton.[64] The
additions during the 1910s and '20s reflected a change in social relations.
People were not just coming to Winnipeg Beach to gaze at the lake or to
socialize within their community. Men and women were coming for the
opportunity to promenade and dance in public.[65] The crowd and excitement
that went along with those activities became the entertainment.[66]

The early advertisements for Winnipeg Beach moved back and forth
between the section for travel advertisements and that for entertainment
advertisements. Was going to Winnipeg Beach equivalent to a trip to
Vancouver, or was it similar to going to the theatre? Or was it both? As the
CPR's advertising developed from simple lists of departure times, it came to
reflect the fact that what the CPR was selling was a heterosexual adult experience. In this, Winnipeg Beach was similar to Coney Island and Blackpool,
already home to well-developed amusement areas, where it was adults
rather than children who crowded the rides in the first half of the century.[67]
Winnipeg Beach advertisements reflected a typical gender construction
of recreation areas. Images of women were used to sell the resort to its

Winnipeg Beach's original Dance Pavilion; more modest than the Dance Palace, its plans suggest that it was built to host distinct groups at the resort. There was an open hall with an eating area in the back.

imagined customers, who were expected to be male, white, and heterosexual, and who would be moderated and vitalized by the presence of "respectable women."[68] While children and families did periodically appear in the CPR's advertisements, most often it used images of a dancing couple, or, in the 1940s, a woman sitting on the beach in a bikini. As one large CPR advertisement featuring dancing and the Moonlight trains intoned in 1920: "Oh, Boy! Let's Go. The board-walk a-quiver with life and gaiety.—Every attraction in full swing.—The trees, the grasses, the breezes and the crowd—all invite you. Make it a real holiday."[69] The product was the heterosexual experience, encouraged by the presence of nature and sanctioned by the support of companies such as the CPR.

Given that adults were paying customers, whereas children travelled for free, the CPR's profit depended on ensuring that adults wanted to come to the beach. Children were useful to the railway primarily as a lever to draw ticket-paying adults; otherwise, they were simply taking up space. Even when the town of Winnipeg Beach began running advertisements in 1938 to help draw people to the resort (and the expectation was that people would drive rather than take the train) it used imagery that focused on young men and women.[70]

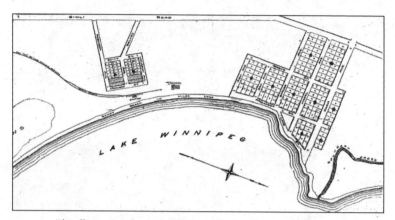

This illustration shows the CPR's initial plans for Winnipeg Beach.
The business section was behind the train station; The CPR moved the train station
behind the business section in 1911.

Winnipeg Beach thrived on its lakeside location, which offered the "trees and breezes" that the CPR referred to in its advertisements. Yet if the resort was to make the CPR money, passengers had to be able to reach the beach quickly. The CPR's market broke down into three segments: picnickers, cabin owners/renters (also known as *campers*, presumably because in the early years many of them were), and day trippers. Speed mattered for all of these groups. The CPR upgraded its rail bed in 1908 in an effort to get trains from Winnipeg to Winnipeg Beach in seventy-five minutes.[71] By 1915, it was claiming that trains could make the trip in seventy minutes, and Victor Martin, a CPR fireman who worked on the Moonlight, says that on the late-night trips home they probably did a little better than that.[72] For the day trippers and picnickers, speed was essential to enable them to get there, enjoy the day, and get back into Winnipeg. For the campers, it meant that they could commute efficiently. The steamships that had initially trundled people to Lake Winnipeg's beaches from Selkirk could never match the train's speed.

The trip was a foundational part of the Winnipeg Beach experience. Historian Wolfgang Schivelbusch has argued that the train creates its destination. It focuses passengers on the departure point and the arrival point, while the space in between is unused or even "destroyed." When passengers did look outside, they found themselves encountering a panorama of passing landscape rather than a place.[73] Contrast this with the experience of the *Telegram* reporter who journeyed to Winnipeg Beach in 1901. The round trip took about thirty-six hours, and while the reporter discussed the resort—the destination—the vast majority of his commentary was consumed with the conditions of the terrain between the beach and Winnipeg and the difficulties in traversing it. For him, the journey was all about the space in between, rather than the destination.[74]

But while the train destroyed the space between Winnipeg and Winnipeg Beach, it created the time and social space of the journey. And this time and social space was not unused. Indeed, it is the use of this time—to build excitement in children awaiting their arrival at the beach, or to provide a moment together for couples returning on the Moonlight special—that provides many of the foundational memories of Winnipeg Beach. For many people, the journey to Winnipeg Beach was as significant as the destination. The journey to the beach also set the Winnipeg Beach experience apart from that of other resorts, such as Coney Island. There the gap between New York and the sea shore was bridged by a number of rail lines and, later, subway lines.[75] Everyone had to travel to get there, but the journey was not a shared experience, in contrast to Winnipeg Beach, to which, particularly in the earliest years, there was only one route.

The first trips to Winnipeg Beach were called "excursions." The term is defined as a short trip to a place and back, for pleasure or a purpose; a group of people taking a short trip; or a temporary deviation from a regular course or pattern. All three definitions applied to the activities in Winnipeg Beach, and we can add that for most of the trips the term was also code for "working-class or middle-class events."[76] Almost immediately after the construction of the beach line, social, work, religious, and ethnic groups began to use the opportunity of an "excursion" to Winnipeg Beach to solidify or maintain their own social boundaries. The CPR started taking bookings at the beginning of the year, and in 1913 the *Free Press* noted that between forty and fifty picnics were expected—a list that included a wide range of church and social groups, such as the Canadian Order of Foresters, the Rome-Italian society, the Orangemen, the Stovel Mutual Club, and the Vulcan Iron Works.[77] The picnics would remain a staple of Winnipeg Beach into the 1950s. The Caterers' picnic, perhaps the most famous and one that had predated Winnipeg Beach, quickly made the beach its own.[78] It was also among the last major picnics at the beach; it used the CPR train as late as 1961, after regular passenger service had ended.[79] Some picnics attracted

This advertisement illustrates the key ingredients of a night out at Winnipeg Beach; a young couple, nature, and the train.

only a few hundred people while others, such as the CPR's picnic in 1911, drew 2,500 people. The Caterers' picnic could easily draw a crowd of 6,000 people.[80] The list of activities for the CPR's picnic illustrates how these events were very much about maintaining social networks. Competitions included distinct categories for married and single men and women, and focused primarily on adults rather than children. [81] The races offered an opportunity for women to perform in front of men and for men to perform in front of women. In the early part of the century, when courting was restricted to the home or social network, it was these sorts of events that helped provide

opportunities for courtship. For the most part, the picnics were limited
to the guests who came up on the train, but as Winnipeg Beach resident
Lawrence Isfeld recalled, there was always a group of local youngsters
prepared to break through those boundaries and take part in the festivi-
ties. Sometimes they were allowed in, other times they were shooed away.[82]
Winnipeg Beach was, of course, far from alone in being a hot spot for
these sorts of picnics. Grand Beach was a competing site across the lake,
and Toronto Island, accessible through a quick ferry ride, offered a similar
refuge for picnic groups in the city of Toronto.[83]

The picnics were a way of maximizing the profitability of the beach
line for the CPR. But they also added to the excitement of Winnipeg Beach
by ensuring that there was always something going on. Nestor Mudry can
remember travelling to the CPR picnic in 1934, when he would have been
about thirteen years old.[84] The family did not have a cottage, and vacations
were limited to the odd Sunday, all of which meant that going to the CPR
picnic was an event. "It was exciting. I remember being in the station and
'Are we going, are we going yet?' Then of course they had young boys selling stuff on the train, Cokes and Crackerjack and all of that sort of thing,"
Mudry recalled. "That was the main outing, oh that was a good thrill for
us. Especially when the train was coming along and oh, we could see the
lake. 'Oh, there's the lake! Oh there it was.' So it was a pretty big deal for us
kids."[85] Seats on at least some of the CPR trains could be moved. They could
be oriented to face forward, similar to bus seats, or they could by spun
around so that people could sit with each other in groups of four. When
Mudry travelled with his family, the seats were orientated so that kids and
parents faced each other in a not-too-subtle use of space as regulation. "We
pretty well stayed with the family. My parents didn't like us wandering off,
so we pretty well had to stay put," Mudry remembered.[86] The picnics continued throughout Winnipeg Beach's life as a resort area, but, as in other
resorts such as Toronto Island, they did decline in both importance and
numbers.[87] That decline worked in tandem with the growth of the resort's
public entertainment zone and suggests something of how people who
used to socialize within the closed circle of the group were now doing so in
mass-entertainment areas.

The CPR's travel time permitted Winnipeg Beach to become a commuter
community, with businessmen setting up their families at the beach while
they travelled back and forth to the city on the train. This was the genteel

middle-class public face the beach wanted to project: earnest businessmen commuting into the city to work, while their families enjoyed the summer in this suburban retreat.[88] At a cost of $1.20 for a round-trip fare, at a time when an early-twentieth-century labourer's salary was twenty cents an hour, or a skilled tradesman's sixty-five cents an hour, this daily commute was beyond the budget of all but the very affluent.[89] But it was marketed to wealthier citizens, with advertisements pointing out that businessmen— and it was always men—could commute on the train. Areas such as Matlock advertised that their location nearer to Winnipeg could shave a half hour off the daily round trip.[90] This gendered commute was laid out officially as the "Daddy's train" in CPR advertisements, a terminology that suggests workers were male, married, and with children. Indeed, the terminology was probably created by the travellers and then picked up by the CPR. A 1 June 1917 advertisement in the *Manitoba Free Press* touted four trains that would be leaving for the beach on Saturday—each of them with its own particular market. The Afternoon special headed out at 2:00 p.m., the Daddy's train left at 5:20 p.m. (a reminder that Saturday was often a work day), the Moonlight special left at 6:45 p.m., and the Last Chance train headed out at 10:30 p.m. The Last Chance was aptly named because until 1923 the CPR's beach train could not run on Sunday. The 5:20 p.m. Daddy's train was a staple of beach life until train travel died out in the 1950s.

The popular image of the Daddy's train was of fathers commuting on a daily basis, but the reality was that most fathers spent the week working in the city and the weekends at the cottage. Winnipeg Beach was not alone in this. "The husband train," as it was also sometimes called, played the same role in vacation spots throughout the world until it was replaced by the car. And cabin life see-sawed between the long spells with mom as the single parent to the frenzy of activity and excitement that would accompany the return of dad.[91] We have to keep in mind that for most people in the first half of the century a phone at the beach would have been an impossibility, which reduced communication to letters during the week or a few lines jotted down on a postcard—a prospect that no doubt increased the feeling of "being away" when one was at the resort. At Winnipeg Beach, the train station became the focal point for weekly family reunions and departures. Ina Drummond stayed at the beach in the late 1940s and early 1950s. Her mother and aunts would rent a cottage and her father, a CPR employee, joined them on weekends. "[The Daddy's train] used to come down Friday night and go back Sunday. So while the mom and kids were down at the lake, dad would be at work and he'd come down Friday night and spend the weekend," Drummond recalled.[92] Technically, the Daddy's train ran at 5:20 p.m. on weeknights and Saturday. But Drummond's memories remind us of how the train became linked with the coming and going of her father, and in that sense it was the Friday train that mattered. "We couldn't wait for that Daddy train to come down on Friday.... I remember one day my dad when he came down, I was so happy to see him that I went tearing in the gate to tell my mom dad was here and I closed the gate behind me and my dad got it right in the bridge of the nose. It didn't break anything but afterwards he had a little lump on his nose and after that whenever I did anything wrong he would say, 'Remember?,'" Drummond remembered, pointing to her own nose.[93] The train gave Drummond's excitement a temporal and spatial focal point—one that was critical to the construction of Winnipeg Beach. Drummond's father later served as CPR constable at the beach, which allowed the family to stay at the beach together throughout the summer. But many families had the same weekend reunions. Jessica can remember her father joining the family at the lake on the weekend. On the flip side, Orest could remember growing up in the city's north end and seeing the rail commuters roll into the city for work in the morning, as much a part of summer as going to the beach itself.[94]

Indeed, Winnipeg Beach was so much a suburb of Winnipeg that, in 1946, officials with the Wartime Prices and Trade Board worried city residents who had moved to the beach for the summer would not be able to find housing in the city in the fall.[95] Toronto faced a similar problem during World War II, when Toronto Island's summer homes were called on to provide extra housing for families.[96] American writers have discussed how housing in American suburbs was designed for white, young, middle-class families with the father as the assumed breadwinner and the mother as the housekeeper. In that sense, the gender imbalances of the nineteenth and twentieth centuries flowed through housing developments as well as the labour market and society.[97] This process was at work on a seasonal basis in Winnipeg Beach in the first half of the twentieth century. Ethnicity did play out in Winnipeg Beach, in a concerted effort to imprint it as a "British" enclave—illustrated by the resort's ubiquitous Union Jacks. But despite the sea of flags, Winnipeg Beach emerged as an ethnically diverse resort, as we will see when we turn to the tourism infrastructure.

Nestor Mudry would have travelled on this train, or one very similar, when he went to Winnipeg Beach for the CPR Employees' Annual Picnic.

Memories of the Moonlight specials are a staple of Winnipeg Beach lore. The Moonlight encapsulates the Winnipeg Beach experience as a location for dating, providing in a few short hours the journey to somewhere else, the collective and performative experience on the boardwalk and dance hall, and the return, accompanied by the creation of private and hidden space. The Moonlight represents a different use of the train from the picnic trains, which would have seen distinct social groups going to the beach together, and the Daddy's train, which provided a male gendered experience. The Moonlight train, in contrast, was conceptualized as a heterosocial affair—with men and women travelling together. Howard Dundas provides us with perhaps the most graphic description of the Moonlight trains in his book *Wrinkled Arrows: Good Old Days in Winnipeg*. He offers a striking illustration of how the trains and Winnipeg Beach represented an opportunity to escape the regulation of the city and to enter a locale on the other side of the boundary line that separated "proper" behaviour from the possibility of sexual expression. Dundas is explicit in arguing that, when it came to stepping on the Moonlight trains in the 1920s, "sexual ignorance abounded and the cool of the evening beckoned."[98] Dundas was born in 1905, and his book was published in 1980, although the chapters appear to have been written over several years. He begins the chapter "Go to Sleep, Sweetie, It's

Arrival of the Canadian Pacific Railway train, 1925. The train allowed workers to commute from Winnipeg Beach to Winnipeg on the Daddy's Train; more often than not, however, the daddy's bunked in the city during the week and came out on the weekends while their families stayed at the beach.

Just the Moonlight Going By" with the statement, "Sex wasn't bandied about very much in those good old days when I was young."[99] In fact, Dundas portrays his entire youth as an effort to find out more about sex in the face of numerous rebuffs at the wall of regulation. "The Moonlights ended all this," he writes.[100] He credits economic competition with launching the Moonlights, believing that the CPR and CNR, each trying to maximize profits on their beach lines, did not quite know what they were getting into when they added the Moonlight specials.

In fact the Moonlight specials had been running to Winnipeg Beach long before Grand Beach was opened in 1916. But there is still some truth in Dundas's argument. I believe that, as with the Daddy's trains, the term *Moonlight* was added to the excursions in the years after they started running. While the "Moonlight" trains are mentioned in social columns beginning in about 1906, the term does not appear in CPR advertisements until about 1910, when it is listed as a "Moonlight Excursion."[101] Either the term *Moonlight* was added by the patrons and appropriated by the CPR, or it had been used unofficially by the CPR and was added to advertisements after the company realized it could be used to help sell the train ride. This progression was amplified after the CNR opened its Grand Beach line. Not coincidentally, the CPR began advertising Winnipeg Beach more aggressively, and advertisements for the Moonlight trains included pictures of dancing couples, suggesting how romance had become a commodity to be marketed.[102] The Moonlight excursion would go on to be known as the "70-minute Moonlight," reflecting the fact that Winnipeg Beach could be reached more quickly than Grand Beach, before finally becoming the "Moonlight special" in 1920.[103] Similarly, Winnipeg Beach advertisements completed their shift from appearing among travel and excursion advertisements to the entertainment section of the newspaper, a transition that reflected both a new role and the growth of mass entertainment. The language and emphasis given to the Moonlight trains reflects the growth of a dating culture. Heterosexuality had come out of its own closet by the 1920s, becoming the focal point of social relations.[104] But people still had to play by a set of rules that dictated how men and women should behave with one another.

Dundas kicks off his Moonlight ride with a description of the trips up both sides of the lake. On the west side, "commuting members of the Establishment" detrained along the way and gave the Winnipeg Beach–bound passengers the opportunity to see "the younger members of the Establishment in their yellow and black St. John's sweaters and the U. of M. brown and gold blazers and white flannels playing brisk games of croquet through the twinkling leaves of the aspens, or just sauntering up and down the station platform looking debonair."[105] The people in Whytewold, Ponemah, and Matlock were clearly considered elite Winnipeggers by Dundas, and they were marking their own territory with their station-side stroll.

In contrast, at Balsam Bay on the Grand Beach side, train patrons were "stared at rather enigmatically by a few score of Indians sitting or loitering in the station's shade," and, says Dundas, a discussion on the battle of Seven Oaks ensued.[106] We can see again how Aboriginal people are considered outside the experience of colonial subjects such as Dundas. And by locating them within Canada's past, at the Battle of Seven Oaks, he neatly cuts them out of any activity in Canada's present. The trip was a build-up to adventure, but Dundas is doing more than providing narrative. He is using class and race to form a boundary around the beaches. In their journey, working-class riders on the Moonlight trains travelled through a moat of class and race to reach an area beyond the regulation that Dundas encountered in the city.

The CPR Pier decorated with Union Jack flags; the flags helped give the resort a British-Canadian identity even if the reality was more complex.

This boundary between Winnipeg Beach and the city was a constant fixture of the resort. A 1910 incident illustrates how the concept of distance was keenly felt at the beach in its early days. The Winnipeg Beach social column of 12 July noted that "between 40 and 50 people got left at the beach after the last train pulled out on Saturday evening. Some wanted to walk to Winnipeg, but upon being warned by Station Master Eby that they would most certainly be eaten by bears on the trip, thought better of it and chartered the launch, 'River Queen,' owned by Mr. Watson of St. Louis, who took the tardy ones safely into Winnipeg. The home journey was enlivened by music and singing."[107] Until 1923 trains were not permitted to run on Sunday, which meant the beach was cut off from the city. But the incident illustrates how the train was expected to transport people through the "wilds" between Winnipeg and Winnipeg Beach.

Dundas gives scant attention to the actual stay at the beaches before putting his passengers back on the train. That is not surprising, given that he sees the train ride as an opportunity for circumventing sexual repression. Dundas continues: "On both sides of the lake the train's departure was heralded by the ringing of a loud bell, and was followed by a clamorous rush to the trains for the return journey. Both trains high-balled at twenty-three hours, and between Balsam Bay on one side of the lake and Ponemah on the other, the youthful passengers vied with the trainmen, putting the lights in the cars on and off eight times. Youth always won, and the trainmen left the cars in darkness, said 'the hell with it' and went into the baggage car to play Euchre."[108] And what happened after "youth" had won and created this darkened space? "There were squeals of laughter, poignant silences and sudden shrieks of indignation, cries for help and soft sighs of happy reciprocity; the ringing slap of palm and the brisk crack of knuckles shadowed the train's passage through the night."[109] As if the metaphor of the train as a centre of illicit sexuality were not enough, Dundas adds, "In the sleeping farmsteads along the railway's right of way mothers soothed and calmed awakened children and said, 'Go to sleep, sweetie, it's just the Moonlight going by.'"[110] Darkness, with its implicit link to the night, has traditionally been conceptualized as an area for transgression: "The night time has been the right time, a fleeting but regular period of modest but cherished freedoms from the constraints and cares of daily life."[111] It was the potential for this role, this flexibility, that helped make the late-night Moonlight trips back to Winnipeg so enticing for the youthful passengers.

Dundas's portrayal of the Moonlight journey replicates standard expectations of sexual roles, with the male as pursuer and the female as defender of virtue.[112] It also offers a spatial analysis of the return journey: "The Oak Bluff whistle warned the young men there was only another twenty miles left for sweet talk and gentle persuasion, and their young ladies to dig in anew at this threat of a new ambush.... The Transcona warning wail gave them their last chance to try something they hadn't thought of since Ponemah or Balsam Bay, and their girlfriends, by now feeling it was safe enough, to let [the men] cop a miniscule feel, so they wouldn't feel too let down from their hopes of the earlier evening, and to ensure a date for next Saturday."[113] Dundas is tapping into a familiar theme here, suggesting women used their sexuality to ensure that their date would foot the bill for the outing. The question of how far women would go to earn their night out was one that ensured the surveillance of moral reformers at the beginning of the twentieth century.[114] Dundas goes on to describe "weary and dishevelled" youth finally leaving the trains and catching a ride home on the streetcars.

The clamour of the returning Moonlight train, like the arrival of the commuting daddies, was part of life in Winnipeg in the early part of the century. In 1967, Jocelyn Square wrote an article for the *Winnipeg Free Press* detailing her childhood in the Royal Alexandra from 1923 to 1928, during "the years of the Roaring Twenties. And the old Royal Alex did roar in those days.... Each Sunday from May 24 until after Labor Day, I was usually awakened around 1 a.m. by the opening of the great wrought iron gates on the Main Street side of the hotel. A great surge of people, all laughing and talking, pushing their way down the incline from the station platform heralded the return of the weekly Moonlight train to Winnipeg Beach."[115] Despite his colourful description of the trip, Dundas pulls back at the end of his tale to say, "I don't think anyone ever made the 'supreme sacrifice' on the Moonlights.... Virginity was pretty highly thought of in those days, and premarital trial runs being more the exception rather than the rule."[116] In the end, even Dundas cannot resist regulating sexual behaviour. In fairness, his recollections of the 1920s are seen through the lens of the 1970s, when his book was published. The rarity of sexual activity in the past has been exaggerated, but the openness that Dundas sees in the present seems to prompt him to recoil from the contemporary world, as he sees it, and to insist on the greater virtues of an earlier age.

Dundas is mythologizing the Moonlight experience. His description of events on the train fits neatly into the script of how men and women were expected to behave: men were to be initiators of sexual activity, women the moderators and regulators of such activities. And at the end of the ride, the men were expected to listen when the women said "enough."[117] Although far less graphic, other male descriptions of the Moonlight trains follow a similar pattern. These rules of behaviour encouraged both men and women to create private space under the cover of darkness, where, it was assumed, they could push the limits of acceptable behaviour. Of course, those opportunities also created fear about what the young travellers might be up to.[118]

In a series of letters, Helen Sigurdur, Dorothy Lynch, and Agnes Walker recalled journeying to the beach on the Moonlight train in the 1930s and 1940s, often to meet dates or a boyfriend.[119] Lynch's recollections make it clear that she was travelling to Winnipeg Beach with female friends, with the goal of meeting men. "We would be back in Winnipeg by midnight, on a coal-fired train. How our mother[s] worried about their young, innocent daughters, arriving home early Sunday morning, having been out with boys unknown to them. They waited up for us, listening to the wireless radio, or pacing the floor," she recalled.[120] In contrast, Val Kinack, a summer camper,

Stovel and Co. brought its workers to Winnipeg Beach for this picnic in 1906; kids were on hand but most of the participants were adult workers at the company.

can remember dates travelling on the train to meet her in the 1940s.[121] Orest travelled on the Moonlight special to Winnipeg Beach in 1956, its final year. But the routine was much the same as it had been twenty or thirty years earlier. "Winnipeg Beach was summer time. A chance to get out of Winnipeg, it was something different," Orest said.[122] He travelled with a friend or two and the goal was simple—have a good time and, he hoped, meet a girl. We can look to these groups and note the flexibility and protection that train travel gave them. "If you were nineteen years of age, you didn't go out with your date. So you'd go out with your girlfriends," Myrna Charach recalled. "The girls would go up, four or five girls out together to be at somebody's cottage and naturally the guys would come up separate. They'd get together there. But you never came out…. You told your mother you were going with your girlfriends. [Laughs.]"[123] Barney Charach remembered these unisex groups descending from the train. In this they were following the pattern of behaviour seen at other recreation facilities, with people arriving with members of their own gender, but fully expecting to couple up after they had arrived.[124]

Of course, not everyone headed to the beach in same-sex groups. Izzy and Mary Peltz travelled to Winnipeg Beach with a group of friends, before they were married.[125] The group of friends offered the same protection that the same-sex groups did. Certainly in the early years of the Winnipeg Beach experience, the safety of the group would have been necessary. Concerns about white slavery in North America had led to the creation of laws such as the United States' 1910 Mann Act, which ostensibly was created to prohibit "interstate traffic in women" but was often used to harass and detain unmarried couples travelling together.[126] The Mann Act did not apply in Canada, but it suggests the atmosphere that people had to operate within during the first years of the twentieth century. There were CPR officials aboard to ensure proper behaviour on the Moonlight train rides, but as Dundas and even some of the interview subjects discovered, they were prepared to leave the passengers to their own devices on the trip home.

The evening began when passengers stepped on the train and men and women flirted back and forth: "The good looking guys and the good looking chicks hit it off pretty fast and the normal looking guys had to kind of see what they could find," Orest recalled. Ina Drummond had only a limited experience with the Moonlight train, heading to Winnipeg Beach as a teenager a few times to join her family. But even then she could see that people began flirting the moment they stepped on the train, rather than waiting until their arrival at the dance hall.[127]

In many ways the experience of travelling on the Moonlight special has taken on the role of a regional myth: a complex of symbols and images embedded in a larger narrative with predictable rhythms.[128] That role does not make the experience any less real. But it does mean that individual recollections of the trip are likely to tap a familiar list of experiences. For example, many interview subjects remember the lights being turned off, but they never claim to have turned the lights out themselves. Orest remembered the lights being extinguished as a regular part of travelling on the Moonlight special. "The CP cops and the conductors would just go crazy because they wanted the lights to be seen as the train was going by, otherwise if it's dark they could get into trouble," Orest recalled. And why did people put the lights out? "To neck. [Laughs.] Or smooch or whatever you want to call it," he replied.[129]

Izzy Peltz recalled similar incidents in the late 1930s when he and Mary travelled to Winnipeg Beach. The couple headed up with friends, all of them young and dating. And as with Orest, his story, too, contained a reference to the lights being extinguished on the trip home. "Most of the guys got into a corner and were smooching. [Laughter.] Because they were all still single dates. Some of them would go and turn the lights off on the train," Peltz said.[130] We should not miss the laugh that comes with both these admissions—fifty to seventy years later, Orest and Peltz are still of the view that people were being just a little bit naughty on the train ride home. Turning the lights off created a symbolic—and very real—moment of freedom.

Victor Martin worked as a fireman on the Moonlight special on several trips. While he did not have to deal with it directly, he certainly heard stories of what people were doing in the coaches: "I know a few times some of the conductors were frustrated because [the passengers] were always turning the lights out in the coaches and in the end they would give up. [Laughs.] You know, I mean I'm talking people our age, that were supposed to be the wild ones in those days, water fights, cinders coming, people would get them in the eye, people always hanging out the windows, you couldn't stop them, but trains in those days were the mode of travel and nobody paid any attention to that stuff. It was the only way you travelled and you did what you wanted or tried to get away with as much as you wanted," Martin recalled.[131]

Nestor Mudry performed in a band at the Dance Palace, Winnipeg Beach's signature dance hall, in the summer of 1941, but he made a few Moonlight trips to the dance hall with friends on his own time: "I remember going [on] the Moonlight coming back, and here's all these guys necking with their girlfriends and turning off the lights and the poor trainmen, these guys are turning off the light and the poor trainmen were trying to put on the lights. A lot of them, they weren't electrical lights, they were gas lights. Anyway, that was kind of amusing," Mudry recalled. "They were doing their romancing and they preferred it to be dark." But Mudry was careful to clarify that people limited their activity. "In those days they didn't carry the love making quite that far, it was pretty tame compared to today's standards," Mudry said. What could they do? "Just smooching was all. There was no love making, not in those days. That was a no no."[132]

As Dundas suggested, there was a point beyond which people were not allowed to go, although there was speculation that some did break the conventions. Some of the trains had been used to transport immigrants into Western Canada prior to being put on the Moonlight line and came with bunk beds that could be dropped down for a snooze. Dr. Paul Adams said there were always rumours that bunk beds were put to use as spots for love making.[133]

Not all recollections of the Moonlight special are quite as exciting. "I remember taking the ride back when my girlfriend and I took the Moonlight.

It was very quiet. People were tired after the weekend or couple of days there," Jessica recalled. "Did couples have a chance to be together alone on the train? They might have had a chance to be alone on a seat but there were always people around them."[134] Val Kinack expressed similar scepticism as to what couples could do together on the train: "I sincerely don't believe couples ever had a chance to be alone on that train. That train was so packed. I mean they were not.... They didn't have the sexual freedom that they have today. I don't honest to Godly know for sure; but I sincerely doubt that anybody would have thought of something like that."[135] Myrna Charach voiced similar views on what women would have been able to do:

> See on the train would have been parents and even if you were a couple you wouldn't want to demonstrate it in front of.... You have to remember that in those days, and I'm a heck of a lot younger, I can just begin to imagine what it was like with the girls. The girls didn't have the freedom. There was no birth control. There was nothing. Girls were not running around. So it was heavy petting and kissing and all of that. There was always the girls that you knew were loose. But that was no different in 1960, it was no different in 1950 and it was no different in 1940. Girls didn't have the freedom that the girls have today. You know?[136]

It would be easy to argue that the recollections of the Moonlight train follow the expected gender patterns, with men recalling the chase and women recalling the limits. There is an element of that. However, there is not a simple division along the gender line. Dorothy Garbutt wrote a column in 1961 for the *Winnipeg Free Press* recalling her experiences at Winnipeg Beach in the summer of 1919. As in Peltz's story, Garbutt's recollection included a reference to groups of young people taking excursions to Winnipeg Beach. And, as in some of the other stories, when they begin the return journey on the Moonlight special, "for some mysterious reason, none of the group you came with was able to find seats together and so you paired off, apart from the others, and if a little ... well, it was the Moonlight, wasn't it?"[137]

The *Winnipeg Free Press* and *Lethbridge Herald* tell us that, at the very least, the lights did go out on the Moonlight special. In a 1946 article headlined "Putting out Train Lights Brings Fine for 2 Youths," the *Free Press* quoted Magistrate D.G. Potter stating that "Young people making a nuisance of themselves on Moonlight Specials from Winnipeg Beach will be fined the maximum penalty in the future." In this case, Winnipeg youths George Burke and John Kupskay received a ten-dollar fine for turning out the lights.[138] Potter was even crankier in August that same year when he laid down a fine of twenty dollars for turning off the Moonlight lights and threatened to increase it to forty the next time someone came into his court on the charge. The *Lethbridge Herald* carried the story through the news wire under the headline "Warns Romeos"—an interesting turn of phrase given the difficulty Romeo and Juliet had in getting together. The article noted that "Romeos who turn off coach lights, thereby providing themselves with a better atmosphere for their pursuits, will be dealt with more severely in future, Magistrate D.G. Potter warned."[139] In 1950, the same sorts of charges showed up in juvenile court, although the language surrounding them was less sympathetic. The *Free Press* article entitled "Young Hooligans on Beach Trains Get Warning" noted, "Young people who create disturbances on moonlight and special beach trains were given a warning by Judge Emerson J. Heaney in juvenile court Thursday. Judge Heaney fined one youth $25 and costs for turning out lights on a moonlight train coming to Winnipeg from Winnipeg Beach over the week-end. Juvenile court authorities and Canadian Pacific railway police said the fines would be continued if more hooliganism occurred on the beach trains."[140]

The news articles, and in particular the "Warns Romeos" article in the *Lethbridge Herald*, neatly follow the script laid down by male interview subjects and Dundas, with men being charged for seeking darkness in which to create "a better atmosphere for their pursuits"—the pursuits being women, of course. Men and women did seek out dark spaces on the Moonlight trains, whether by turning out the lights or snuggling up in a seat. What they did under the cover of darkness is a matter of speculation. Did they look at the stars rolling by, as Susan remembers; doze quietly, as Jessica remembers; smooch, as Orest remembers; or pull a muscle in the throes of passion, as Dundas writes?[141] In the end, the tally of acts is less important than the pattern demonstrated. We can see the standard scripts of behaviour in descriptions of the Moonlight train, with men as aggressors and women called upon to be a moderating influence. The train was a space in which the rules could be challenged and renegotiated, not only on the rare occasions when the lights went out, but also when they stayed on and couples leaned back into their seats to steal a kiss, hold hands, or let their heads rest on each other's shoulders.

But when the lights flickered out on the Moonlight special, was it only men and women getting together? David B., interviewed for the Gay and Lesbian Oral History Project in 1990, recalled travelling to Winnipeg Beach with his father on the Moonlight special to meet his mother, who was already staying down at the beach. "That was the thing to do in those days," David B. recalled. "I can remember getting up, going through the train to see if there was people I could talk to. I met one young man, and I didn't realize at that point that that was what I was doing, but I felt very attracted to him."[142] We can look to David B.'s experience and point out that in some ways the Moonlight special was a place where men and women could flirt back and forth, but that it also, much like the Daddy's train, would have been filled with men heading to the beach to meet dates, girlfriends, and wives, or perhaps even male friends. It is tempting to push David B.'s transgression of heterosexual space and imagine these two male strangers flirting on the Moonlight special and even imagining possibilities of their own for the evening, all while heterosexual activities went on around them. The train was available space. In her study on Niagara Falls, Karen Dubinsky describes two gay couples who managed to spot each other among the primarily heterosexual crowd on the train, and quickly became travelling companions.[143] However, on this particular Moonlight special, heterosexual space was not so easily transgressed. "Of course I didn't have any hope that anything sexual would come of it," David B. recalled. "I was just acting on instinct, I had a very strong feeling that I wanted to meet men. This was one of the things that was driving me."[144] This "instinct" played out in, and perhaps was remembered because of, the anticipation of the Moonlight special.

Whether it was a picnic train, Daddy's train, or Moonlight special, the trains all rolled into the Winnipeg Beach station. Long-time Winnipeg journalist Val Werier has argued that the trains provided the rhythm for Winnipeg Beach: "When the big steam locomotive shsshed and panted into the station it was alive with people. Meeting the train was part of beach life, seeing who was arriving or going."[145] The train station was the hub of the community and a window into the activities of Winnipeg Beach. The trains kept regular schedules, but if people had not checked their watches they would have been drawn to the station by the sound of the train. Jessica remembered the train whistle as a rallying cry: "We'd all go down to the train station because the Moonlight was coming in. Now the Moonlight

Young men and women coming to Winnipeg Beach spent their evening at the Dance Palace before catching the late-night train back to Winnipeg on the Moonlight Special.

was a very exciting time; even if you weren't expecting anyone, you would go down to watch the people coming off the Moonlight in case there was someone there you knew that you could go down to the pier with," Jessica recalled. "And all the men who came off the train were carrying sausages and breads and you could see all this food coming out of bags that they were bringing for the weekend. Plus, I'm sure, a couple of bottles at the bottom."[146] An interview subject who self-identified as a retired CNR employee stayed at the beach as a youth in the 1950s and would bike down to meet the train: "It was very exciting with the people; it was like they almost couldn't wait to get off the train, and a lot of fun was going to happen during the weekend."[147]

The train station was a critical hub. When "Kid" took a vacation at Winnipeg Beach in 1908, she sent a string of postcards to Ethel McKnight in Winnipeg to send greetings, make requests, and query when McKnight might be coming up. In a postcard dated 25 August 1908, Kid noted, "Missed you Saturday. Had a great time yesterday. My nose is peeling today. Only three Moonlights this week Tuesday, Thursday and Saturday. We'll meet them all. Hope you will come."[148] With the postcards communication was only one way. So Kid would make a regular stroll down to the train station to see if anyone she knew had come up. Sometimes a meeting might occur, other times they would miss each other in the crowd.

Trains were greeted by a swarm of children eager to do everything from hauling luggage to buying and selling tickets. Lawrence Isfeld said it was the train station where he and other Winnipeg Beach kids cut their teeth in business. "When I was a kid, eleven or twelve, we would run down to the station and grab the *Free Press*," he recalled.[149] They could buy a paper for a nickel and then sell it on the beach or at the entrance to the beer parlour for a dime or a quarter. Isfeld would not be alone when he rushed to the train station. "There would be another ten kids with the same idea and then you would run as fast as you could to the beach [to sell the papers]." The work was not limited to people who were locals. Children on vacation joined in. Barry Anderson and Barney Charach, who were both campers, flipped stubs for a profit.[150] The stubs were the second half of a fifty-cent Moonlight return ticket. The Moonlight tickets were generally sold at fifty cents for a return trip, under the assumption that people would head up for a few hours of entertainment and then return to Winnipeg that same night. But often, people would buy a ticket for the Moonlight train with plans to spend the weekend. In that case, they could sell the stub from their ticket to a young middleman who would then go on to sell it to someone planning to return to Winnipeg that night. M.W. Bennett, the Winnipeg Beach station agent between 1927 and 1950, recalled in 1964, "This was illegal, of course, and we tried to stop it at every opportunity. But there were hundreds of people on the platform for arrivals and departures—why, some people would even try to sell me a stub while I'd be talking over schedules with the train conductor."[151] At times the CPR pressed charges against people, but more often the company appears to have looked the other way.[152] It was a competitive business, and to get an edge people like Charach would head up the tracks to beat the crowds: "We would either hitchhike or walk to Ponemah, jump on the train when the conductor wasn't looking and then go up and down the train yelling, 'Does anybody got any stubs for sale?' and people who weren't returning that night would say, 'Yes, I'm not going back tonight.' So we'd give them fifteen or twenty cents for the stub and sell it for a quarter or thirty cents."[153] The hubbub was a natural part of relying on the train for transportation; across the lake at Grand Beach the story was much the same, with children hustling luggage around the train station.[154]

Val Kinack could recall racing down to meet the train as a child. Sometimes she would buy a stub for a grown-up who was planning to catch the train back to Winnipeg, but more often than not she was just there to be part of the excitement: "Omigosh, we were all down at the station. We were so close we could hear it tooting down at Netley. So we'd all run down to the train, just to see who was on it. Oh yeah, everybody loved the train. We'd stand and wait until it chugged past." As she got older, the train station was a place to meet dates. It was even where she met her husband for the first time, although not as the usual romantic script would have it: "I went down to meet someone else that was coming out for the evening for a date. And my husband was a friend of … my girlfriend's boyfriend and they had just bought a new car. He just bought a new Cadillac and they said, 'Oh, do you want to go for a ride?' … I looked over and I thought, 'Oh my God, I'm supposed to meet this guy.' I looked at this Cadillac and I said, 'Sure, let's go for a ride.' So they drove us all the way to Nick's out here in Headingley. So that was the whole evening shot. But there were a lot of romances broken up that way. You'd meet someone else and toss the other one over. And that's how I met my husband."[155] Kinack's casual dismissal of her would-be date also speaks to the dating culture that evolved around Winnipeg Beach. As she noted, she and her friends always travelled in groups when they toured the boardwalk and dance hall. No doubt her date was part of a group and went on to the dance hall and found some new dance partners of his own.

Kinack's car ride to Winnipeg reminds us that while the CPR might have created Winnipeg Beach, it was not able to maintain its monopoly on the resort's travel links. Discussions about completing a provincial road to Winnipeg Beach were taking place as early as 1909, and by 1910 the first cars had started to make the journey to the beach.[156] There is something of the explorer in these early trips, with drivers ferreting out the best routes and then sharing their experiences in the *Free Press*. Manitoba's drivers did not wait for roads to open, they actively promoted auto travel. In 1914 the Manitoba Motor League awarded Sadie Grim a gold medal for reaching Winnipeg Beach via motorbike, an act that proves the CPR's monopoly on travel to Winnipeg Beach was challenged early and actively by promoters of motorized transport, and that women like Grim were part of the effort.[157] In 1925, seventeen trains made the trip to the beach for the July 1 holiday, but while it was estimated that 14,747 people came to the beach by train, including 2,000 people on three Moonlight excursions, an additional 20,000 people were believed to have come in an estimated 3,700 automobiles.[158] For drivers in 1925, the long weekend probably warranted a special trip. But by 1938 a full-page advertisement in the *Free Press* for Winnipeg Beach

WINNIPEG BEACH.

A crush of people meet the CPR train in 1915; the expanded station had far more room than the CPR's original beachfront location.

used roads and cars to illustrate how people should reach the resort.[159] Winnipeg Beach benefitted from having one of the first provincial highways. Pictures from the 1920s and 1930s show that plenty of people were reaching Winnipeg Beach by car. But the period after World War II was the tipping point for car use: in 1941 less than half of Canada's suburb-dwelling residents owned cars, but by 1961 a large majority of them did.[160]

The car opened new landscapes for exploration, and ones that did not require a dedicated rail line to reach. Giving people the option of a seamless journey from home to destination point, the car changed what people expected out of transportation. Schedules were no longer acceptable when drivers could set the schedule themselves.[161] This competition was felt acutely at Winnipeg Beach, with other government-sponsored provincial parks—complete with new highway links—rightly blamed for cutting into the crowds.[162] The car also changed the social aspect of travel. When Nestor Mudry travelled on the train as a child, his parents required him to stick with the family. But even then, he could still take in the events happening around him, experience the crowd, or buy refreshments for the trip.[163]

For some children, the train let them shed their parents for a trip to Winnipeg Beach. In 1944, for example, seven-year-old Irene and four-year-old Billy Feasey trooped out from their Elmwood-area home and caught a Sunday morning train to the beach. Their disappearance set off a panic among their parents and police, but the children spent the day at the beach blissfully unaware of what was happening at home and caught an evening train back to Winnipeg. On neither trip were they asked for tickets, reflecting the fact that the CPR was not interested in children as a market.[164] (A precocious child, Irene tried to stow away on the SS *Keenora* as well.) But the ease with which they could make the trip shows the power of public transportation. In contrast, the automobile created "the family pack," with families able to travel independently and within their limited social group.[165] People travelling in vehicles found their own ways to add interest to the trip, and Selkirk no doubt benefitted from the number of people who stopped in for an ice cream or other treats on the way to Winnipeg Beach. The automobile, in other words, atomized the travel experience, disrupting the collective social space that had existed on the trains, including the Moonlight experience and the myth making that had gone along with it.

Yet the train maintained a tenacious hold on the imagination of Winnipeg Beach. In 1942 there were still 11,000 people taking the train to Winnipeg Beach on a busy weekend, and in 1943, when a busy war-time schedule forced the CPR to cut back to one Moonlight special on the weekend, it still expected to sell at least 1,600 tickets for the trip.[166] The train continued to be a focal point for the crowd at Winnipeg Beach into the early 1950s, even though the majority of people would have been coming to Winnipeg Beach via car. And while Val Kinack's family typically travelled to Winnipeg Beach by car in the 1940s, it was still the train station where she met a date and to the train station that her friends came when they wanted to find her. Even for the people who were not riding it, the train was a physical presence in the community. Given that Winnipeg Beach's target market was the adult male, and that the Moonlight special was intimately tied to the heterosexual experience at Winnipeg Beach, that physical presence was a masculine one. This aspect has not been missed by other people considering their experiences at Winnipeg Beach. In 1965, Christopher Dafoe, grandson of the *Free Press*'s John Dafoe—who had made one of the first trips to Winnipeg Beach during a press junket in 1902—recalled spending his teen years at Winnipeg Beach in a fruitless quest for the heterosexual experience. Not surprisingly, he concludes his failure to find female companionship with the departure of the train: "At midnight, as The Moonlight panted out

Group Winnipeg Beach   *Sept 1926*

*The car was a popular option for getting to Winnipeg Beach by the 1920s. Here the
McDonald family arrives for their stay at the resort.*

of town, we always made our way back to Ponemah Beach wondering what
it had all been for."[167] The image of a spent Moonlight train pulling out of
town in tandem with the disappointed males is an almost irresistible one.

Orest was taking the Moonlight train to Winnipeg Beach in the 1950s.
For him, riding the train was shorthand for the entire experience, which
is why when the train had stopped running and the amusement area had
been removed, the community had no resonance for him. "During the '70s
and '80s, I used to go to Winnipeg Beach, my sister's got a cottage there, but
that was just for Saturday for supper and then head back. I never stayed.
Just to do some visiting. I would never go into town at Winnipeg Beach,"
Orest said. "But the train ride, the Moonlight, yes."[168]

Chapter Two
Staying at the Beach
TOURISM INFRASTRUCTURE

This study of Winnipeg Beach touches on three different systems of court-ship, and the transition between these systems shows itself clearly within the recreation infrastructure. The resort's roots in middle-class Winnipeg society are tracked in social columns, which provide extensive details on who was staying at the resort and how successful private parties were. In this period, which lasted roughly until 1915, there are traces of the calling system of courtship being played out in the gatherings and meetings at the beach. The Daddy's train aided in all of this by helping men of Winnipeg society establish their families at the resort. While a dance hall was there from the beginning, much of the socializing in this early period at Winnipeg Beach would have been taking place in the parlours and verandas of private cabins. But as the approach to courting shifted from calling to dating, Winnipeg Beach transformed as well. However, we have to be careful not to see the boundaries between these different approaches to courting as being concrete; people still courted in private settings after 1915, but the rise of public opportunities for being together was clear.

The beach's location near nature made it an attractive haven from the stresses of the city, but its position as a liminal point between land and sea also gave it a particular allure as a place for men and women to meet. Winnipeg Beach became an industrial saturnalia for working-class men and women. With crowds growing to 40,000 on a busy weekend, an elaborate tourism infrastructure evolved to house, feed, and entertain the people coming to the beach. The train allowed men and women to travel to the beach in same-sex groups, and the wide range of accommodations

Swimming pool in the Tourist Park, 1927. The natural setting helped draw people to Winnipeg Beach.

allowed them to maintain that respectability during their stay at the lake. The close relationship with the proprietors ensured a certain moral code would be observed, while the wide range of private spaces gave opportunities to transgress those boundaries. The tourism infrastructure's role in housing young singles was breaking down by the 1950s, as competition drew people elsewhere and those who had made a living renting rooms quit the business. Winnipeg Beach's history contains hints of the more sexually permissive system of courting that has been tied to the cultural changes of the 1950s and 1960s, but by that time most of the crowds had moved on.

The CPR again plays a role in tourism infrastructure. The company was in business to make money by moving people. Its motives were not merely to build a community at Winnipeg Beach but also to ensure that as many people as possible could go to the beach. In Winnipeg's ethnically diverse community, that meant that being able to purchase a ticket or rent a cabin trumped ethnic bias. The tourism infrastructure is where Winnipeg Beach's ethnic relations stand out in high relief. The resort was a meeting place—or boundary zone—for Winnipeg's cultural mosaic. Indeed, restrictions at the other resorts around Lake Winnipeg ensured that it would be. But the pot melted uneasily, and while people seemed to set aside their ethnic differences when they promenaded in public on the boardwalk—or frolicked in "the people's playground," as Winnipeg Beach was called—tensions simmered when they returned to the private space of the tourism accommodations.[1]

After it bought its lakefront property in 1901, the CPR made a conscious decision to lease the land for cottage lots rather than sell the property. The goal was to keep speculators from snapping up the property and then sitting on it, hoping to turn a profit.[2] That was a legitimate concern, given the speculative boom in land prices occurring across Western Canada at the time, and a concern that was proven to be valid when word went out in 1905 that the Canadian Pacific line would be extended to Gimli: almost immediately some 200 lots in Gimli were snapped up by speculators.[3] Given that the CPR made its profit from moving people to the beach, it had no use for land that was sitting undeveloped. The Winnipeg Beach lots could be leased for a term of twenty years at a rental rate of five dollars per year, and people could purchase the cottages on their lots.[4] The company's approach ensured that the core of Winnipeg Beach was made up of leased property. That was in contrast to the property around Winnipeg Beach, including Boundary Park, Beach Grove, Ponemah, Whytewold, Matlock, and later Sandy Hook, which was sold outright.[5]

The Village of Winnipeg Beach was incorporated in 1910, pulling territory from the rural municipalities of Gimli and St. Andrew's.[6] The village limits reflected the CPR's original land purchase, which included the cabin area south of Boundary Park and the downtown area.[7] During its first election in 1910, permanent residents were already outnumbered by cabin owners, which illustrates how much Winnipeg Beach was a resort town.[8] The lack of permanent residents in Winnipeg Beach led to a change in provincial law that allowed people to vote in a community based on property ownership or—and this is where the CPR's system of lease agreements no doubt played a role—a leasehold property, rather than simply tenancy.[9] The village became a town in 1914, and the limits were extended north in 1921 towards Sandy Hook, south in 1923 to Stephenson's Point, and west in the 1950s to include the West Beach area.[10] The large number of cabin areas drawn into the community ensured that, with the exception of the first few years, Winnipeg Beach's council was under the control of cabin owners rather than residents. That political reality created a degree of resentment between residents, including local business owners, and cabin owners. The divide was still alive and noted by provincial officials in the late 1960s when the province was taking over the former boardwalk amusement area.[11]

Winnipeg Beach was the focal point for recreation on the west side of Lake Winnipeg for much of the twentieth century, providing entertainment for Matlock, Ponemah, and Whytewold to the south, and Gimli to the north. Residents of the southern cottage areas also received free train service from their cottages to the beach—the rationale being that the CPR won back its fares through the money spent at the recreation facilities.[12]

When the CPR established Winnipeg Beach, the town joined a long tradition of seaside resorts. As Brighton was the "lungs" of London, so the CPR hoped that Winnipeg Beach would be the lungs of Winnipeg.[13] This discourse had a particularly Canadian interpretation, one that saw racial, moral, and social degeneration as linked to the city, and the country as a healthy, pure alternative. Canadian moral reformers went further to link their efforts to Canadian nationalism, arguing that Canada was particularly suited to lead the world due to its pure northern climate.[14] The undertone to this argument makes it clear that when people spoke of leading the world it was assumed that it should be British Canadians doing the leading.[15] The idea of the country as cure for the evils of city life can be clearly seen at work in Winnipeg Beach. As one promotional piece for Winnipeg Beach noted in 1919, "Transplanting children in the summer from town to the beaches is like transplanting little plants from the hotbed to the fresh and strengthening soil of the garden. It is the summer days spent in pure outdoor air that make children sturdy and big and strong and no air is purer than that which blows over the great waterways of Canada."[16] Similarly, when lots for Sandy Hook were being sold in 1912, the advertisements argued that "every right-living man wants to take his family out to the lake shore for the hot weather; every mother wants her babies to get tanned, strong and healthy from playing in the sand that is washed by the sparkling water of Canada's greatest lake. That is what Sandy Hook offers. It offers you this within easy daily reach of the city, with desirable neighbours—and desirable neighbours only. The title deeds to Happiness go with every cottage in Sandy Hook."[17]

Sandy Hook's environment was beneficial due to its rural location, bunched up against the natural in the form of Lake Winnipeg. It was the duty of responsible fathers and nurturing mothers to ensure that their children had access to this environment. This sort of discourse depicted Winnipeg Beach as an ideal home for a range of summer camps aimed at children, women (through the Young Women's Christian Association), and recovering World War I veterans (through the Red Cross Hospital).[18]

During World War II the Winnipeg Beach Cadet camp was opened to provide cadets with two weeks of exposure to the beach after which they could return to Winnipeg "bronzed and healthy."[19] The summer camps also appealed to ethnic groups in the province because they were able to draw the community together. Growing up in a rural community, Myrna Charach recalled that one of the primary reasons her parents sent her to the B'nai Brith camp north of Winnipeg Beach was so that she could meet other Jewish kids.[20] The camps helped ethnic communities maintain the web of relationships that held them together. But children also found a way to turn their stay into an opportunity to mingle with other ethnic groups; Barney Charach could recall spending time at the same B'nai Brith summer camp, but he took the opportunity to sneak out when he could and tour the sights and sounds of Winnipeg Beach.

This equation of health with the beach was not limited to the turn of the century. Val Kinack can remember being sent to Winnipeg Beach in the 1930s and 1940s in an effort to get her away from the polio threat in Winnipeg. "They couldn't get the kids out of the city fast enough," Kinack recalled. "We had some terrible epidemics in the city. They closed everything. They closed the theatres, they closed the movie houses. They closed swimming pools. There was nothing open. Nothing."[21] Even after the polio scare was over, Kinack said the idea of summer equating to beach equating to health was still deeply ingrained in people. In her case, the trip to the pure environment of the beach did not help. She was afflicted with polio when she was seventeen years old, and it caused some damage to one of her legs. Kinack's infection came in 1946, the beginning of another spike in incidences of the disease in Manitoba.[22]

The first decades of the twentieth century marked a movement in courtship from calling, where courtship took place within the home or other controlled social settings, to dating, where couples courted in public.[23] Winnipeg Beach thrived as a location for young men and women out on a date, but its roots were in the calling regime. As Jim Blanchard has noted in *Winnipeg 1912*, the society columns in Winnipeg's newspapers tracked the activities of the middle-class campers with the same precision it used to report their Winnipeg activities, neatly transferring social structures and hierarchy to the beach.[24] The social columns noted the location of society's eligible singles, providing a useful tool for bachelors looking to call on young women at the beach.[25]

The Tourist Park, 1927. For many people, tenting was the way to go at Winnipeg Beach.

We can expand our notion of calling to understand that what it really entailed was courting within controlled social groups, and it is in this light that the picnics and house parties at Winnipeg Beach tell us that Winnipeg's genteel middle class and its various ethnic communities were using the beach as a place to meet.[26] In 1904, for example, "the sergeants of the 90th regiment were entertained to a trip to Winnipeg Beach on Saturday evening by Sergeant Major and Mrs. Morley. A private car was attached to the train which left for the beach, for the accommodation of the soldiers, and after a very pleasant trip down, a good time was spent with music and dancing. In spite of the weather, which was threatening."[27] In 1905 the "Rough House Boys," Dan, Little Dan, Spike, Shine, Reuben, Billy, and Leeflets hosted seventy-five guests at their cottage, which was named Grovenonk. The *Free Press* announced that their "at home was a great success" and listed some of the guests in attendance. While not complete, the names that are on the list tell us that these house parties were social mixers—the guests listed included just four married women, but some twenty-three single women.[28] Ideally, for the male suitors an invitation to visit the house of some of these female cottage guests would have followed the "at home."[29] Similarly, when Privates Lechly, Phillip, James, McDonald, and Hunt, members of the 43rd Battalion, spent three days' leave at the Pinniwig Cottage in Winnipeg Beach (the home of Mr. Baxter) during the middle part of May in 1915, their visit was "brought to a close by a social evening and dance."[30] In Winnipeg these large gatherings would have taken place in the parlour of the house, but at Winnipeg Beach the parlour was replaced by the veranda.

As the *Free Press* noted in 1906, "Every train now brings a party of cottagers and the summer homes all over the beach are decked with flags and other decorations. Verandahs are the scenes of very lively parties as everyone eats out of door, particularly those cottagers who overlook the lake."[31] And to round out these experiences, a 1910 article sized up the weekend social landscape by noting that "several house parties have been arranged and scarcely a cottage is without guests. Many prominent Winnipeg business men, with their families, are already settled here for the summer. The refreshing lake breezes and the delightful scenery of this natural garden spot and the perfect beach are enough to make any visitor feel glad he came."[32] As I have mentioned, those expansive summer homes wore British flags to illustrate the status of the homeowners and to stamp the resort as British terrain.

As an example of what an upper-middle-class cabin would have been like, we have the *Manitoba Free Press*'s description of Winnipeg alderman Henry Sandison's cottage in Whytewold, which was built in 1905, as "A Pretty Summer Home"; the article goes on to say, "The main feature of the structure is the living room, which is 18 feet wide and 16 feet long…. The end of the living room towards the verandah is constructed with folding door so that when the weather is favourable the room and verandah can be made into a room 40 feet long, all screened in. The floor of the room and verandah are level, so that it can be utilized for dancing when required for that purpose."[33] We can see that these summer homes had a far broader role than simply putting a roof over a person's head.

The CPR had a dance hall at Winnipeg Beach almost from day one, and it functioned as a "rendezvous point for the campers and their friends."[34] The beach, of course, attracted crowds to take in the regattas and various events. But the elaborate leisure zone that would evolve at the beach did not exist before World War I. In 1906 there was a merry-go-round there, but it was primarily used by children.[35] The lavish bar of the Empress Hotel would have provided a meeting place for men, but likely men only: the presence of women within the bar would have been frowned upon.[36] So, for many people travelling to Winnipeg Beach during this period, stepping out for an evening's entertainment meant stepping into a social gathering held in a cottage.

Winnipeg Beach was integrated into Winnipeg's middle-class land-scape. The phrase "desirable neighbours only" that turned up in the Sandy Hook advertisement reminds us that the resort was also integrated into Winnipeg's ethnic landscape. Implicit in this phrase is the notion that people buying property in Sandy Hook were being vetted. Sandy Hook marketers were even clearer in a *Winnipeg Tribune* advertisement that read "Your home in Sandy Hook is protected by restrictions that will perma-nently ensure its freedom from undesirable associations."[37] The "undesirable associations" would have been other ethnic groups, and the goal would have been to keep the Sandy Hook area a British enclave. Across the lake, the *Victoria Beach Herald* was explicit about who should be barred from buying property when a Jewish family expressed interest in purchasing a cottage in Victoria Beach in 1943. In an editorial, the newspaper wrote, "You have an obligation to your neighbours at Victoria Beach. Remember, you have an obligation to see to it that those unwanted people who have over-run beaches on the other side of Lake Winnipeg are not permitted to buy or rent here ... up until this year we have been able to keep our beach free of them, maintaining a rule, unwritten, but unanimously approved and observed for more than twenty-five years."[38]

In their article "Ethnicity, Religion, and Class Elements in the Evolution of Lake Winnipeg Resorts," John C. Lehr, H. John Selwood, and Eileen Badiuk have confirmed what the *Victoria Beach Herald* was stating, that Jewish people could access Winnipeg Beach but not Victoria Beach. The Winnipeg Beach and Victoria Beach electoral and tax rolls from 1981–82 (which reflect in part the effects of the original ethnic make-up of this area) show that the ethnic breakdown of cottage owners in Winnipeg Beach in the early 1980s included 11.5 percent Jewish ownership, 23.8 percent Slavic ownership, and 44.5 percent Anglo-Saxon ownership. Victoria Beach dur-ing the same period was composed of 70.2 percent Anglo-Saxon ownership, 8.8 percent Slavic ownership, and 6.8 per cent French ownership. Given that the majority of the French ownership was focused in neighbouring Albert Beach, the percentage of Anglo-Saxon owners in Victoria Beach proper would have been even higher than the 70.2 percent figure suggests.[39]

Lehr, Selwood, and Badiuk go further, tracking where cabin owners lived in Winnipeg to get a sense of the class dimensions of the cabin resorts. Their study relies on equating neighbourhood to wealth, a less than perfect approach that nevertheless provides at least a sense of the class base of the different resorts. Victoria Beach owners were focused in East Kildonan and North River Heights, suggesting they had upper-class status. In contrast, Winnipeg Beach owners were scattered across the city, suggesting that people from a wider range of classes used that resort. Ethnicity trumped class in pushing people towards Winnipeg Beach. "Exclusion from Victoria Beach pushed those Jews wishing to purchase a cottage on Lake Winnipeg shores, or anywhere else in Manitoba for that matter, toward the less discriminating environment of Winnipeg Beach."[40] The study cannot say what the degree of Jewish ownership or tenancy would have been in Winnipeg Beach during the heyday of the resort; instead, the figures drawn from 1981/82 represent an echo of the ethnic relationships that would have existed in the 1920s and 1930s.

But, as the Sandy Hook advertisement illustrates, the situation is even more complicated because Winnipeg Beach was not a homogeneous territory. Beach Grove, located west of the CPR's Winnipeg Beach property, told buyers in 1911 that they could "secure a lot in the new SELECT, RESTRICTED subdivision for Summer Cottagers and Judicious Investors" and went further to note that Beach Grove was "the only close-in and restricted subdivision on the market."[41] Adjacent Sandy Hook was also created with restrictions on ownership and advertised as an alternative to Winnipeg Beach. It meant that within and around Winnipeg Beach ethnic boundaries were maintained. Born in 1939 in Winnipeg Beach, Lawrence Isfeld could remember the downtown area being the focal point of the British residents, with the Icelandic and Ukrainian residents living to the west of the downtown. The Jewish cabin owners were limited to a space roughly between Ash Avenue and Boundary Park. "The Jewish people couldn't own north of Boundary Park," Isfeld recalled. "They were only allowed that one little pocket."[42] Izzy Peltz also remembered Boundary Park as the limit to where Jewish people could purchase cottages until roughly the 1950s.[43] It is not coincidental that this "pocket" includes the original CPR cabin territory. When it came to leasing property, the CPR was clearly more concerned with having willing renters and passengers than it was with ethnicity.

Estimates provided by interview subjects of the percentage of Jewish cottage owners or renters within this "pocket" before 1950 have ranged as high as 75 to 85 percent, making it truly an ethnic enclave.[44] The business opportunity of catering to this ethnic enclave was not lost on people setting up shop in Winnipeg Beach. As one example, Lillian Teel began operating the Park-A-While boarding house on Park Avenue in Winnipeg Beach in approximately 1927. At that time her sister was already operating a boarding house at the beach and tailoring her business to a specific market. As Teel recalled, "It was the heyday, my sister had a very big clientele, Jewish, very wealthy, hers was the 'Linger Longer.' She sent the overflow to me. She said, 'Lil, give them nice beds and good bedding.'"[45] Teel relied on word of mouth and return customers for her business rather than advertising. It was a practice that helped her be selective about whom she took in. "I didn't take gentiles in because I didn't want to mix the two together," Teel recalled. "The people with the money were the Jewish people and they were good, very good for the rooms and regulations of the house."[46] In that sense Teel's business fell directly within the Jewish community, but her own presence and that of her family ensured that the Jewish clients who were coming to Winnipeg Beach were also going to be exposed to the British community and potentially other ethnic groups. It is not surprising that Jewish people were a lucrative niche market, given that restrictions elsewhere pushed upper- and middle-class Jewish people to Winnipeg Beach—unlike wealthier British citizens, who could go elsewhere, such as Victoria Beach.

Lillian Teel and her sister were not the only ones tapping this ethnic market at the beach. Mildred Kelly remembered Winnipeg Beach drawing a wide range of ethnicities, enough to lend it a "colourful" atmosphere, but she could recall that the percentage of Jewish people stood out. It was a market her family did not miss when they were doing business: "There was more Jewish people. I imagine they were the ones that no one else would take in, that's why mother took them. They saved their pennies and nickels to come to the beach, best people in the world," Kelly recalled.[47]

While Teel and her sister courted an upper-class market, Ziporah and Pesach Torchinsky targeted working-class Jewish patrons. Interviewed in 1991, their daughter Doris Margolis recalled, "My father was well versed in Yiddish, capable, but never seemed to be able to make much of a living, so when my sister Shirley returned from a sojourn she decided that my mother should go into a business."[48] Shirley was thirteen years older than Doris and seems to have played the role of matriarch in the family. "So it was that in 1926 or 27 that my sister rented a large rambling cottage at Winnipeg Beach, filled with what ever dishes, pots and pans she could find. Duplicate dishes for everything, one for meat, one for dairy. Kosher law. Not easy at the beach without running water. The hope was that people who were observant

Winnipeg Beach's harbour. The building at the end of the harbour was the Red Cross Hospital for World War I veterans and later the resort's Aquatic Club, which at certain times was off limits to Jewish visitors.

would come flocking to our door," Margolis recalled.[49] The Torchinskys' clientele varied from factory girls out for a week's vacation to families.

Eventually, the Torchinskys were able to purchase their own cottage. It was called the White Rabbit Lodge and able to hold twenty guests. Not surprisingly, it was located on Spruce Avenue, within the ethnic enclave. Margolis recalls spending her youth and teen years at the resort every summer and being surrounded by people from her own ethnic group: "We were like in our own environment. We only had Jewish people in the cottage, only had contact with Jewish people in the neighbourhood." [50] They did do business with local Ukrainian farmers who supplied produce for the business, but here the fact that Ziporah Torchinsky could speak Ukrainian helped make the relationship run easier. "Around us were mainly Jewish people, we had no other contact, there was just the odd neighbour who wasn't Jewish, he'd smile and be friendly, but there was little contact."[51]

Other interview subjects also recalled little social contact between the different ethnic groups in the community.[52] In some cases that division was enforced. For example, the former Red Cross Hospital for war veterans became the home of the Aquatic Club in the 1930s but was not open to Jewish patrons; in this it followed a trend that included the Manitoba Club, the Winnipeg Winter Club, and other private clubs in Canada.[53] For

Lillian Teel, a member of the Aquatic Club, catering to a Jewish clientele while being part of the British community—in other words, existing in the boundary between groups—meant careful navigation between two sometimes competing interests. Teel's three boys spent their summers at the beach and grew up with the business's Jewish clients. As Teel recalled, "My boys would take some of the young Jewish people over [to the Aquatic Club] to swim, and I got wind of it. I'd say, 'Ross, why take Dick over there? You know it's against their rules. It'd be embarrassing if they came out and said something in front of Dick.' He said, 'Mother, I never gave it a thought.' 'Well,' I said, 'You had better. You had better.'"[54] Similarly, when she heard that some of her young Jewish house guests were throwing water on people washing outside the Lady of the Lake church, Teel was quick to lecture them: "I would tell them to have respect for that religion, even though it's not mine or yours." Teel was probably more aware than most of the ethnic boundaries in the community. And she knew that her three sons, bridging those boundaries, were often the peacemakers. "Many a time Garth would stop a fight [between the Jewish boys and] the locals, the locals knew him," Teel recalled. "He would say to me, 'Mother, I think this is awful, these boys can't walk down the street.'"[55]

Garth Teel served as a lifeguard at Winnipeg Beach from 1952 to 1954. Between that position and his home life at the Park-A-While, he had the distinction of dealing with most of the different ethnic communities in Winnipeg Beach. As he recalled when interviewed in 2008, they did not always get along. "The problem arose from the people who lived here permanently, called the locals: the Icelandic fellows and the Ukrainian fellows. I guess they banded together and took a great pleasure in harassing the Jewish kids. And quite often it would be fisticuffs, and gangs meeting at the park right at the end of our street," Garth Teel recalled.[56] Teel and fellow lifeguard Tom Evans would step in to break up these fights. "We were always the mediators," Garth Teel recalled. His own view was that there was a class aspect at work in the disputes: "See, you're talking about a fairly wealthy type of population, Jewish folks, that came down and spread a lot of money and the locals, majority were fisherman, some were in the milk delivery system, service, the majority were fishermen and it's a tough life, they didn't have the pleasures that these people coming down for the summer might have so there certainly was and still is [resentment]."[57] Of course not all the Jewish people who came to Winnipeg Beach were wealthy, but given that the Teels catered to a wealthier clientele, many of the people who stayed at the Park-A-While would have been.

Jack London spent the summers of his youth, in the late 1940s and early 1950s, at Winnipeg Beach, where his family ran the Playland Arcade and a series of other businesses. He was Jewish, but like Teel his position as a summer worker at the beach allowed him to bridge the gap between the various groups. His role as intermediary also meant that he felt the tensions between the groups clearly. Other residents like Margolis, who were embedded in their own communities, were able to more easily tune them out. Given that the fights Teel described were inevitably happening between groups of males, there is probably an element of territorial masculinity to the tensions between locals and Jewish campers. London, who was thoroughly in the boundary zone between ethnic groups, recalled, "We summered here but it was our place of business. I tended to associate or spend time with all of the groups at the beach. I felt privileged. I was accepted into all of the cultures, that was important later in my life." London continued, "I would spend time with each, as a mascot of the beach boys—local residents—and then socializing with the Jewish kids, which is my own culture, particularly on weekends, with parties, and at the tennis courts."[58] The tennis courts, unsurprisingly, were where the young residents at Lillian Teel's guest house also hung out.[59] London also believed the local beach kids, who spent their summers working, felt jealous of the Jewish kids who came out to play. It was a jealousy he found easier to understand given that he, like the local residents, was using Winnipeg Beach as a place of employment rather than a place of pleasure.

To a degree, ethnicity probably provided the language to express these frustrations, rather than being the actual reason for them. In *On Holiday: A History of Vacationing*, Orvar Lofgren sees similar conflicts playing out in Swedish vacation areas. Lacking the ethnic dynamics of Winnipeg Beach, Sweden's conflict seems to be entirely class based. The discourse linking resort areas with nature also plays a role; locals are described as closer to nature than the urban visitors, who come with a cultural taint.[60] This view dovetails with London's description of the "beach boys" relying on their physical prowess to defend their honour, and even with Christopher Dafoe's recollections in 1964 of the time when "the Dew Drop Boys, a band of roughnecks from Winnipeg, arrived in town looking for trouble and were put to bloody rout by a company of farmhands fresh from the

The Empress Hotel was renowned for its lavish bar in the early years of Winnipeg Beach; but prohibition would have shut that bar down in 1916.

muscle-building harvest fields."[61] Winnipeg Beach's lifeguards and RCMP detachment also played a role in running the Dew Drop Gang out of town, but it is not surprising that Dafoe uses the incident to illustrate the urban/local divide, with the natural environment of the lake area strengthening the locals.

At Winnipeg Beach, the ethnic conflicts followed a particular territorial pattern. London said the fighting was at its worse in the 1930s and '40s, before he was born, and that he grew up on legends of "fistfights at Boundary Park and the government pier between the Jewish kids from Winnipeg and the Beach boys." Boundary Park, of course, was the literal boundary point between where Jewish people could own cottages and where they could not. The adults set the boundaries by deciding who could buy property, but it was the teenagers enforcing those boundaries on the ground. Garth Teel's recollections are of fights happening in the park and tennis court area at the end of Park Avenue, where the residents of Park-A-While used to hang out, and at the Aquatic Club, which was adjacent to the government pier.[62] The Aquatic Club was again in a boundary area between where Jewish people were allowed and where they were not. However, the leisure zone—whether the dance hall, boardwalk, beach or CPR Pier—was not recalled as a conflict zone. It would seem that the "public space" of Winnipeg Beach, which was frequented by all ethnic groups, was considered an open territory, at least to a point. Manitoba writer Allan Levine has noted that Winnipeg's Jewish community knew to hang out at the Londons' Playland Arcade rather than the neighbouring arcade, where they would have been less welcome.[63] It is worth noting that the anti-Semitism at work in Manitoba occurred in other parts of Canada as well. Attempts were made to exclude Jewish people from Toronto Island, and swastika gangs were said to have roamed the boardwalks of the Toronto waterfront.[64]

Winnipeg Beach's contemporary, Coney Island, had its own form of regionalization when it came to ethnicity. The diverse ethnic groups of New York City each staked out a bay along the beach to call their own. Within the recreation infrastructure of Coney Island there were also distinct ethnic enclaves, housing Irish, Greek, Hungarian, Jewish, Italian, and African American residents. As with Winnipeg Beach, these divisions seemed to disappear when people entered the crowd that thronged the amusement areas.[65]

Winnipeg Beach's ethnic tensions, embedded in the tourism infrastructure, rarely made headlines. However, in 1963 a couple of incidents did warrant mention in the *Winnipeg Free Press* (formerly the *Manitoba Free Press*) and *Tribune*. The first incident, on 30 June, involved a man driving through the streets of Winnipeg Beach with a loudspeaker making statements such as "This is Adolph Eichmann speaking ... all Jews get off the street." The *Israelite Post* reported that the car was covered with placards carrying anti-Semitic slogans. The twenty-two-year-old driver, who eventually pleaded guilty to causing a disturbance, maintained that the signs had been advertising a dance. The car probably was outfitted with a speaker system to advertise the dance, and the equipment gave the driver a chance to make some anti-Semitic remarks at the same time. In doing so, he was trying to enforce Winnipeg Beach's ethnic boundaries: he was telling Jewish people not to come to the dance.[66]

The second incident occurred in the middle of July 1963 and warranted a government press release outlining how the province was going to respond. This time a fourteen-year-old boy was roughed up, a store was smeared, and a cottage and synagogue were painted with swastikas. Two people were charged with disturbing the peace and fined fifty dollars, although a government spokesman speculated that there was a small group of people behind the activities. "Such acts have no place in Manitoba," the government statement went on to say.[67] Such acts probably were not without precedent in Winnipeg Beach. Kathleen Rees could recall a sign going up just before World War II at the entrance to the community telling Jewish people to stay out.[68] What was unprecedented was the attention the incidents received in 1963, which was significantly different from what might have happened twenty years earlier.

Despite the high-profile headlines, ethnic tension was probably on the decline in Winnipeg Beach by 1963. Even in the 1950s, London said that, rather than fighting in the streets, the Jewish boys and beach boys—inevitably male—had decided to take out their frustrations on a different field of battle: "We had an annual football game in the park between the Jewish boys from Winnipeg and the boys who lived in the beach. And we would annually get together and have this game, competitive and very rough. We looked forward to it always. Sense of frustrations of two cultures meeting and competing with each other, once of the essence of Winnipeg Beach experience for all of us, this was a benign way of working itself out on the football field, and then afterwards camaraderie."[69] London's football game is perhaps the best example we could ask for of a boundary zone between ethnic groups; here they could come together.

The ethnic dynamic was changing. Land covenants that had allowed property owners to discriminate against Jewish people and other ethnic groups were declared illegal by the Supreme Court of Canada in 1950.[70] By the 1950s, the unspoken covenants were also breaking down around Winnipeg Beach. Izzy Peltz recalled the transition this way:

I have the story on that. I don't know if they'll let me repeat this story in public. That was when I was already practicing as a chartered accountant. And one of our clients was a very successful businessman in the soft trade business, coats and cloths, and he was in partnership with another gentleman, who was not Jewish, in the metal business. And he tried to buy a cottage [past Boundary Park] and they wouldn't sell to him. And he told me the story afterwards. So his partner said, "What do you mean they wouldn't sell to you?" … "You want a cottage out there?" And he said, "Yeah, I'd like one." So [his business partner] said, "Sure, I'm going to go and buy one." He went out and he bought one and of course they sold it to him and he, in turn, sold it back to our client. That broke the ice. And then the door was open for everybody.[71]

Peltz bought his own cabin on Maple Avenue, past Boundary Park, in 1960. He recalled that similar restrictions in place south of Winnipeg Beach were coming down at the same time. He said his family had no trouble fitting in: "[the children] made friends who were not necessarily Jewish. They got to know them. You know how kids are, especially when my son was teaching them swimming lessons."[72] Teaching swimming lessons would have meant Peltz's son was interacting with the community in a similar fashion to London and Garth Teel. Teel also recalled that the ethnic tensions between Jewish campers and Winnipeg Beach residents were easing—although not disappearing—by this time. Probably the Jewish enclave that Doris Margolis remembered from growing up at Winnipeg Beach during the summer began to wane as Jewish families exercised the option of moving elsewhere. Mildred Kelly recalled meeting a former guest years later in Winnipeg; he said, "Now we can afford to go where we want, but we still remember having our best times at Winnipeg Beach."[73] For Jewish people it probably was not merely a question of being able to afford to go where they wanted, it was having the option as well.

A Safe Place to Stay

The discussion about ethnicity introduced landladies such as Lillian Teel and Zaporah Torchinsky. Before 1910, going to Winnipeg Beach meant staying at one of the two or three hotels at the beach. A postcard booklet from 1907 shows a number of private and, presumably, guest cottages that people might have used for accommodation.[74] Pitching a tent was also an option. Indeed when some of the early guests were establishing themselves for the summer, they were doing so in a tent. When Presbyterian minister James Savage summered at the beach in 1914, for example, he was living in a tent.[75] But the growing popularity of Winnipeg Beach ensured that a lively rental market sprang up to meet the demand. Many of the people being served were families who either could not afford their own cabins or were simply looking to take advantage of vacation time that was increasingly becoming available to North American workers.[76] Val Kinack can remember travelling to Winnipeg Beach in the 1930s, when the family would always rely on Pickles Tent and Awnings for a rental cabin on Pleiades Avenue.[77]

Pickles was not the only rental business in town—most of central Winnipeg Beach was built with the rental trade in mind. Looking back to the 1940s, Lawrence Isfeld recalled,

> There was tons of these little cottages that are all gone now, they're torn down now. On a lot there would be 12 of these little cottages. They were 12 by 12 and a family would rent that and they'd all be in on a lot. I remember Eddie Walker had a bunch of them on Ash Street and Kelly's had a bunch of them on Oak by the lake and they rented these cottages out to people and they would come for maybe a week or two weeks. And of course they were very cheap. I think they probably charged thirty dollars a week or twenty dollars a week. There was Wood's cabins right in town and these people they all cooked with wood. There was about three families that sold ice and wood.[78]

There was also a host of lodges and rooming houses. In her study of Niagara Falls, Karen Dubinsky tracks a gender divide between the larger hotels in town, which were invariably owned or operated by men, and tourist homes, which were most often run by women.[79] In 1937, Mass-Observation—an eclectic British research group that included artists, students, journalists, and non-academic social scientists who believed that the best way to understand human behaviour was through close observation—set out to discover how lodgings were conducted in Blackpool. The group found that of a sampling of eighty-six lodging houses, three were run by men, ten were run by couples, and the remaining seventy-three lodges were headed by women.[80] The situation was repeated in other vacation areas.[81] At Winnipeg Beach, Wood's cabins and Walker's cabins, along with Richie and Pickles, were businesses headed by men. The Kelly family was an exception to the rule. Headed by Hannah Kelly—or Mrs. Sam Kelly, as she appeared in advertisements after 1919—the family operated the Winnipeg Beach Hotel, the Ash Grove Lodge, a series of cabins, a store, and a restaurant, and they could house between 700 and 800 people at any given time.[82] Fitting the trend shown elsewhere, many of the rooming houses and lodges at Winnipeg Beach were headed by women. A perusal of the classified ads in 1920 reveals Mrs. Cox running Uneeda Rest and Ash Grove, presumably before the Kellys took over the latter, and Mrs. Banfield's Rusticana, which offered a sleeping veranda and furnished rooms. Mrs. Locke was

A middle-class cottage at Winnipeg Beach in 1914. People could enjoy a rustic, yet comfortable stay at the lake.

advertising in 1918, and Mrs. Waddy, who was running the Lake Park Hotel, joined Mrs. Booker, Mrs. Main, Mrs. Walier, and Mrs. Cox in advertising accommodations in the classifieds in 1929.[83] We have already mentioned Mrs. Teel and Mrs. Torchinsky.

Women's work in the early twentieth century was "regarded as an extension of work that women had traditionally done in the home," and running a tourist home would fall in that category.[84] Lillian Teel took over the Park-A-While lodge in 1927 during what she called the "heyday" of Winnipeg Beach. In peak season the lodge would hold between 60 and 70 people. The owner of the lodge was already renting the Linger Longer lodge to Teel's sister and asked her to recruit Teel into the business. "He said, 'You have a sister. Why not have her come down and take Park Street over?' So I had the three boys and I thought, 'Well, maybe I will,'" Teel recalled in a 1991 interview.[85] "My husband never liked it, he never liked me being in this business, he said, 'Why go into this? Why not go into ready to wear?'" Teel recalled, supplying an example of what were considered the options for a married woman seeking employment in the 1920s. And indeed, it would appear that the female hostesses were always married or widowed. The title of

"Mrs." was probably a necessary ingredient for stepping into the profession.

This lively rental market shows how Winnipeg Beach was growing in popularity, but the people who came and what they did also illustrate how the resort's crowd was changing by the 1920s. The private "in house" gatherings that punctuated the first years of the beach had been replaced by the singles and groups who came to the beach to participate in the public amusements. Harry Simpson could recall staying with Mrs. J.B.Vickers at the Zephyr Lodge, on the corner of Prospect and Spruce, and at Mrs. Kale's, across from the bandstand, in the late 1930s and early 1940s. Vickers offered space for about eight lodgers, with two of the bedrooms, including the one Simpson usually rented, located on the veranda. Simpson would have been in his teens and early twenties when he was heading to the beach, and the other lodgers were usually about the same age. "There was a station agent, a young lady my age working downtown somewhere, transient people in for the weekend. I always used to write [Mrs. Vickers] and she'd always reply. She didn't have a telephone so you'd have to do it all by postage," Simpson recalled. "She was a grand lady, old style, ran a grand place, fussy about who she took in."[86]

These landladies played a role in the chemistry of Winnipeg Beach that went beyond simply supplying a room. By being "fussy" about who they accepted, they acted as moral watchguards at the beach, or at least they were perceived that way. In a way they also provided moral sanction to the people who were staying with them. In Blackpool the landlady was considered "the matriarch, the time clock, and the booking clerk," and a direct impediment to lodgers seeking sexual pleasures or other joys.[87] Meanwhile, in Niagara Falls the "female space" of the tourist houses carried the reputation of being a safer place for young women on a trip than the hotels.[88]

At Winnipeg Beach, Lillian Teel was also fussy about whom she took in, not just in attempting to keep Jewish people from mixing with gentiles but by sizing people up when they came to her door to see if they "looked like trouble."[89] This meant that people had to behave and dress the part if they wanted a room. Teel deliberately targeted young singles out to enjoy a weekend or a vacation at the beach—the exact market that would have been using the beach as a dating place. She served as a parent figure to the youth when they were at the lake. "I'd say so and so is coming down and she's your friend, explain to her the rules of the house, and they were very good and they would," Teel recalled. The lodge also brought people together into micro networks, and while the leisure zone was the focal point of the resort, these micro-groups also carved out their own social spaces. "My young fellows and girls who stayed here, before I changed my business, everyone met at the tennis courts … if you went down to play tennis, and weren't at Teel's you weren't part of the gang."[90] Teel's mention that she "changed her business" refers to her decision in the late 1950s and 1960s to stop targeting young singles and focus more on families. It is a period that coincides with the decline of Winnipeg Beach as a location for dating culture. The young singles were not coming anymore, at least not to the degree they had.

The lodges that were used as boarding houses at Winnipeg Beach had been converted from cabins to suit their new task. As with Vickers's Zephyr Lodge, the veranda at Teel's—an ideal place to host a social gathering or "in home" during the early years of Winnipeg Beach—was converted into a bedroom area during busy weekends for guests who were intent on stepping out and enjoying the leisure zone at the beach. At the Torchinsky guest house, the veranda was also put to work; it was divided into independent rooms with private doors that allowed the guests to come and go as they pleased. There were thin walls throughout the cabin, so privacy was at a premium. A warm summer night offered better options for privacy. Margolis recalled heading home one evening with a date and using the doorstep and a bit of darkness for a kiss goodnight.[91] Given that people came to Winnipeg Beach to play, late returns to the cabin were common and, as Margolis recalled, sometimes comedic:

> My sister rented out a double cot on the veranda to two spinsters, my mother not aware that the cot was spoken for rented it out to two young men who came to spend the night, she told them that when they came home late not to make a noise and to slide into the cot. You can well imagine what took place. When the men came in they quietly slipped out of their shirts and pants and crawled into bed. The girls started to scream and woke up the whole cottage. Pandemonium reigned and one woman trying to placate the girls said, "Why are you making such a fuss, God knows when you'll get such a wonderful opportunity again."[92]

The accommodations were often a homosocial affair; men were happy to share beds with other men, and women with other women, and then use the public space of the leisure zone to mingle with the opposite sex. But we

The interior of the cottage shown earlier. Note the British flags scattered about the veranda; there was a conscious effort to mark Winnipeg Beach as English territory. But, despite that, the beach grew to have a cosmopolitan flavour.

can also look at the above situation and ask if the spinsters and young men in question were really looking for the "wonderful opportunity" of being thrown together. Just as the homosocial nature of alcohol regulation in the 1930s and '40s—made most visible in the all-male beer parlour—could be an entry point for same-sex behaviour, so too could bunking with someone of the same sex in Winnipeg Beach.[93]

There is no way to comment on the sexuality of the Torchinskys' guests, but the Gay and Lesbian Oral History Project shows that at least some of the young men and women who went to Winnipeg Beach were gay or lesbian and not interested in the heterosexual opportunities. George M. Smith and Gerry, interviewed in 1991, provide two windows into this world. "In summer we had a place at the lake. My friend had a place not too far down the road that his mother owned, but she was not often there," Gerry said, recalling a period in the 1950s. "We had quite a few parties, some of them turned orgieish."[94] The lake was a place for sexual encounters and simple sociability for Gerry and his friends. But they did not confine their activities to the cabins. Gerry could recall his friends arriving in a convertible with one of them dressed up in drag and riding on the hood. His father, home at the time, was none the wiser to the drag queen's actual gender or to his son's sexuality. Gerry's father was, however, more on the ball when it came to spotting the sexuality of a lesbian couple who came to the beach year after year to rent an adjacent cottage. He would say, "Here come the girl fruits," Gerry recalled.[95]

George Smith spent time at Winnipeg Beach and Grand Beach. The Grand Beach Hotel at the time was owned by a "Bertha" Green, a gay man and "tough little bugger," which made the hotel, at least, gay friendly. But, Smith said, "We preferred Winnipeg Beach, it was more fun. We went there for a week's holiday. About six of us could rent a cottage."[96] Smith does not say what went on inside the cottage, but he and his friends were not afraid to venture outside: "We used to walk around in drag just in the area where we lived, which was silly, and this one time, one night we came home and we're in the room and a bunch of fellows and girls outside were throwing rocks at the roof.... I had seen *Secrets* with Mary Pickford and I was always dramatic, and I said this is just like *Secrets*, we're being attacked by Indians." The use of the term *Indians* to "other" his attackers is interesting. Smith was relying on the cultural tools of the time, which provided Native people as the available "other." But Smith's use of language is more interesting given that Native people were cast into the role of the natural in a European script that had cowboys conquering the West. In that sense, Smith was appropriating this language and casting himself and his friends as the cowboys venturing into the natural heterosexual terrain of Winnipeg Beach. The cottage area at Winnipeg Beach was expected to be heterosexual, and the people throwing rocks at Smith's cabin gave a clear indication that they were prepared to defend that heterosexual space. But they had more than rocks to work with. Gay and lesbian people would have faced a heterosexual gaze at Winnipeg Beach in the form of every man and woman holding hands, every wife making dinner, and every husband returning home from work. This gaze is made tangible through the comments of Gerry's father and the sort of treatment that was meted out to Smith and his companions when they punctured this space. And yet, Gerry and Smith were transgressing the heterosexual space, challenging it, and subverting it for their own purposes. Winnipeg Beach, with its pictures of men heading out together in boats or women relaxing next to each other on the beach, is filled with what-ifs.

Gerry and Smith remind us that much of the activity at Winnipeg

Beach—that is, the activities in the cabins—went on behind closed doors. As we might expect, those activities ran the gamut, from children playing games on rainy days to wives socializing while their husbands stayed in or commuted to Winnipeg. Nestor Mudry played the beach as a member of Leonard's Casino Band in 1941, when eight of the band members bunked in a cabin all summer.[97] He was twenty years old at the time, and the summer was as much play as it was work. "It was good. Lots of fun. We had all kinds of laughs. We'd go out on the beach and have parties and all that sort of stuff," Mudry recalled. "After, 'specially on Saturday night after we'd played out, after one o'clock we'd all kind of head back to the cottage there and we'd party until about four or five in the morning."[98]

The thin walls of the Torchinskys' guest house probably made it a poor place to bring a date. Cabins did open up few more options, as they had for Gerry and his friends. So did the hotel. While the discourse at the time was that unmarried sex was inappropriate, Mildred Kelly's recollections of working at the Winnipeg Beach Hotel in the 1930s and '40s suggest people were breaking the rules. She could recall working in the hotel in the 1930s and getting the "shock of her life."[99] What was the shock? "Things that today people don't blink an eye at, I hadn't seen it or hadn't been brought up that way. I didn't think people did that sort of thing and left the door open to make it obvious, like I said, after a while I got quite used to it, you didn't blink an eye sort of thing, but you still asked where they had to write down they were man and wife when they went upstairs, you were to make sure and after that they were on their own.... You could have rented the rooms many times over, that was during my time, I'm talking about."[100] Clearly, not all guests were husband and wife. But Kelly went through the motions of asking and they went through the motions of saying they were, and on paper the script of appropriate behaviour was followed to the letter.

In the early years of Winnipeg Beach, the hotels offered a place for men to drink. The Empress Hotel, for example, was famed for its "lavish bar."[101] Women were discouraged from taking part in this male-oriented drinking.[102] Given that, alcohol consumption was primarily a concern for what it might do to men's behaviour. Cabin owners requested a local constable for the beach in 1905, for example, citing the need for protection after the province granted liquor licences to two hotels in Winnipeg Beach.[103] In 1914 divinity student James Savage sent a letter to the *Free Press* taking the province to task for its lax enforcement of liquor laws at the Empress Hotel and the King Edward Hotel. Savage argued that "Winnipeg Beach seems out of the jurisdiction of the license department at the present time." He went on further to argue that the Empress Hotel was keeping its "barroom open seven days a week, and almost twenty-four hours every day" and added, "I wonder if the parents of Winnipeg are aware that young men are being debauched in the Empress Hotel this summer, many of them mere lads, not long in their teens."[104] Savage's efforts eventually led to Empress Hotel manager Edward Windebank's being charged with selling alcohol after hours.[105]

In the tense years leading up to Prohibition (which began in 1916 in Manitoba) Savage's campaign against drinking at Winnipeg Beach also led to a confrontation with Windebank. The enmity between the two escalated to the point that Windebank threatened Savage and then, with two friends, paid a late-evening visit to Savage's tent on 18 August 1914, ostensibly to talk things over. In the fracas that ensued, Savage managed to bean Windebank with a coat hanger and fight off the other two men. Everyone involved ended up in court facing a series of charges and counter-charges.[106] Savage, the divinity student who squared off against three people and won, was a darling of the *Free Press* and won accolades from his own Winnipeg Beach congregation, which published the following statement: "We, the congregation, worshipping during the summer months under the ministry of Mr. Savage, the Presbyterian student, do express our admiration of the manly stand he has taken in giving publicity to the flagrant law breaking in connection with the liquor traffic at Winnipeg Beach, thereby rendering himself liable to annoyance and assault."[107] Savage seemed to drive home the notion of "muscular" Christianity that was so prevalent at the time. While the confrontation seemed violent, the court trial reduced it to a case of boys being boys. The trial included witty exchanges between the lawyers, who, with a crowd of women among the spectators, must have felt they were putting on a performance. Certainly, reducing the experience to absurdity was probably in Windebank's favour. But we should consider seriously the notion that it was dismissed because the judge interpreted it as a case of errant masculinity, harmless if no one is permanently harmed. The *Free Press* reported that "Among the amusing replies to questions was one made by Windebank when he was asked what he did when Savage yelled for help after hitting him over the head two or three times. I said, 'You don't want any help. You're getting on all right.' He said that three thoughts ran through his mind while he was being beaten. They were; 'Why did he tear my coat open?' 'What is he hitting me over the head with?' and 'I mustn't let him make a fool of himself.'" R.W. Craig, who was acting for Savage, spoke of the "deep psychological reverie" that Windebank indulged in while being struck.[108] The judge dismissed the case, stating that he did not want to create any more animosity between the two. They probably did not shake hands and call truce, however; the next year Savage helped pass a petition calling on the province to deny the Empress a renewed licence.[109] Windebank had his own challenges. By 1915 he was involved in arbitration with the CPR over the ownership and worth of the Empress Hotel; the CPR would eventually win control of the hotel.[110] (Windebank, however, seems to have been able to move on; he joined the World War I effort and his contribution was significant enough that when he died in 1925 the *Manitoba Free Press* ran a notice on the front page.)[111]

Savage's complaints suggest Winnipeg Beach was on the regulatory edge, both in its being out of the city and in its contravening of provincial laws. Publicly, at least, it was also a place where young men went to play. As interesting as what was in Savage's original letter is what was not in it: he raised no concern about the safety of women at the beach due to the presence of alcohol. Clearly, alcohol was considered to be within the male domain, and the men going to the hotels were engaged in male sociability. This public sociability ended in 1916 when Prohibition was enacted in Manitoba. The rules were relaxed in 1923 to allow for the sale of liquor in government-run stores, and then again in 1928 to allow public drinking in licensed male-only beer parlours.[112] The male-only beer parlours, and Winnipeg Beach did have one on its Main Street after 1928, made clear that liquor regulation was a gendered affair, with regulations predicated on fears that mixing men, women, and alcohol would lead to immoral behaviour.[113] It was not until 1957 that mixed-gendered public drinking establishments were allowed in Manitoba.

Prohibition pushed alcohol consumption and sales into the recreation infrastructure at Winnipeg Beach. The *Free Press* shows a steady stream of Winnipeg Beach people being charged with contravention of the Temperance Act. Those being charged with bootlegging, or selling liquor, reveal that the practice was embedded in the tourist trade. Anne Zelinitsky was "charged with illegal selling at that favourite resort on June 18, 1927."[114] Zelinitsky and her husband challenged the charges and the judge gave her "the benefit of the doubt and told her to keep heed to her ways in the future."[115] Mike Urich faced a fine of $150 and two weeks in jail after the provincial police raided his Blue Star Lodge in Winnipeg Beach on 16 July 1927.[116] Similarly, Mrs. J.M. Cox, the "proprietress" of a boarding house at Winnipeg Beach, was convicted on 18 August 1927 of the illegal sale of liquor, fined $200 and sentenced to two weeks in jail.[117] Bella Jetta was fined $300 and sentenced to two weeks in jail for illegally selling liquor in Winnipeg Beach on 11 June 1927. However, her jail sentence was suspended when it was put forward by her defence attorney that she was "the sole support of a family of small children, with a husband sick and unable to work."[118] No doubt some rooming house and lodge owners supplemented their income, and the appeal of their facilities, by the sale of liquor. Lillian Teel did not sell alcohol, but the guests were not stopped from acquiring their own.[119]

Liquor charges fell under the purview of the provincial morality squad rather than the local police, which meant that the authorities had to travel to the resort to enforce the law.[120] It was widely believed among Winnipeg Beach residents that the railway was the corridor for regulation. Recalling the era, Lillian Teel noted, "Sometimes word would go around that the boys are in town."[121] While regulation came from outside, it took an informant from the community to let it in. "The spotters were sent out by the government in Winnipeg, they came out on the train, you could spot them when they got off. They used to come out on the Moonlight, they had the names," Kathleen Rees recalled. "How would they know if they were two strangers off the train? Someone must have informed them."[122] And indeed, in her view, scores in the community were settled by calling in the authorities on a neighbour engaged in bootlegging.

Into the 1940s, Lawrence Isfeld could recall bootleggers being scattered throughout his neighbourhood: "There was bootleggers around in Winnipeg Beach where I lived, within three blocks there was seven bootleggers, people who sold homebrew, or, there was an Englishman, who used to sell government liquor. There was the Ukrainians, you could go sit in a home and have a shot of homebrew and it would cost like thirty cents. There was lots of that."[123] The bootlegging houses were more than simply places to swill a glass of alcohol. They were places to socialize and play a hand or two of cards with friends and neighbours. They followed their own code of ethics, such as not selling their products to children.[124] The bonds of ethnicity determined, for the most part, who stopped at which bootleggers for a drink, and campers probably had a tougher time gaining access to the booze. Many of the houses directed their sales to residents they knew to avoid being caught by provincial police. But others, like Mrs. Melbourne, were familiar names among residents and campers alike. "You'd go up there on a Sunday afternoon and you'd have a ball," Lil Teel recalled of a period that would have been in the 1930s and '40s. "And she was very proper, everything had to be just so."[125]

Mildred Kelly's family ran the beer parlour at the Beach Hotel, but she viewed Melbourne as a community member rather than competition. "You'd never know that she sold her own drinks, as far as I'm concerned she was the same as us," Kelly said.[126] When Kelly almost lost a child to Rh disease and had to be taken into the city for medical help, it was Melbourne who drove the vehicle during the five-hour trip. "When she took me to Winnipeg that night, she was in her 80s, and she told me dirty jokes all the way in," Kelly recalled.[127] But as Teel's afternoon visits show, Melbourne was providing a service that the Kelly family's men-only beer parlour could not. Women participated in the drinking and they participated in the marketing. In fact, based on the couples Isfeld can remember who were bootleggers, bootlegging was very much a wife-and-husband affair, with bootlegging supplementing the family income along with the sale of vegetables or other farm products. Charges for the improper sale of liquor at Winnipeg Beach persisted into the 1960s, and when a cabbie was busted for selling two mickeys of alcohol in 1963, the Crown attorney noted that bootlegging in Winnipeg Beach had reached "serious proportions this spring."[128] The incentive for these businesses was providing ease of access and setting for the consumption of alcohol.[129]

The discussion around the guest houses and the bootlegging businesses provides a hint of just how well the tourism infrastructure at Winnipeg Beach was integrated with the leisure zone during the first half of the century. Servicing the crowds coming to Winnipeg Beach was big business, and the gendered division of labour ensured that many of these service positions were held by women.[130] Domestic servants underpinned upper- and middle-class household labour in the first part of the twentieth century. When a *Free Press* reporter quizzed women staying at the Empress Hotel in 1910 about why they did not buy their own cottages, they answered that they would, but they found it impossible to get their maids to come to the beach.[131] Often, the daughters and wives of local farmers and fishermen were recruited into the positions. When Lillian Teel was searching for workers, she would turn to the local community for help.[132] But, recalling the 1940s, Lawrence Isfeld could remember domestic servants coming from Winnipeg: "A lot of the cottagers used to get girls working, they brought them out to look after their kids, and do their housework. These girls would be sixteen years old, they'd come out and they'd be at these dances. It wasn't like ten, it was like maybe a hundred of these girls…. Oh when I got older, when I was fifteen, we loved it. These girls were just great for us. A lot of them were German girls, good looking, blond," Isfeld recalled.[133] If Winnipeg Beach was advertised as a destination for men, this workforce ensured they were greeted by women when they arrived.

John Reykdal and his sister Mrs. R. Thedrikson (née Reykdal) were interviewed in 1991 about Winnipeg Beach.[134] Their grandfather had emigrated from Iceland and settled in the Winnipeg Beach area in 1875. While the men in the family farmed or fished, the women supplemented the family income by working at Winnipeg Beach. During the 1910s their mother earned about twenty-five cents per hour doing laundry and cleaning cabins for people at the beach. Thedrikson joined the paid labour force when she was sixteen, working in the bathing house at Winnipeg Beach in the 1920s or 1930s. The bathing house rented bathing suits to day trippers and campers who did not have a suit of their own, a not uncommon situation in the first half of the century, when going for a swim might be a once-a-year event. Thedrikson was one of six women who worked in the bathing house cleaning and drying swimsuits after every use and ensuring they were ready for the next customer. Despite having 300 suits on hand, Thedrikson said a busy weekend would see them all rented out and would tax their ability to get the returned suits ready for the next customers.

Olive Sielski was also drawn into the Winnipeg Beach labour force at a young age.[135] She grew up in the Foley District, some fifteen kilometres away from Winnipeg Beach, and went to work at Charlie and May Sutherland's Lakeside Café—located just down from the railway station—in 1943, when she was thirteen years old. During the summer, Sielski would bunk with the other workers in rooms above the café, making the nine-mile walk home on her days off. "We were kitchen girls, we had to peel potatoes, haul water in garbage cans with the little wagon, make chips, bring wood in. There was no electric stove, Mrs. Sutherland had a wood stove," Sielski recalled. There was no running water either, so workers headed down with a wagon to the town pump. The amount of manual labour involved in running the restaurant, just one of many in downtown Winnipeg Beach, required a large female staff. "There were four kitchen girls, cooks, then there were the waitresses, then the girls that worked in the hotdog stand. There was sixteen of us, anyways."[136] Sielski was paid five dollars per week for her efforts in the kitchen.

Work at the Lakeside Café moved to the tempo of the trains. Just down from the CPR station, the café was often the last stop for people headed out. "There used to be three, four trains and then everybody is running to catch the train back to Winnipeg at midnight and they're, 'Quick, bag of chips, Quick, a hotdog, drinks!' … We stayed open until the train left. Oh there was thousands of people," Sielski recalled.[137] She is not exaggerating: a single Moonlight train could move 1,600 people, and a busy evening might see two or three trains transporting people.[138] Of course, not everybody who went up on the Moonlight came back on it. "Some of them would miss it, then they'd have to, they'd just sleep in the park," or on the beach, or even in the change house or picnic pavilion.[139] After the train left, the workers at the beach would catch their breath. Sometimes there was a late-night campers' dance. Other times the band would drop by after its last set for a late-evening meal. As with the lodgers at Teel's, the workers at the Lakeside Café formed their own social network, reminding us that while Winnipeg Beach was a crowded resort, it was composed of these smaller micro-groups in which people of different backgrounds could come together. Sielski remembered, "We used to have fun…. Then after the restaurant closed down, we'd all be in the kitchen. We'd all have hot chocolate or a piece of pie or something. Mr. Sutherland would go put all the money away and he used to go and take a frozen wiener and [touch it against the leg of one of the workers and] they'd scream. Mrs. Sutherland [would say] 'Charlie, what are you doing?'"[140] Surrounded by a female workforce, Charlie was probably reinforcing his own masculinity through his actions, which would certainly be read differently today. But while Mr. Sutherland handled the money, it was Mrs. Sutherland who was the authority when it came to the all-female staff. Sielski recalled, "Mrs. Sutherland was very strict, we weren't allowed out, we had to be in at nine o'clock because we were underage. One girl says, she's not going to know and when she comes home it was ten o'clock. The door was locked she had to come knock on the door for Mrs. Sutherland. So Mrs. Sutherland opened the door. [The girl] didn't have no day off for two weeks and her pay was held back for two weeks."[141] Sutherland was

Campers at the Wildwood Tourist Park and people staying at cabins at Winnipeg Beach would have turned to local residents for vegetables, firewood, and ice during the first half of the century. That business relationship ensured that local people had a vested interest in the tourist trade.

acting as a surrogate mother to her underage workers, and she took the task seriously. But her actions tell us that while Winnipeg Beach during the day was acceptable terrain for her young workers, the leisure zone after dark—focused as it was on bringing men and women together—was not. Sielski stayed up late to serve the last batch of customers rushing to catch the train, but if she was not working she was in her room by 9:00 p.m. However, with the leisure zone just entering high tide, Sielski and the other girls her age still found a way to participate in the spectacle: "We'd go to the older girls' bedrooms and look out the front windows. And we'd see a couple walking hugging and we'd go get a pitcher of water." Which they promptly dumped on the couple below. "[And they would say,] 'Where in the hell did that come from?' [Laughs.] Oh no, we'd go to look out the front, and see everybody walking."[142]

From the Lakeside Café, Sielski went on to work at a number of Winnipeg Beach businesses—everything from other restaurants, to cabins, to the local liquor commission in the 1960s. She was also part of a team of eight or nine women who cleaned the dance hall every day in preparation for the next dance. With the exception of a few years off when she had her children, Sielski never had any trouble finding work during her time at Winnipeg Beach, a period that lasted from 1943 to 1947 and then resumed again in the 1950s and 1960s. Her husband worked too. But unlike Sielski he often sought opportunities outside the community. Sielski explained, "He did everything. He worked construction, he worked for Dan's transfer, he worked brush cutting and plumbing. He did everything. I think about five or six years he worked for Dave Funk in Winnipeg. He used to work up north and he worked for Cosie [a Winnipeg Beach business], he used to go long haul driving like to Ohio, he used to go pick up the big caterpillars and that. And he used to work on construction, building roads and everything."[143] Unlike Sielski, he did not beat the dust out of mattresses for the Lake Lodge Hotel, or work in the restaurants, or do any one of numerous other resort-oriented jobs meant to be filled by women. Their career paths stuck to the gender restrictions of the time, and that meant that Sielski's husband sought opportunities outside the community, either because there were better jobs elsewhere or because there simply were not enough opportunities in Winnipeg Beach for male workers. Of course, some jobs were decidedly male. Victor Martin worked with the CPR, including on the Moonlight special, and was part of the predominantly male rail trade. The "honeyman," the person who came around to empty the outhouses at Winnipeg Beach, was inevitably a man. Similarly, the iceman was a man, and one who had a lucrative business until the coming of electricity and electric refrigerators.[144] Winter pictures from the era show roads leading to the lake for ice cutting and teams hard at work chopping out the blocks, which were stored for use during the summer.[145] Most of the basic supplies in Winnipeg Beach would have come from local people. Val Kinack can remember her parents buying a range of goods from local people, everything from ice, wood, and vegetables to pickerel fillets. "We looked on the Ukrainians and the Polish people as the providers. They're the ones who we bought stuff off to survive on," Kinack recalled.[146]

The leisure zone was staffed by locals and campers. While the boardwalk amusements were run by Beach Attractions Limited—but owned by the CPR until 1952—the Main Street businesses, like the Londons' Playland Arcade, were independently run affairs. The boardwalk and Main Street amusements created two sides to the boardwalk "oval."[147] As with Lillian Teel, the Kelly family, and other business owners at the beach, the notion of a traditional male breadwinner and female homemaker did not apply to the

London family—an interesting contrast to Winnipeg Beach's target market, which was expected to be headed by a white, married, heterosexual male. "I come from a matriarchal family," London recalled. "My mother and father owned the business jointly, but my mother was the driving force of the business, they would work from eight in the morning until two in the morning, from May 24 until mid October, it never stopped."[148]

And that included Sunday. Businesses at Winnipeg Beach were supposed to be closed on Sunday. But, just as James Savage had complained in 1914 about liquor sales on Sunday in the male-dominated hotels, the arcades and boardwalk businesses in the public leisure zone flouted the Sunday closing law during London's time in the 1940s and '50s. "Our largest day of business was Sunday, all of the Sunday business laws were being [ignored] during this time," London recalled.[149] Businesses were breaking the law, and the municipal council was going along with it by licensing the businesses. "The RCMP would periodically and symbolically come in and appear to enforce the law," London recalled. "And every couple of years my parents would pay a twenty-five-dollar fine for operating on a Sunday."[150] On one occasion, the RCMP even broke apart a pinball machine to drive home the point. But the Londons and other businesses owners would be up and running again the next Sunday—or even later the same day. The Lord's Day Alliance complained to the provincial attorney general in the fall of 1951 and again in 1952 about businesses in Winnipeg Beach operating on Sunday in defiance of provincial law. "We are living at a time when a persistent and vocal minority appear to be determined to flout the laws they do not like. Some of this stems from individual and corporate greed, and a determination to exploit the public on Sundays for their financial profit," the Alliance said in its brief to the province.[151] It is not surprising Winnipeg Beach became a lightning rod for their frustrations. When the first parts of the resort were being built in 1905, cabin owners were criticized for engaging in manual labour on Sunday.[152] And in 1923, when the province finally passed a motion allowing trains to run on Sunday, access to Winnipeg Beach was held up as a reason for the change.[153] Winnipeg Beach was at the regulatory edge in a number of ways.

As with workers at the Lakeside Café, the people in London's businesses came together in their own social network. London recalled, "We would get together after close, the people who worked, mostly residents of the beach, at one to one thirty in the morning, almost every night, my mother would

Cutting ice on Lake Winnipeg provided winter work for residents and summer ice for campers at the resort.

make toast, jam, peanut butter, hot coffee, we would just relax and come down, laughing, a quite incredible coming together of a family of the people who worked in the business, very different origins, culture, a real melding, under the auspices of my mother who was so dynamic, she would bring this group of sometimes five, sometimes twenty people together."[154] These workplace gatherings were critical to how people constructed Winnipeg Beach. It was experienced as more than just a recreation area.

Lawrence Isfeld grew up in Winnipeg Beach but came away with similar memories. His father was a commercial fisherman who had worked in the dance hall in 1927 when he was first settling in the area. Isfeld was at the train station as a child to sell newspaper and flip train tickets. By the time he was twelve years old, he was working in the dance hall, and when he was fourteen he was plying his talents on the boardwalk, trying to lure patrons into the games. "All the kids were doing something enterprising," Isfeld recalled. "I wouldn't have wanted to grow up any other place. It was really a great experience. All the guys I went to school with have all done really good in life and many opened their own businesses."[155]

Dance hall and boardwalk positions were generally divided by gender. Teens or young men such as Isfeld guided dancers on and off the dance floor or routed them in and out of the building. Men such as Nestor Mudry provided the entertainment—though there were a select number of female musicians at the time—while women such as Ina Drummond and Val Kinack provided the refreshments in the dance hall.[156] Drummond's father worked as the CPR constable in the early 1950s, giving her an "in" for a job with the boardwalk amusements, despite her being only eleven or twelve when she started. She recalled, "My father became very friendly with the manager of the boardwalk and I think I worked on every place on the boardwalk that a female could work."[157] Women could sell tickets for the rides and concessions, and could pass out cards in the bingo tent. They did not run the carnival-style games, leaving that to males such as Isfeld. But lines did blur when required. While pin setters in the bowling alley were typically male, Drummond said she could recall filling in when the regular setter was sick. Similarly, Bill McIntosh remembered cleaning the board-walk and setting up the concession areas in the morning.[158] The running of rides like the roller coaster was left to male professional workers.

The boardwalk hummed to the tempo of the trains, and Drummond said on the weekends they knew that when the train arrived they were going to get busy: "You were going to get busy and you never know you might see somebody that you know. You wonder who might be coming down this weekend. Especially the girls when you got a little older, you wonder if a certain guy is coming down and the guys wonder if a certain girl is coming down."[159] For workers the line between being on the job and getting caught up in the excitement of the tourist resort could easily blur.

Working on the boardwalk was fun, but it was not the area that Drummond enjoyed the most. "The one thing I really remember is that I worked in the concession stand in the dance hall and that's where I learned how to jive. I taught myself how to jive by watching all the dancers on the dance floor," she recalled.[160] Drummond and the other workers had to stay in the concession area—but that did not stop them from dancing behind the counter. They sold chips, chocolates, cigarettes, and soft drinks. Val Kinack spent her summers down at Winnipeg Beach as a kid, and like Drummond she picked up work at the boardwalk and dance hall: "We were all students, and … at sixteen we could go down there and get a job." She always had a particular job in mind when she went down to look for work.

"[The owner would line us up and say,] 'You go there, you sell tickets there, you go there, and I always tried to sort of hang back so he'd say, 'And you go in the dance hall.' I just loved it there. That's where you met. You saw, oh there's all your friends."[161]

Winnipeg Beach became even more focused on the dating crowd as the 1930s transitioned into the 1940s. In a letter to the *Winnipeg Free Press* in 1941, Winnipeg Beach mayor T.C. Knight wrote that over the past ten years roads and new tourism options had drawn people away from Winnipeg Beach. Winnipeg Beach had thrived as a natural location outside of the city. But by the 1940s that role had been usurped by Riding Mountain and the Whiteshell region, which had opened for tourism and were reachable by car. At best, Winnipeg Beach could promote itself as easy to reach.[162] But while the vacation crowd that had come to rent a cabin for a week or two at Winnipeg Beach during the summer began to erode, the dating crowd did not. Knight wrote, "An analysis of tourist groups shows that visitors of week-end and 24 hours duration have shown a rapid increase, while those in the other brackets have diminished." [163] The town responded by trying to cater and advertise to the weekenders.[164] If anything Winnipeg Beach's efforts to attract young people out on the prowl increased.

Winnipeg Beach's core had adapted to serve the rental crowd, but that changed over time as the long-term stays decreased and people began purchasing their own cottages. Kinack's family purchased a lot from Pickles just before World War II and had North American Lumber construct a cottage for a cost of about $500.[165] When Kathleen Rees purchased her property around the same time, it came with three small cabins on the lot—likely rental cabins—that she combined into one cabin.[166] The Torchinsky family sold their guest house at the beginning of World War II: "With family members and friends in a position to rent or buy their own cottages, business wound down, we stopped taking on boarders, just family or rent to people with cooking privileges," Margolis recalled.[167] The decreasing enforcement of ethnic boundaries mattered. As options to buy opened for Jewish people, they were no longer forced into Winnipeg Beach's ethnic enclave. Teel stayed in business into the 1970s, but she noted her own business changed from taking in young singles to taking families vacationing at the beach. They were older than the young singles had been and used the cabin facilities to do their own cooking. It was a change in clientele that went hand in hand with Winnipeg Beach's decline as a dating centre.

The decline of Winnipeg Beach's boarding houses and the matronly figures that went with them was felt in the 1950s, when concerns started to be raised about the beach becoming too "honky-tonk."[168] Amid complaints in 1955 from property owners in Winnipeg Beach—both cabin owners and permanent residents—came statements from people like Stephen Juba, a camper, member of the legislative assembly, and, later, mayor of Winnipeg from 1957 to 1977, that dilapidated cottages were being rented to juvenile groups from Winnipeg for "wild week-end parties."[169] Winnipeg Beach councillor George Black addressed a public meeting and echoed Juba in stating that cabins were being rented to juvenile delinquents and that the cabins were "unfit for human habitation."[170] The statement earned him a quick rebuke from Edwin Walker, who defended the quality and reputation of his rental cabins. But even into the 1960s Christopher Dafoe recalled stories of "secret and, perhaps, highly questionable pleasures" taking place in the cabins.[171] And yet questionable pleasures had been taking place at the Winnipeg Beach Hotel for years and people had looked the other way. This discussion illustrates a moral panic regarding juvenile delinquency that occurred in the post–World War II period, with delinquency being tied directly to sexual behaviour.[172] Toronto's waterfront came under a similar spotlight, with teens accused of unsavoury behaviour.[173]

However, the changes happening in Winnipeg Beach also help explain why youth behaviour was increasingly a matter of concern. The decline of the boarding-house culture meant a similar decline of the maternal surveillance—and the perception that there was such surveillance—that had gone hand in hand with the boarding houses. It is hard to imagine wild weekend parties going on under Mrs. Teel's watchful eye. The removal of the watchful eye offered by the landladies gave people the opportunity to offer their own interpretation of what was happening. Significantly, as former rental cabins and boarding houses became private family houses or cabins, the integration of the tourism infrastructure and the leisure zone began to break down. Weekend visitors were not paying customers anymore, they were irritants.

Similarly, by the 1960s Beach Attractions Limited was renting the boardwalk concessions for the season, leaving it to the renter/operators to turn a profit on them and cutting down on the jobs available for residents and campers who had lined up on the boardwalk to find work in Kinack's time.[174] In other words, the new approach destroyed the networks of

By the 1960s many of the rental cabins and large boarding houses had been shut down at Winnipeg Beach. What remained were single-family cabins whose owners had little interest in the tourist trade.

employees that had underpinned the beach. Finally, the transition from train to car atomized traffic at the beach and scattered the weekend population throughout the town as they sought parking spots, creating yet one more irritant for the cabin owners.[175]

As much as it was a place apart, then, the beach was also an extension of the social networks that existed in the city. Indeed, the first years of the beach gave it the role of retreat for Winnipeg's upper- and middle-class-society members. Cabins were seldom without guests, and they acted as the focal point for private social gatherings. But an elaborate public entertainment area developed, reflecting a social change that saw dating move from the parlour, or veranda in the case of Winnipeg Beach, to public areas. The tourism infrastructure in Winnipeg Beach reflected this change, with cabins being converted into boarding houses and verandas being turned into bedrooms for guests who now did their courting on the boardwalk. Just as the train allowed people to approach the beach in safe public space— as both same-sex and mixed-sex groups—the boarding houses allowed people to stay in safe public space. Women and men were willing to share a bed in a rooming house, with the understanding that their pursuit of the opposite sex would be contained in the leisure district. That they were renting their bed from responsible married women only helped ensure propriety. Of course this homosocial living space, of men bunking together with men and women bunking with female friends, also opened opportunities for gay and lesbian people looking to stay at the beach.

The transition to this elaborate tourism infrastructure was aided by the ethnic composition of the beach. While Jewish people faced ethnic roadblocks when they tried to stay in other beaches around Lake Winnipeg, they were able to secure space in the heart of Winnipeg Beach, an opening that owed as much to the laissez-faire attitude of the CPR as it did to the competitive nature of the Winnipeg Beach boarding houses, whose owners were, often, though not always, more interested in renting a room than turning away paying customers. The growth of this tourism infrastructure helped pull local people into the job market to staff the hotels, restaurants, and amusement businesses that serviced the young couples and groups out for an evening's entertainment. The train played its role in all of this by providing the rhythm of the tourism infrastructure. If locals and campers sometimes rubbed shoulders uncomfortably, they at least shared in the benefits of Winnipeg Beach's popularity. However, as the popularity of the beach declined, the elaborate tourism infrastructure that underpinned it was transformed again. The boarding houses returned to their role as family cabins; the rental cabins that had hosted visitors were sold to private owners; and the overall number of people engaged in running the beach declined. By the 1950s, many people living in or owning cabins at Winnipeg Beach had no interest in whether the crowds continued to come and were just as happy to see them go elsewhere.

Chapter Three
Playing at the Beach
THE LEISURE ZONE

The leisure zone was the heart of Winnipeg Beach in its role as an industrial saturnalia, a place where people could seek "a release from the 'rules' of urban/industrial life."[1] My interest here is (as it was in both the transportation corridor and the tourism infrastructure) in how the leisure zone evolved as a meeting place for men and women during the first half of the twentieth century. The beach, of course, was there from the beginning. The first dance hall was constructed almost immediately after the Canadian Pacific Railway ran its tracks up to Winnipeg Beach. The rest of the leisure zone emerged more slowly, filling the space between the train station and the beach. At Winnipeg Beach the notion of being released from conventional behaviour and the restraints of daily life was made possible by the resort's critical location next to the lake. In recalling the appeal of Winnipeg Beach, Jessica pulls all of these elements together:

> Alright, there was the boardwalk. There were the rides. There was the sand. The smell of the lake. People were very informal. They were ... by looser I don't mean ... they just acted a little bit differently than they did at home. They were very informal, let me put it that way. You had to dress differently in the city. You had to act a little bit differently in the city. And somehow when you were out there you were on holidays or even for the weekend you were on holiday. It's mostly that you were more relaxed and very very informal.[2]

Winnipeg Beach's crowd in 1910 looked anything but carefree in their suits and long dresses. But their posture and the occasional loosened tie or casual hat suggests that they were relaxing when they came to the beach.

Jessica was recalling her experiences from the 1940s and 1950s. Pictures from the turn of the century seem to show a different experience, with people heading out to the beach in formal dresses, suits, and ties. But by taking a closer look at the well-dressed New Yorkers who crowded the shores and amusement areas at Coney Island, John Kasson has illustrated how they were letting their hair down at the beach, whether through a loosened tie or less rigid body posture.[3] We can see the same thing at Winnipeg Beach, with people sitting back on the beach or wading into the water with their trousers rolled up. They might have been dressed up, but they were kicking back and relaxing.

Winnipeg Beach's leisure zone grew in the first decades of the twentieth century in tandem with the emergence of a dating culture—or what writers have called a sexual revolution.[4] Dating moved from the parlour, veranda, and social gatherings of Winnipeg Beach's picnics and into commercial locations.[5] Places such as Winnipeg Beach's dance pavilion offered "opportunities available no where else to spend time with the opposite sex. For the women especially, there was safety in the anonymity of the dance floor. They could flirt, hug, even hold hands if they chose, without parents, teachers, employers, or family friends looking over their shoulders."[6] There was also a communal aspect to the dancing. People went out not simply to dance, but to dance in public.[7]

As Dorothy Garbutt reminisced in a *Winnipeg Free Press* article, "the world suddenly went dance crazy" in the years following World War I.[8] Similarly, it is no surprise that when Winnipeg author and musician Owen Clark put together his book *Musical Ghosts: Manitoba's Jazz and Dance Bands 1914–1966*, he took 1914 as the starting date. World War I could be considered a rough transition point between calling, a system of courting embedded in middle-class society, and dating. The period witnessed the creation of a mass-culture entertainment industry that both reflected and pushed the changes in courting. It was a change that also reflected the growth of a working-class culture in contrast to the genteel middle-class sensibility that had prevailed throughout the nineteenth century.[9]

Winnipeg Beach provides an opportunity to see this evolution because the resort was launched in 1901, when much of the public entertainment structure that fed the dating approach to courting did not exist in Winnipeg. At Winnipeg Beach the changes in courting can be tracked through the use of the beach, by people promenading on the boardwalk and dancing in the dance hall. This was a distinctly heterosexual area with expectations of proper masculine and feminine behaviour from men and women. But it was also where people pushed the limits of what they could do and carved out their own space to transgress the boundaries of the time. The beach and the rest of the leisure zone were the public stages of performances, but just as critical were the spaces immediately off the boardwalk and out of sight. As we have already seen on the train ride to Winnipeg Beach and on the doorsteps of the cabin areas, "the night offered a measure of freedom from the regulation of daily life."[10] The dark corners of the beach, the woods behind the dance hall, and even the piers were spaces just a step back from the leisure zone, and all of them had their roles to play in how Winnipeg Beach was experienced and how it was conceptualized.

It is tempting to view the beach as a constant in the Winnipeg Beach experience. As Christopher Dafoe remarks in *The Lake: An Illustrated History of Manitobans' Cottage Country*, "Only the beach remains—the long sandy curve sighted by Sir William in 1901—and on hot summer weekends it is packed with people from the city and the surrounding countryside. Times and tastes change, the pleasures of 1920 do not appeal in 2000. On the great lakes of Manitoba only the lake and the sand are exactly as they were."[11] Physically, the beach has changed dramatically at Winnipeg Beach over the past century. Much of that long sandy curve that Whyte spied in 1901 has been swept away in the last half of the century. But Dafoe is not just speaking of the physical appearance of the beach; he is talking about the beach's conceptual role. The appeal of Winnipeg Beach that drew the CPR to it at the turn of the last century was its natural setting, in contrast to what was seen as the urban disorder of the time—a theme repeated throughout this discussion. The beach acts as the focal point of this discourse, and it is that particular role that Dafoe is really referring to, rather than its physical construction.

John Fiske views the lake as the "natural"—a turn of phrase intended to capture the lake's construction as raw nature in contrast to controlled culture. The lake is a socio-cultural construction, it is only "uncontrolled" because we conceive of culture as being controlled. To put it another way, the lake is simply a large body of water. It only becomes "uncontrolled" when people become involved. Frances Russell illustrates this discourse in her book *Mistehay Sakahegan the Great Lake: The Beauty and the Treachery of Lake Winnipeg*. Russell kicks off her work with a description of the three sisters, an Icelandic term for a set of three waves tumbling over each other in the lake. "These three sudden, stealthy, lethal waves, rising out of nowhere, can swamp an unwary boat, regardless of size. They capture the essence of Lake Winnipeg—its inscrutable capriciousness and awesome power," Russell writes.[12] The rest of her work is focused on tracing the character of that lake, its interaction with people, and the man-made (cultural) threats to its natural beauty and power.

The beach sits in the shadow of Lake Winnipeg's discursive power. Fiske describes the beach as an anomalous zone, a boundary place between the natural and cultural, a place where people might transcend the cultural and embrace the natural.[13] He goes further to read his meaning directly onto the beach, sketching out a conceptual transition within the physical attributes:

> The move from culture, the city, on the right to nature, the sea, on
> the left is effected through a number of zones. First there is the
> road, the public site of transition, and the boundary beyond which
> the car, that crucial cultural motif, cannot pass. Next comes grass,
> or more typically and significantly, lawn.… The edge of the lawn
> is marked by an esplanade, a concrete flat-topped wall that marks

This gun-powder beacon would have been used to light up the beach for a regatta in 1909; the beach was the seating area and the lake the stage for many events in the early part of the century. Later, as the tourism area developed, it would be the crowd itself that provided much of the entertainment.

the boundary beyond which the sea is not allowed to come.... By crossing the esplanade we reach the beach, the anomalous category between land and sea, but on the nature side of the nature/culture opposition—the fit between the physical and social is good, but significantly not perfect. We need, it would appear, to conceptualize the beach as nearer nature than culture: the beach is natural, whereas the lawn is cultural.[14]

Fiske's description comes close to the experience that Dafoe is trying to capture. But Fiske is not the first person to appreciate this transition from the cultural to the natural. It was precisely this anomalous zone that the CPR was hoping to exploit when it ran its line to Winnipeg Beach in 1901. And it was precisely that transition point that Gabrielle Roy was looking to capture when she took her characters Christine and Monsieur Saint-Hilaire to Winnipeg Beach in *The Road Past Altamont*. The two had struggled through a "fairground" of rides, noise and jostling people, frustrated by the cultural artefacts, but:

> Gradually, we left the odour of frying and the cries of the fairground behind us. We were still going along streets but now they were of sand. Then the sidewalks also ceased. The cottages on either side became more and more hidden among spruce and firs, which smelled good in the sun ... at that moment there came from somewhere ahead of us a fresh breeze that was even brisker than the air of an open prairie. This brisk air took us by surprise. We raised our heads, looking at each other as we drank it in. "That's its breath," the old man told me. An instant later he stopped me with a hand on my shoulder, "Listen. You can hear it." That was true. Before we saw it, we could hear it—a great regular beating like hands applauding in the distance ... at last we came to a long beach of a sand that was as tender to the feet as to the sight. Ahead of us, from one horizon to the other, as the old man had said, was the lake. Nothing but water.[15]

The cultural/natural encounter theme can be extended to include tans: "A tan is an anomalous category between skin (human, culture) and fur (animal, nature). A tanned body is a sign to be read by others, particularly others in the city. It signifies that the wearer, a city dweller, has been into nature and is bringing back both the physical health of the animal and the mental health that contact with nature brings into the artificiality of city life."[16] This should be familiar language: the city/nature contrast and the ability to avoid the "city's turmoil" was one of the ingredients that helped draw the CPR, excursionists, and cabin owners to Winnipeg Beach in the first place.[17]

In 1907 the *Manitoba Free Press* noted that Winnipeg Beach was "famous for its broad level stretches of sandy beaches where children may roll and tumble in the sand or wade and splash in the gradually sloping waters to their hearts' content, coming back for the opening of school with a tan which would do credit to a plains Indian."[18] This is not an idle reference to Aboriginal people having darker skin than European people—a suggestion that in and of itself could be challenged, given that neither group is homogeneous. Rather, the use of the term *Indian* here plays into the notion of the "noble savage" as someone who is at one with nature. This discourse, while not new, flowed across Canada at the turn of the twentieth century, showing itself in others areas such as medical discussions about childbirth, where doctors fretted that European women struggled through childbirth because civilization had physically taken them away from nature, in contrast to Aboriginal people, who were believed to be closer to nature and thus had an easier time with childbirth.[19] Winnipeg Beach children, through their exposure to the beach and acquisition of a tan, might also claim this oneness with nature and the health benefits that could come of it.

The discussion around tans says something about how Aboriginal people were incorporated into the Canadian colonial society. The journey to Winnipeg Beach took people into a natural setting—another sort of contact zone—where they might briefly take up some of the attributes of Aboriginal people.[20] But in making that journey, Manitoba's ethnically diverse population imagined itself in contrast to Canada's Aboriginal people. In that sense, Aboriginal people were used to help create a homogeneous European identity which, in turn, helped mask the divisions between the ethnic groups that were encompassed by that identity. In addition, identifying Aboriginal people and their presence with the past helped bolster the idea that Canada was a progressive country moving forward through the hard work of European settlers.[21] This identifying process can be seen in a *Free Press* article in 1924 that noted, "A local touch was given by the presence of some Indians and their squaws, who had dressed up for the occasion. They spent an enjoyable day watching the white folks lose their money on the wheel."[22] The English, Jewish, Ukrainian, Icelandic, and myriad other ethnic groups that came to Winnipeg Beach all became "white" when in the presence of Aboriginal people. Winnipeg Beach was not unique in this respect; it provided just one more example of the fact that colonialism is a process involving far more than signing treaties and creating reserves.

We can also observe the notion of skin colour at work in Bess Kaplan's novel *Corner Store*, set in the 1930s. As Becky, the protagonist, reaches the

19   Shooting the water shoot at Winnipeg Beach, 1906

The chutes would have been a popular ride in the early years of Winnipeg Beach before the boardwalk was fully developed. This 1906 image shows the earliest version of the CPR Pier in the background.

beach she comments, "I saw brown bodies, red bodies, and like ours, white bodies, the giveaway that they had just arrived at the beach. The white ones looked pale, sickly, and I didn't want to be one of them. I wondered how long it would be before we were the right color for the beach."[23] Roy's Christine and Monsieur Saint-Hilaire also see the distinction of a tan in *The Road Past Altamont*: "We looked exactly what we were, little folk from the city who were unaccustomed to the ways of beaches and had come there only to dream. More and more people overran the beach. They were for the most part young, bronzed, and laughing: they ran barefoot over the sand or went to throw themselves into the water with a great resounding splash."[24] We can see in both these references the familiar theme of the beach being a place away from the city, with the tan providing another signifier of this distinction and its health-promoting benefits. Demonstrating Roy's almost ceremonial treatment of the beach, Christine and Monsieur Saint-Hilaire stare outwards and contemplate this construction of the natural, while the young bronzed people around them go racing past and embrace it. The youth become, for a moment, one with the natural.

There is a class element in all of this, with the ideal beach tan—one that includes a body-wide, even bronzing, in contrast to the working-man's "farmer's tan"—requiring extended periods of leisure time that would be unavailable to people without financial means.[25] At Winnipeg Beach, particularly during the first half of the century, a tan would have differentiated campers from day trippers, those who could afford a cabin from those who could not. To people such as Victor Martin, who rented a bathing suit to swim at Winnipeg Beach, getting an all-over tan probably was not an option.[26] Lounging in the sun was a special event for a lot of people at Winnipeg Beach in the 1920s and 1930s. The brisk business that Mrs. R. Thedrikson (née Raykdal) could remember doing as a worker in the beach's swimsuit rental business suggests that many visitors to Winnipeg Beach were in the same situation as Martin.[27] In *Corner Store* the beach also carries a distinctive class element, with protagonist Becky linking it to a wealthy classmate who was able to make annual jaunts to the lake shore. No wonder she was in such a hurry to acquire a tan, which would be the colour of nature and the colour of the upper class, during her two-week stint at the beach.[28]

This talk of tanning raises the obvious question of what people were wearing when they went to the beach. The bathing suit that Victor Martin rented in the 1930s, which stretched from his knees to his shoulders, had changed little from the turn of the century, although more stylish suits for men were starting to increase the amount of skin that showed.[29] For women, as we will see, hemlines were on the move when, in the 1930s, tanning was starting to come into fashion.[30] That trend was noted by Jessie in 1930, when she sent a postcard from Winnipeg Beach to Miss Jeanie Mulholland in Scotland: "Dear Jeanie—Spending the last few days of my holidays here and having a wonderful time. The weather is very favourable and just ideal for getting the fashionable 'sun-tan,' Love Jessie."[31]

In the earliest years of Winnipeg Beach, when people were socializing more exclusively within community networks—with men "calling" on women, to borrow the middle-class phrase—instead of dating, the beach was an excursion point. People were content to use the lake as something to be admired or to take in an event that might be happening on the water. They were spectators when it came to entertainment.[32] While articles in 1904 and 1905 readily refer to children paddling in the water, their parents are most often positioned as beach-bound spectators, a scenario that fits neatly with pictures from the period that show couples, although relaxed, idling on the shore in dress clothes and dresses.[33] The goal was neither to tan nor to swim, but rather to promenade in this natural setting. At least, that was what they did at Winnipeg Beach, where the beach was, thanks to the efforts of the CPR, an area open to men and women.

Other swimming locations at the same time were open to men only, a situation that shaped how people behaved. Winnipeg's *Morning Telegram* ran an article in 1901 describing the public baths in Boston:

> 'The spectacle here on a warm day is really one of the sights of the world—thousands of men and boys disporting in the water or enjoying air and sun baths on the beach. For a picture of pure physical enjoyment it would be difficult to match it. And that the absence of costume requirements of any sort is appreciated by the patrons is shown by the fact that fully 90 per cent of the bathers dispense with all raiment and appear in Greek simplicity.' How long will it be before something similar can be written of Winnipeg?[34]

Indeed, swimming was often something men and women did in separate groups and was a clothing-less activity in the nineteenth century. On Toronto Island men staying on the island could nip into the water before 9:00 a.m. for a nude swim; the women in turn knew to avoid looking out towards the beach during that time.[35] The trend started to change in the first years of the twentieth century. In an Eaton's advertisement from 1911 the sales pitch for bathing suits states: "'COME ON IN FELLERS, THE WATER'S FINE.' Trust the boys to make the most of their bathing privileges during vacation days. Rules and regulations, however, enforce the wearing of Bathing Suits."[36] The use of the word *privileges* is probably entirely accurate in implying just how much swimming was a male privilege at the time, particularly when it came to swimming without clothes, and yet the reminder that bathing suits are a necessity tells us that that privilege was undergoing adjustments. Other articles also suggest that the era of swimming without clothes, something that clearly had gone on in semi-public areas, was passing. In 1912 the *Free Press* reported that "Percy Carson was fined $5 and costs in the police court yesterday for bathing in the Assiniboine River at River Heights without a bathing suit. Residents in the vicinity have been troubled very much lately with naked men bathing in the river, and it is likely that other arrests will follow."[37] The river swimmers were likely doing what they could to get a bath in the city. Private spaces, where access could be controlled, helped maintain the "clothing optional" approach to men's swimming up until the middle of the twentieth century. Male swim-team member Garth Teel can remember nude team practice at the YMCA as a

Swimming was a pretty modest affair in 1912, with clothing covering most of the body.

normal routine in the 1940s.[38] But Winnipeg Beach was not this sort of space. It was constructed to be a heterosocial public space, and swimsuits were part of the requirements if men and women were going to enter the water together.

The initial swimsuits people, and women in particular, wore in the first ten years of the twentieth century left nearly everything to the imagination, swaddling the body from head to nearly toe in clothing. These bathing suits had little to do with bathing and everything to do with protecting the virtue of women at the beach. Men also faced regulation. In 1910, for example, eight young men were arrested for wearing tight-fitting "Parisian" style swimsuits at Coney Island.[39] But just as public space was being opened for the heterosexual dating experience in the first years of the twentieth century, the physical boundaries of swimwear were being renegotiated. There was a practical aspect to this renegotiation. As women entered swim competitions at the start of the century, they needed swimwear that they could actually swim in. The trend towards more practical swimsuits caught attention at the international level in 1906 with the notoriety of swimming champion and later vaudeville star Annette Kellerman, who popularized the one-piece bathing suit and was promptly charged for appearing in one at Boston's Revere Beach.[40] Female swimmers won the right to compete in the 1912 Olympic Games in Stockholm. But attitudes followed more slowly: the New South Wales Ladies Amateur Swimming Association initially demanded—although it later backed down—that men not be able to view the female competitors at the 1912 Olympics.[41] Rose Scott, the president of the association since its inception, resigned in protest over the matter, saying, "I think it is disgusting that men should be allowed to attend ... I think it is horrible. We cannot have too much modesty, refinement or delicacy in the relation between men and women."[42] She might have added "distance" to her list, because the clothes, as much as the locations where men and women could associate together, were about controlling contact between the genders. While the Australians sent a female swimmer to the Olympics in 1912, the American amateur sport boss of the same period was adamantly opposed to women and men being in the same pool.[43]

The beach, as much as dance halls and public amusements, attested to the transition from homosocial to heterosocial behaviour, or from men and woman socializing separately to their playing together. In extolling the virtues of swimming lessons for girls and young children, a social column in the *Manitoba Free Press* noted in 1910 that "The old idea that swimming is a man's exercise has been dispersed, 'Everyone for herself,' says the maiden of today."[44] Bringing men and women together on the beach was not an easy transition. Mrs. George Harrison served as "matron" of the municipal public baths in Winnipeg for twenty-two years. When she retired in 1933, she recalled the challenge of launching the first women's swim club at the Pritchard Avenue public baths some twenty-plus years earlier. The women swam in private at the Pritchard Avenue baths, but they had their public debut at Winnipeg Beach. The *Free Press* reported Harrison's recollection this way: "'I remember it yet,' said Mrs. Harrison, with a twinkle in her eye: 'We were to take the girls to Winnipeg Beach for an exhibition and it was the first time girls ever put on such an exhibition in the province in one-piece bathing suits. I'm afraid there was a lot of comment.'"[45]

This regulatory discourse slowly shifted over the next forty years. American papers in 1921 still described "seamstresses with pins, needles, thread ... stationed at Chicago beaches ... to censor the bathing suits worn by women and sew in those wearers who violated prohibitions."[46] Similarly, at Coney Island in the 1920s, "women caught without stockings were escorted from the beach and 'one piece swimsuits' with less than five inches of skirt were deemed immoral."[47] A Canadian Press photo in 1941 shows a beach censor checking the measurements of a woman's swimsuit in Ventnor City, New Jersey. Ironically, the illustration of regulation flouted the goal of regulation by presenting a picture of a man running a tape measure up a woman's leg.[48] And again, these restrictions were not limited to women. In the 1930s fines of up to fifty dollars and sentences of up to ten days in jail were handed out to men at Coney Island Beach who wore topless bathing suits.[49] Zipper suits had become fashionable and allowed men to zip down their top when they were in the water and then zip it up when they were among people on the beach. However, such suits were taboo at Manitoba beaches in the 1930s if men tried to wear them with the top down.[50]

The shifting ground of what people could do is illustrated by an article that appeared in 1932 under the "News of Winnipeg Society—Items of Interest to Women" section in the *Free Press* describing how police forces had "gone modern" with their views on bathing suits: "'It's all in what you get used to,' one police officer, who preferred not to be mentioned by name, declared. 'If a girl appeared on the beach a few years ago with a few inches of bathing suit above the waist and not much more below, she would certainly have been indecently clad, and so would be subject to arrest. Today, you see those kinds of suits everywhere, on the stage, on the screen, in the magazines, so why bar them from the beaches?'"[51] The reference to stage and screen illustrates how mass culture in North America could have an impact on social mores at the local level. Yet this modern turn came with several caveats. For all that there was a more relaxed attitude, it was confined to the beach. The article went on to note that bathing suits were restricted to the lakeshore and riverbank. Similarly, there was concern that beach attire worn for "promenade" on the boardwalk rather than the beach was showing too much skin.[52]

The discussion around beach attire—and where it was appropriate—prompted an opinion piece in the *Free Press* entitled "Morals and Geography." The article observed, "It seems plain, then, that if [bathing suits] are not considered indecent now, the indecency we formerly attributed to them was solely in our own minds!" The article went on to point out the incongruity of allowing people to watch men in trunks box on TV but not allowing men to zip down their tops on the beach. It also noted that restrictions about limiting beach wear to the beach, "provides a pretty

By 1935 men were starting to lose their tops and women were starting to show a little more skin at Winnipeg Beach.

geographical angle to morality. Why is a bare back chaste at Grand or Winnipeg Beach and improper on Portage Avenue? And how many feet, or yards, or miles, away from a lake shore or a river bank is one permitted to go and yet remain within the circumstance of official purity?"[53] The article argued, "there is a line somewhere between a beach and a city that defines the moral from the immoral. The problem is to find it." Recalling Dundas's vivid description of a train ride back from Winnipeg Beach, one might argue that the line between immoral and moral was drawn the moment people stepped off the train in Winnipeg. But at the very least, these remarks remind us that people considered beaches a unique terrain. Indeed the shorthand use of the word *beach* to stand for the Winnipeg Beach resort town illustrates how the conceptual and moral geography of the beach filters throughout the entire resort.

This territorial appropriateness of clothing played out at beaches across North America. At Coney Island, beach-goers could be fined if they walked on the boardwalk in their bathing suits.[54] Similarly, Pauline Ketch could remember Mr. Quincy, the Winnipeg Beach police officer in the 1930s, taking a girl in a bathing suit off the Main Street and stating, "You are not allowed walking on the Main Street."[55] Assuming Ketch is remembering the period correctly, it fell before such strictures were cast into law at Winnipeg Beach: in 1943 the town council passed Bylaw 359, which insisted that

"Persons over the age of 12 years must be clad from shoulder to knees while promenading upon public highways, in business districts, or entering stores or other public places in the town of Winnipeg Beach."[56] The law stipulated a fine of twenty-five dollars for those who broke it. The council's decision earned it a rebuke from the *Free Press* in an article entitled "Queer Edict." There is nothing of the moral in the *Free Press*'s response, which argued for allowing beach-goers to move around the resort in their swimsuits as a matter of convenience.[57] However, in a letter to the editor, Mildred Carter Smith supported the new bylaw, noting that it rightly insisted that bathing suits be used for their "original purpose only." She goes on to add, "We are created by God and in His image and it is unseemly to desecrate our bodies in action as blaspheme Him in word."[58] Clearly to Smith, even God was willing to make allowances for people on the beach.

As the principal resort in Manitoba at the time—and arguably in all of the prairie provinces—Winnipeg Beach became synonymous with this sort of change, a fact that was seen even from newsrooms in Alberta. In an "On This Date" article in the *Lethbridge Herald* in 1936, the author recalled that when a circus came to the new city of Winnipeg in 1878 there was consternation over pictures of the trapeze artists in tights. He went on to ask, "what would they have said if they could have seen some of the bathing 'suits' worn at Winnipeg Beach nowadays?"[59]

There was one place where bathing suits were allowed, at least during special occasions: the Winnipeg Beach Dance Palace, where women and children participated in annual beauty pageants. Again, this was part of an international trend. Although women had appeared on stage in the nineteenth century, the first Miss America beauty pageant was held in 1921 in Atlantic City—not coincidentally, a seaside resort like Winnipeg Beach.[60] Toronto's Sunnyside Beach joined the fun in the 1920s with the Miss Toronto competition. The introduction of the beauty contest illustrates both women's ability to appear semi-clad in public without fear of sanction and the gender dynamics at work in women displaying themselves for men.[61] If the heterosexual experience was a marketable product, did that mean that the sexuality of women became a product as well?[62] There was also a moral geography to this; the beauty contests were acceptable at Winnipeg Beach because the dance hall, as the CPR had intended it, sat adjacent to the beach.

By the 1930s, beauty contests were an annual event at Winnipeg Beach, and pictures of the winners were routinely run in the *Free Press* from then

If bathing suits represented a boundary between men and women, then clearly by 1953 that boundary had been reduced, with bathing suits little different than today.

into the 1960s. The number of competitors in the 1930s ranged from 50 to 125, and the number of spectators ranged from 1,000 to 2,000, numbers made more impressive by the fact that at the time contests were held in the middle of the week. Commentary around the beauty contests is fairly limited, although the *Free Press* did tag the cutline for one picture in 1950 with the phrase "Here are five excellent reasons why there were more cases of eyestrain than sunburn at the Caterers' picnic Wednesday at Winnipeg Beach."[63] For adults, the pageants were a way for men and women to connect. Orest can remember getting one girl's address during a pageant held during the Caterers' picnic at Grand Beach in 1959. "She lived in the West End. I had a car at that time and I did take her out a couple of·times," he recalled.[64] But the contests also linked the community into that dating culture. Children were allowed to participate, and for Jessica, who could remember entering a contest as a child, the beauty contest was a taste of the adult world at Winnipeg Beach.[65] The contests were part of the dating scene at Winnipeg Beach, and it is no surprise that they, like the dating scene, petered out in the early 1960s.[66]

All this talk of bathing suits and tanning addresses the public face of the beach. At night, the darkness allowed people on the beach to bend the rules that restricted them during the day.[67] An amusing story from 1906 gives us a window into this night-time world. One summer evening two cottagers headed to the beach to go skinny-dipping or, as the *Free Press* column put it at the time, for a swim in their "home bath-room regulation garb." The skinny-dipping that had taken place in the rivers around Winnipeg did continue at Winnipeg Beach, but it went on under the cover of darkness. A few minutes after the men had entered the water:

> Two couples looking for a quiet spot to spoon wandered down almost to the lake shore and seated themselves, comfortably on an up-turned boat. The bathers bathed and frolicked, and then, like all good things, the bath came to an end and the bathers turned their faces homeward. Discovering the people quietly sitting on the upturned boat where their clothes rested, they called, hoping it might be members of their families; they called again but got no reply, and then shivering and with teeth chattering they rushed for the shore, whereupon the spooners bolted amid the shrieks of outraged femininity.[68]

The article goes on to note that the bathers and a few others had gone on to form "the Curfew Bathers club" and had picked out a less frequented part of the beach for their frolics "when no one should be looking, but the wise and silent old man in the moon."[69]

There is something of a territorial masculinity in the telling of this story, with the male bathers taking possession of the lake around them through their bodies and the very act of skinny-dipping. They created an all-male space that would be extended when more members were invited into the club. It was a move that was approved of even by the "old man in the moon." The spooning couples were also using the darkness to seek out a little freedom from the constraints of daily life. The "shrieks of outraged femininity" that the column recounted suggests that the female "spooners" behaved appropriately when confronted by naked men. Indeed, the use of the word *femininity* suggests it was the proper response for their entire gender, let alone these individuals. During the first ten to fifteen years of Winnipeg Beach, most courting went on in private, controlled settings. But these couples were heading out into the cover of darkness to get some time alone.

Were they properly married? The article provides no answers and does not seem terribly concerned about the question. Even in 1906, the beach was opening space for transgression.

Two weeks after the skinny-dippers and the couples had their encounter, the CPR announced plans to string electric lights along the beach front, "making the shore at night as light as day, which will add greatly to the enjoyment of the evening crowds from the city."[70] But was it really about enjoyment, or was it about controlling night-time behaviour? The timing might have been coincidental. But "morality lights" were often employed in recreation areas.[71] If darkness meant freedom, then lights would signify control. Certainly the addition of lights would have changed the experience of the beach. Both the skinny-dippers and the couples had sought out the darkness. Their experiences would not have been possible without it.

These night-time transgressions would continue to be a part of the beach experience. In mid-century, Bill McIntosh could recall skinny-dipping down by the water tower after the glowing boardwalk had shut down for the evening.[72] Trish Jones could also remember skinny-dipping at Winnipeg Beach as a child. The family would hire a transfer truck to take them out to Winnipeg Beach, a long arduous process that might not land them and their belongings at their rented cabin until eleven or twelve o'clock at night. But getting there made it all seem worthwhile: "It was wonderful when you first came down, everything was so fresh, the air, it was wonderful as a child, it seemed like hundreds of miles away. It seemed magical." Skinny-dipping was a late-night adventure for the family. "Mother would go down with a flashlight and we'd go skinny dipping, it was wonderful on a hot summer night," Jones recalled.[73]

For men and women, the public space of the beach could provide a safe, acceptable place for private moments, and not just at night. For Jessica, the beach provided the space for an encounter at the edge of World War II. As she recalled:

> I think one of the most pleasant days that I can remember was at Winnipeg Beach. There was a boy that I went to high school with. He was a boyfriend of a girlfriend of mine. I happen to bump into him on the government pier and we were talking and talking and then we decided to go for a walk along the lake and we found a little cove and we sat on the sand and talked and looked at the sky

The amusement area during its heyday in the 1920s with a crowd of people pushing along the boardwalk. Note the cars crowded among the amusements; even in the 1920s many people were driving to Winnipeg Beach.

and made pictures. He never touched me. Not once. Not even to hold my hand. And I had never talked to this man before, except to say hi or in a group. We went back to the pier and he said he had joined the navy and that was the last I saw of him. I mean he was just, it was just an incident. That was all it was.[74]

She received a letter from him during the war and wrote back. But they never made contact again. "I don't know if he died or changed his mind about corresponding or whatever. But that day at the beach was a very beautiful day. So that's all. Just a little story."[75]

Jessica's meeting on the pier reminds us that this extension of "land" into the water also provided a different environment from the beach, a place away from the sand and the bugs and the shoreline. If the lake was the "natural," the piers were a chance to extend the cultural even farther into the water. It should come as no surprise that they were a rallying point for young people at the beach and very much part of their territory.[76] When events such as the Wrigley Swim were underway and people crowded the piers to watch, local youths would look on with irritation. "It would be crowded," Bill McIntosh recalled. "We would be thinking, 'Why are all these people on our pier?'"[77]

The pier and the beach often served as the bleachers for many of Winnipeg Beach's performances, a scenario aptly pointed out by pictures of both the regatta, near the turn of the century, and the mile-long Wrigley Swim in the 1930s and 1940s, which show throngs of people lining the shore as events take place in the water.[78] The water, in turn, was a place to prove your worth. The events changed over the years, reflecting changes in class and gender. Sailing regattas were a staple of beach life in its first decades, a mark of Winnipeg Beach's flirtation with the upper class in its early years.[79] The Wrigley Swim competition was held at the beach in the 1930s, 1940s, and 1950s, and had categories for men and women. Winnipeg Beach was also the finishing point for long-distance swimmers proving that they could make the twenty-nine-kilometre swim from Grand Beach to Winnipeg Beach in the 1950s and 1960s. The latter event was most famously a female-led affair. Kathie McIntosh became the first person to swim the width of the lake in 1955. She had tried and failed on an earlier attempt. Her second attempt on Friday, 19 August 1955 brought out five men competing against her to be the first person to cross the lake, but McIntosh was the sole person to make it, garnering a time of sixteen hours and forty-two minutes.[80] The implications of her win were played up handily in newspapers with head-lines such as "She Won Where Five Men Failed."[81] McIntosh's record was knocked off on Saturday, 27 August 1955 when Rudy Shlack, an appliance salesman, crossed the lake in fifteen hours and forty minutes. McIntosh sent Shlack a telegram after he crossed the lake that read, "Congratulations. Glad to have a man in the club." [82] It was a neat statement of the equality of their efforts, and a subtle reminder that he was joining a club that she had created.

Even if there were no events happening, the lake served as the focal point, "sparkling like a great pale sapphire in the sun," as one 1905 *Free Press* article put it.[83] In a 1991 interview Jack London pointed out the lake's power in an almost offhand statement: "The town is on the wrong side of the lake," he noted, "because you can't take in the sunset looking at the water."[84]

The Built Environment

In 1903 the leisure zone consisted of little more than a dance pavilion. The railway, until it was moved further inland in 1911, swung along the lake-shore, taking passengers in front of the small business district and almost onto the beach itself. The dance pavilion was located a short walk north along the shoreline. Behind the dance pavilion was an extended park area for picnics. This design reflected the initial goals for Winnipeg Beach; it was intended to host large homogeneous groups, whether they were at the beach as part of an excursion or picnic or had strolled over from the cottages. The pavilion was built with an open hall and dining room in the back. Plans printed in the *Morning Telegram* in 1901 suggest the open hall was intended to host the excursion groups that were coming down to the beach[85]—most often composed of a distinct social group, whether church members or company employees—or to serve as a "rendezvous point for the campers and their friends."[86] But the natural setting of the lake was the real attraction. Most often, people faced outward to the lake for their public entertainment, whether they were watching a regatta or paddling a rowboat. The men had the option of engaging in the male-centred atmosphere of one of the local hotels, but much of the entertaining in these first years would have taken place in the cabins and on the verandas, away from the leisure zone.

There was a steady growth in attractions at the beach during the period before 1915, but the leisure zone did not really take off until World War I— around the time when Canada went "dance crazy"—and the CPR, egged on by demand and by competition from the new Grand Beach resort, rapidly expanded the rides offered along the boardwalk, adding the roller coaster in 1919. The boardwalk circuit was completed in 1924 when the CPR built the Dance Palace, which came complete with a 14,000-square-foot dance floor, the largest in Western Canada.[87] While the old dance hall sat in a park-like setting, the new dance hall sat at the north end of Main Street and, along with the roller coaster on the south side, created a book end for the board-walk and Main Street. The layout of the boardwalk and Main Street formed a distinctive loop that allowed people to flow along the boardwalk, where the concessions and rides were, and then circle back on Main Street, which hosted a number of restaurants and other amusement businesses, such as the Londons' Playland Arcade.

Winnipeg Beach was not an amusement park in the same sense that Steeplechase, Luna Park, or Dreamland were at Coney Island. Behaviour and even how people dressed when on the boardwalk was policed both by CPR and town or RCMP authorities and by other members of the crowd. But there were no gates to keep people out, and the only admission fee was the price of a train ride between Winnipeg and Winnipeg Beach, assuming people arrived by train. So the sort of control over the crowd that other amusement parks could achieve was not so readily available at Winnipeg Beach.

However, from a spatial arrangement point of view, Winnipeg Beach was an amusement park because the Main Street–boardwalk loop created a distinct area and allowed people to circulate through it, taking in this sensory experience. Amusement areas succeeded because they were able to capture the combination of thrill and intimacy.[88] They were meant to be "different from ordinary experience," not a "journey from urban life but a journey to an intensified version of it."[89] As I have noted, they were intended to recreate the carnival experience by providing an area that allowed for the "temporary suspension of all hierarchic distinctions and barriers."[90] For people going to Winnipeg Beach, this was a seasonal experience; summer was the time to hit the boardwalk and have some fun. The boardwalk also formed a bridge between nature and culture, literally allowing people to look at the games and rides on one side and the lake on the other side.[91] It was also a place where all the crowds could come together; the different ethnic communities merged, and the men and women who were bunking apart in the tourism infrastructure mingled on the boardwalk, allowing numbers to trump concerns that a man and woman alone together might engage in risky behaviour.[92]

Once on the boardwalk, the individual people merged into a spectacle of people, noise, and excitement.[93] The differences that divided Winnipeg Beach's diverse population did not disappear; friends clustered with friends, men and women promenaded in an effort to attract the opposite sex, and ethnic differences remained. And yet everyone was willing to join a collective experience. The boardwalk depended on both the crowd and the commercial amusements to create the excitement. Winnipeg Beach's boardwalk became a place for men and women to date and flirt and play because people brought that expectation into it.[94] Without the people and their urge to have a good time, Winnipeg Beach's spectacular roller coaster was merely a piece of equipment. But with groups of people screaming as they careened around the corners and clutching each other closely it became something more. Being part of the spectacle released people from the conventional behaviour and restraints of daily life, and, like the dance halls, such parks were places where young people could meet "without embarrassment within the sanctioned conventionality of the midway."[95]

The boardwalk linked the dance hall, beach, and rides and was fed directly by the train station. Dr. Paul Adams can remember meeting the trains at Winnipeg Beach in his youth and watching the people flow out of the train station. Many of them would head directly "on to the boardwalk either to spend money there, go on the amusements or to just watch. Because there was excitement there. There was activity."[96] Lawrence Isfeld had similar recollections: "With all the rides going, it was busy, it was like the hype. You know the merry-go-round was going around, the bumping cars, the planes were going, and the roller coaster. Yeah, things were happening. It was, people wanted to be there, because there was action going on."[97] The bumping cars and the roller coaster followed in a proud tradition of amusement park games whose goal, at least in part, was to allow men and women to be "bumped" together, challenging gender boundaries ever so slightly.[98]

Looking back at the 1940s, Val Kinack could recall that "the attractions didn't open until six o'clock, I think. We always knew they were open because there was a calliope that would be down there and it used to start playing and you could hear it all over the beach. So when we heard that we knew things were going. This is when we were younger and we'd high tail it down to the beach."[99] Just as the train whistle would alert people to the arrival and departure of the train, the calliope, a mechanical steam organ, would tell them when the boardwalk had been switched on. The calliope also came to symbolize the beach for Christopher Dafoe when he tried to trace the decline of Winnipeg Beach and argued that, as the area became more of a focal point for men trying to pick up women in the 1950s, "the merry-go-round music of the steam calliope became the slightly obscene wail of the saxophone."[100]

The boardwalk offered a little something for everyone; heading south from the dance hall, patrons could check out the movie theatre or head into the bowling alley, wander past the games of chance and maybe win some chocolate, and then move on to the rides such as the merry-go-round, dodgem cars, airplane ride, small Ferris wheel, or the beach's signature roller coaster. An interview subject who self-identified as a retired CNR worker could recall racing to the boardwalk with his friends on their bikes in the 1950s, and even fifty years later he could remember the distinctive feel of the roller coaster, which was built in 1919 but was still the main attraction in the 1950s when he was going: "It was a wooden structure. It moved. You know when you were going around corners the whole structure moved,"

The Winnipeg Beach boardwalk in full swing; clothing choices were often policed on the boardwalk to ensure that people looked respectable.

he recalled.[101] There was an element of male and female interaction in all of this. Dr. Paul Adams could recall "the young sparks" fishing out change to take their girlfriends on a ride.[102] But it also was simple escapism and performance. Married at just sixteen, Susan travelled to Winnipeg Beach with her husband and a group of friends to take part in the rides and the dance hall. Some of her strongest memories are of being banged about in the bumper cars and of riding on the roller coaster twenty-three times in a row.[103] She was not alone. Victor Martin said he and his friends would start their evening on the boardwalk. The "big attraction for us was riding the roller coaster; you went around and didn't hang on. As soon as you held on you were chicken. That was the biggest thing we got a kick out of," Martin recalled. "Rides were cheap, you just stayed on, I know one guy would go down and just about handcuff himself into [the roller coaster]."[104]

Nestor Mudry, who travelled to Winnipeg Beach in the 1930s and 1940s, could remember the boardwalk being lit up and a corridor of lights running from the boardwalk to the train station, which was also lit up.[105] In this Winnipeg Beach reflected its larger cousins at Blackpool or Coney Island, where Luna Park's "200,000 lights guaranteed decency even as they created feelings of freedom from constraint."[106] Lights helped control the use of space, and at Winnipeg Beach lights equated to public zones such as the boardwalk and the walkway to the train station, while a lack of lights equated to the anomalous zones of darkness, such as the beach at night or the forest of trees that surrounded the dance hall and grew to the south of the roller coaster.[107] Once again, lights provided moral security: the skinny-dipping and spooning that had happened during that summer evening in 1906 would never have occurred had the beach been lit up.

The boardwalk also included other amusements that showcased technology, a hallmark of amusement parks that had focused on attracting crowds through the miracle of technological innovation.[108] Winnipeg Beach did periodically update its rides and amusements, but others remained locked in time at the level of the resort's heyday in the 1920s. In particular, after the CPR sold to J.C. Hewitt in 1952 there were no major improvements to the resort. However, when Harry Silverberg, under Beach Enterprises Limited, took over the resort in 1961, he did make some repairs and improvements to the boardwalk amusements.[109] Dr. Paul Adams could recall an amusement booth that contained picture machines "where you would turn the handle and you would see pictures going by and in those days they were usually sort of cardboard papers that would flash down and make a moving picture." The pictures Adams was allowed to look at included horses running or some sort of adventure, but he also said, "I think some of them were girly pictures but we weren't allowed to view [them]."[110] While Adams's recollections are of the 1930s, Christopher Dafoe could recall similar naughty pictures of women clad in 1920s garb from his own rambling on the boardwalk in the 1950s.[111] It is a subtle reminder that Winnipeg Beach peaked, and many of its amusements were created and remained locked in the 1920s.

The excitement of the boardwalk is captured in pictures of the period showing the boardwalk literally filled with people. Pauline Ketch joked in a 1991 interview, "the crowds were so thick on the boardwalk, if you lost your child on Saturday, you couldn't find him until Monday [when] the crowds cleared."[112] Lawrence Isfeld could recall one evening when three Moonlight trains came rolling in to bolster an already busy summer crowd. The people promptly flowed from the train station to the boardwalk: "It was like a big flood. And of course the town, it's exactly the same. It's like two blocks there. Well those two blocks, you couldn't stand and talk to somebody on the street. The crowd would just move you along."

The crowd was ethnically diverse, allowing Winnipeg Beach to live up to its billing as "the People's Playground." While there was ethnic tension in the tourism infrastructure, the boardwalk was a meeting place for all ethnic groups. Jack London viewed the leisure zone as an ethnic melting pot.

The distinct groups that showed themselves in the tourism infrastructure blended into the crowd of the boardwalk. [113] At Coney Island, too, the ethnic enclaves managed to disappear into the crowds. [114] But as I have noted, there was a limit to this. African American people were rarely allowed into the American amusement areas, or they were segregated into areas of their own that were out of sight of the white patrons. [115] At Winnipeg Beach the racial dynamics were different, with friction centred on ethnicity rather than race. We have seen, however, how Aboriginal people were considered in contrast to the European settlers. That form of separation varied depending on how much Aboriginal people were willing to assimilate to white culture when they entered the resort areas. [116]

But most people remember the inclusions on the boardwalk, rather than the exclusions. Looking back, London said the experience of working in that crowd left him changed for life: "One knew, with the boardwalk, and the atmosphere, you were at the hub of vacation entertainment in Manitoba, because of this tremendous cosmopolitan mix, one had a sense of kind of being world class, growing up, there was no place better to be, it gives you a confidence with you for the rest of your life." [117] Other amusement parks in Canada have inspired similar memories. In the foreword to *I Remember Sunnyside*, Robert Thomas Allen describes the role of the amusement park in his youth, when it was a place to seek adventure, entertainment, and heterosexual love. He ends by noting, "You felt you were somehow at the source of things, a warm and tattered tent of life, convinced that something indescribably wonderful was going to happen within the next few minutes—the very spirit of Sunnyside." [118]

Coming to Winnipeg Beach in the 1930s, Mildred Kelly could recall being struck by the different languages and people. "[Winnipeg Beach was] colourful, yes it was because we had so many nationalities, Polish, Ukrainian, English, Scotch, colourful own way of lifestyle, other than that they got along fine," Kelly recalled. [119] This diversity was probably all the more distinctive for Winnipeggers who grew up in a time when Winnipeg's neighbourhoods were ethnically distinct. For Dr. Paul Adams, Winnipeg Beach's distinctive Jewish enclave stood out so dramatically because he had grown up in St. James, surrounded by predominantly British people. [120] Garth Teel, who grew up playing peacemaker among Winnipeg Beach's factions, and Barney Charach both saw the boardwalk and dance hall as being ethnically diverse places and not places of ethnic conflict. [121] There were, of course, fights in the dance hall and on the boardwalk, and we can speculate that some punch-ups had ethnic undertones. Some business, such as the Londons' Playland Arcade, were friendlier terrain for the Jewish patrons at the beach than others.[122] But I believe we can take the interview subjects seriously when they say that in the public space of the leisure zone, the same sort of conflict that occurred in the more private tourism infrastructure did not play out.

Most recollections of the boardwalk are of crowds and entertainment. But the experience depended on the crowd and the weather. Looking back, Jessica could recall a day in her youth when neither was available: "there was a puppet show on the boardwalk and for a penny you could watch. I remember going there once with another little girl that I was supposedly babysitting. I must have been about eight years old and I had to take this little girl with me. And it was pouring rain. We gave her our pennies. We were the only ones there and finally they just had to close the place and we had to walk all the way back home in the rain. I remember that so well."[123]

Age matters in this discussion. Most of the people recalling the board-walk draw from childhood memories or from memories of their teens or twenties. It was to this young heterosexual crowd that most of the enter-tainment of Winnipeg Beach was targeted, and the people who recall the resort draw their strongest memories from that period in their lives. But the boardwalk was open to all ages, and to a point it managed to serve all people by not serving all of the people at the same time. Heather Manz could recall going to the boardwalk as a child in the later afternoon. While she knew it stayed open late in the evening, she was never allowed to attend then: "the older crowd would go when the younger crowd was shooed off to bed. And that way they could enjoy themselves at the boardwalk," Manz recalled.[124]

But to truly understand the Winnipeg Beach experience we need to pull back from the individual activities and consider what people were really do-ing on the boardwalk. In 1962 a rather inauspicious block of text ran among the entertainment advertisements in the *Winnipeg Free Press*:

WHERE'S MY DOLL?
She was supposed to meet me on the boardwalk at WINNIPEG BEACH. I looked everywhere. In Western Canada's largest indoor roller rink there. I searched the dodgem cars, roller coaster and tilt-a-whirl with no luck. I even checked the new 8 lane bowling

alley and bowled a few games of ten pins, it was real smooth. I'm going back this week-end, maybe I'll find her. They open Friday nites at 7 p.m. Sat. and Sun. at 1 p.m. See you there.

—Ziggie[125]

There is no need to fret over whether Ziggie ever found his doll because, while it does not say so, the text is clearly an advertisement. But if anything, that status makes the text more interesting because it illustrates what Winnipeg Beach was trying to sell. While he—and it should not be surprising that the advertisement was cast in the male gender—provides a rundown of the rides that are available along the boardwalk, Ziggie was not really there for any of those things. He went there to find a woman. In many ways, Ziggie's experience encapsulates what the boardwalk was about. It was less about the individual rides than it was the experience of being on the boardwalk, and the encounters that might come from being there. The recollections of other amusement parks across Canada tell us that they were fuelled by men and women who went to meet and have a good time. In his nostalgic recollection of Toronto's Sunnyside Amusement Park, Mike Filey describes it as "the focal point for our courting and social activities [and a] chance to parade like peacocks our suntanned muscles." In *The Boardwalk Album: Memories of The Beach* Barbaranne Boyer describes children frolicking along Toronto's east-end lakeside amusement parks during the day, but in the evening, "young ladies and their beaus strolled hand in hand through the garden and along the many paths leading down to the shore. The moon and stars against a midnight-blue background provided the perfect romantic effect, living forever in the memories of many."[126] For these writers, there is no question what the beach was about. At Winnipeg Beach this role was even carved into the old dance pavilion, which was still standing in the early 1960s. Etched into the woodwork of the old building were the initials of people who had visited it over the decades, including, "in a lover's knot," the well-worn initials M.H.G. and C.F.W.[127]

Dorothy Lynch detailed her memories of Winnipeg Beach, recalling a period in the 1930s, for the Dance Hall Film Project in 1997. She could remember working a five-and-one-half-day week as a secretary for the marine insurance division of the British America Assurance Company, and after a week of work she was "ready to relax with friends so we'd board the 'Beach Moonlight': And oh, what excitement. We would spend a few hours

The Wrigley Swim gave people a chance to test themselves against Lake Winnipeg.

promenading along the boardwalk, there was the terrifying roller coaster, with its three sky-high peaks and dips and dancing in the pavilion to the music of Marsh Phimister and his Merry Men. We'd waltz, fox-trot and attempt the fancy steps—the fandango or tango. During dancing intermissions, we'd stroll along the boardwalk, our mouths watering, to buy popcorn for 25 cents a bag, and maybe a coke."[128] Jessica had similar memories of promenading at Winnipeg Beach in the 1930s and 1940s:

> When I got older it was just the thing, you went downtown and you walked around in circles all the way around the block and you kept doing that. And we bought chips that were really greasy but oh they were so good and in the evening all of us were sick because I'm sure they used grease that had been used, I don't know, weeks, months.... But that was it. There was nothing else at Winnipeg Beach that you could do. It was a routine. You'll find that with whoever you talk to. It was a routine. You walked around the boardwalk and you went to the dance.[129]

Val Kinack had much the same experience when she stepped on to what amounted to an oval. "[We'd] walk around and around, sometimes we'd stop and have something to eat. Sometimes we'd stop and play some of the games. Or we'd stop and talk to friends, go and have a look at the lake when it started to get darker," Kinack recalled. "We had lots of restaurants on that oval we could stop at. And if you saw one of your friends in there, that was reason enough to go in, sit down and have a coke or something with them."[130] The restaurants and concession stands were part of the experience, allowing people to pull off the boardwalk to talk and interact with one another.

For men the night usually included a stroll on the boardwalk too. For Nestor Mudry, the boardwalk was the first stop after getting off the train. "We went on the Moonlight and then we would get off the train and then go do the boardwalk thing and then end up at the dance hall," he recalled of his jaunts to Winnipeg Beach in the late 1930s and early 1940s.[131] In the 1950s it was similar for Orest when he headed up with male friends: "[We would] get off the train, go to the boardwalk, walk around. Usually go for the roller coaster ride. And I think the dances would start around 8:30 or 9:00 p.m. and they would go to midnight."[132] Barney Charach travelled to Winnipeg Beach as a teen in the 1930s, a routine that was cut short by marriage and service in World War II. As with the others, he can remember people strolling on the boardwalk, both before heading into the dance hall and while taking a break from dancing later in the evening. "They'd walk down to the boardwalk, and they'd start calling the girls' names and before you'd know it they'd double up and those who had a car would drive around and say, 'Hey, hey, you want a ride?' and things like that," Charach recalled.[133]

Charach's comments tell us what he thought this circling was about. Other interview subjects are equally explicit. As a young teenager in the 1950s, Robert Kendall and a friend caught a lift to Winnipeg Beach with his parents but volunteered to walk back to the cabin at Ponemah. On this particular occasion they were wishing to try their hand at the boardwalk: "being young teenagers we tried to hook up with some of the girls that we saw there without any success.… And we played games in the arcades while we were there. And bought hotdogs. Mostly we just eyed the girls and tried to attract their attention," Kendall recalled.[134] And at the end of the evening, "we walked back to Ponemah along the railway tracks after dark." Christopher Dafoe had similar recollections when he looked back at the "broadwalk," as he and his friends had called it. Writing in 1964, Dafoe remembered ten years back, to when he had been a teenager and would stroll down from Ponemah to see what adventures might await at Winnipeg Beach:

> We always went in a group, and there were many other groups just
> like ours, prowling endlessly along the well-worn circuit of Main

Street and the boardwalk, looking, always in vain, for easy girls.…
We went in hope of having the opportunity of sowing wild oats
but always the available female talent was hopelessly outnumbered
by the prowling males. One saw bold-looking girls on the arms of
leather jacketed giants and there were rumours of wild doings in
the beachside tourist cabins, but such secret and, perhaps, highly
questionable pleasures always eluded us.[135]

It should be clear that, at the very least, through their repetitive behaviour—this circling and seeking of opposite gender companions—people at
Winnipeg Beach were stamping the boardwalk as a place for heterosexual
encounters.[136] However, in defining the Winnipeg Beach boardwalk as this
heterosexual encounter area, I do not mean to imply that all the people who
walked on the boardwalk were seeking sex—though some no doubt were—
but rather that the area was ingrained as a place where men and women
could meet. This role is all the more startling when we consider the degree
to which the tourism infrastructure around the boardwalk was segregated
by gender. This role is also situated in time, a product of the dating culture in
which men and women could date in public; in fact, it was their going to the
boardwalk that affirmed it as heterosexual space. The sorts of encounters
taking place on the boardwalk during the 1920s through to the 1950s would
not have occurred in the period when Winnipeg Beach was engaged in
the calling system of courtship. Indeed, in the earliest days, no public
amusement area existed for these encounters to happen in.

Bess Kaplan provides one more description of the Winnipeg Beach
boardwalk in her book *Corner Store*, set in 1937, as seen through the eyes of
her ten-year-old protagonist, Becky Devine:

Gaudy neon signs flicked on and off, and crowds of people jostled
each other. They overflowed the sidewalks, moving sluggishly
through stores and cafes, over boardwalks and against booths,
onto the rides, into the dance pavilion which vibrated with loud
music, between the buildings, where couples hugged and kissed
shamelessly. I stared goggle-eyed till one young Romeo stopped
kissing long enough to growl at me: "Beat it, kid!" Papa walked
along beside Sylvia, looking neither to left nor to right, miss-
ing everything that I found interesting, and Simply Simon and
I snickered whenever we caught sight of another one of those

passionate embraces. Personally, I thought lovers were disgusting, and I couldn't see a) why they had to do anything as sickening as that and b) why they had to do it in public.[137]

We can sink into this description of a vast crowd moving sluggishly through the facilities and of men and women coupling in the spaces between buildings. But while her father tunes out the coupling going on around the family, Becky stares at it "goggle-eyed." Kaplan has a bigger project in mind in bringing Becky to Winnipeg Beach. She is foreshadowing the child's eventual growth into sexual maturity. That goal shows itself in Becky's fascination with the kissing couples, her staring at a swimmer whose breast has tumbled out of her swimsuit, her fascination with her neighbours, the Hannahs, and her efforts to deal with her father's marriage to Sylvia, her new stepmother.[138] In that sense, Kaplan's writing is most interesting because she chose a vacation at Winnipeg Beach as a means to contemplate such a subject.

The interview subjects speak to how the boardwalk was supposed to operate. By wading through the games of chance and bumping cars, it is possible to find that the boardwalk was a patterned terrain for gender display and interaction.[139] It is a display that shows up as clearly through an examination of what was not allowed on the boardwalk. The first example involves a group that called itself the Dew Drop Gang and that visited Winnipeg Beach in the early 1950s. "They were called the Dew Drop Gang and they terrorized the beach for I guess it went on for just about a month until it was finally taken care of. They were hoodlums from the North End, you might say, of Winnipeg. They wore strange fedora hats, that had a particular block in the hats, called the Chicago block, the way the hat was creased, the top of the Stetson, and they wore these things with all strange kind of clothes and chains and things. And they were a pretty nasty bunch," Garth Teel recalled.[140] Teel was working as a lifeguard at the time the Dew Drop Gang came calling. It was a position that lent him and his partner Tom Evans a role of authority. Within the tourism infrastructure, Teel tried to break up fights between the campers and the locals. In a similar role, he and his partner would stroll through the dance hall: "It could be pretty loud. It could be pretty wild. There was no security in the dance hall. Nobody wandering around to break up fights or settle arguments. The lifeguards, my partner and I, would walk around wearing our lifeguard uniform, which consisted of a white long sleeve shirt with a crest on it: Lifeguard ... and white pants. Duck pants they used to call them. They had kind of a flared bottom. And we'd parade around the dance hall in this kind of an outfit, don't ask me why but I would never do it today. But we were young. People respected us, listened to us. We settled a few arguments. We were always the mediators," Teel recalled.[141] There is an element of "good guys wear white and bad guys wear black" in these descriptions. Teel is well aware of how both he and the Dew Drop Gang members were creating their masculine identities through clothing.

The boardwalk had a sense of order, despite all the excitement, with people even being so courteous as to walk in a clockwise motion when crowds were heavy. The circling of men and women, most often in groups of friends, allowed for a little flirting, the chance to play the games and maybe win a prize for your date, and to settle into the restaurants and chat with friends. To this well-managed flow the Dew Drop Gang was a disruptive presence. Teel recalled, "You would spot them on the boardwalk in front of the concessions, just walking from end to end. They really just circled the town, they would walk along the boardwalk that had all the concessions and make a circle through the Main Street of the town and back around on the boardwalk. And that's pretty much what they did and they frequented the dance hall. But they were an ugly bunch of fellows that would just knock people around, off their feet for no reason at all."[142]

The Dew Drop Gang was following the same routine as everyone else. But most people walking in the circuit were trying to impress the opposite sex, or, as Mike Filey has described it with respect to the Sunnyside Amusement Park, looking for a "chance to parade like peacocks our sun-tanned muscles."[143] In contrast, the Dew Drop Gang was displaying an aggressive masculinity focused on bolstering their own sense of identity.[144] They were following a pattern of behaviour that they had already laid down in Winnipeg. The gang gathered public attention in 1949 and early 1950 and drew a series of headlines in the *Free Press* before fading from the public eye.[145] The group of teenagers was based in the North End and was apparently named after a home base, the Dew Drop Inn on Parr Street.[146] In a description that echoes Teel's, the *Free Press* marks Dew Drop Gang members by "their 'Chicago block' gray hats. The particular style of hat block consists of a roll in the crown about a third of the way from the top and one or two ridges in the felt at the very top. The crown slopes from a high peak to a low back."[147] While some gang members were involved in robberies and brandished a weapon during a couple of the reported instances, the group's method of operation in the city was much the same as it would be in Winnipeg Beach. They were "in the habit of trying to break up dances and community clubs all over the city." [148] They dropped into youth canteens, disrupted theatres, and tried to muscle their way into a bowling alley—all places that were, like Winnipeg Beach, spaces for men and women to mingle.

The Dew Drop Gang was primarily about display—even the *Free Press* called them publicity seeking[149]—and their treatment in the local media mirrored the sort of attention that "zoot-suit" gangs were receiving in Toronto at the same time, right down to having their style of clothes described and pictured in the newspaper.[150] Similar gangs made their presence felt on Toronto Island.[151] As in Winnipeg, the media attention the zoot-suit gangs in Toronto received was focused on their distinctive style of clothing. In the United States, zoot-suit-wearing youth received the blame for race riots that occurred in Los Angeles and New York in 1943, but in Canada their flashy clothes marked them as "dangerous to the social order."[152] Viewed alongside copycat groups in other cities we can see that the Dew Drop Gang was not just a group of ruffians in Winnipeg; rather, they were a symptom of the changing dynamics of sexual behaviour.

At Winnipeg Beach, the Dew Drop Gang's hyper-masculine behaviour was so out of script that it could not be allowed to continue. As Teel recalls, a group of local brothers joined forces with the lifeguards and four or five members of the local RCMP detachment to run the Dew Drop Gang out of town. The RCMP faced an interesting quandary—strictly speaking the gang was not breaking any laws, but they were transgressing the accepted norms of the community. "We all sat down and discussed what we could do about it. And there was no reason to arrest this group unless somebody filed a complaint, so it was agreed amongst this family of brothers, the RCMP and the lifeguards, that we would physically knock them around a bit to let them know they weren't welcome."[153] The Dew Drop Gang was lured into a dark area behind the dance hall and worked over by the Winnipeg Beach group. Punches were thrown, but nobody was seriously hurt and nobody, despite the notoriety the Dew Drop Gang had earned in the media, pulled a weapon in the midst of the fight.[154] "It was dark so you couldn't really see who was doing what. But you pretty well knew these guys were going down and after this fracas they just went in their cars and motored back to the city and they never came back," Teel said.[155]

The encounter with the Dew Drop Gang has become part of the lore of Winnipeg Beach—enough that it earned a mention from Christopher Dafoe in 1964 when he was writing his own eulogy for the beach.[156] Interestingly, Dafoe believed the gang had travelled back to Winnipeg on the train: "The corridors of The Moonlight, it was whispered, had seen savage sights on that particular occasion."[157] There is no reason to doubt Teel's recollections of the gang driving back to Winnipeg, but given the train's influence on Winnipeg Beach, it was probably hard to imagine it not being involved.

There were other out-of-script behaviours that were not permitted on the boardwalk. George M. Smith and his friends, for example, received a hail of stones on their cabin after choosing to stroll around the neighbourhood in drag. They also promenaded on the boardwalk and, again, found themselves in trouble when they played with the typical masculine identity. As Smith recalled, "We're walking on the boardwalk, and I don't blame the people, we were wearing these red clogs. They must have been women's clogs. And this dirt came after us. We went into the restaurant and they stood outside waiting for us. And we said, 'This is it this time.' And the fellow who ran it, he was very nice, he said, 'You wait a minute and I'll let you get out the back door.'"[158]

We can assume that the group chasing Smith and his friends did not involve lifeguards or RCMP officers. But again, gender identity was being policed. The Dew Drop Gang had been hyper-masculine, Smith and his group were playing with the feminine, and both of them were doing it in a place coded for heterosocial encounters. The interview with Smith, part of the Gay and Lesbian History Project, spends a great deal of time laying out a terrain of places where gay men in the 1950s and earlier might meet each other in Winnipeg. The interviewer goes on to ask Smith if there were places to cruise at Winnipeg Beach. To which Smith responded, "Cruise. Just the boardwalk. We were such idiots, we would get on the merry-go-round, and we didn't like the merry-go-round, and we would just scream. When you look back it's a wonder we didn't get into trouble."[159] In a way, they were cruising. The lady's clogs—as much a part of their identity as the Chicago Bloc hats had been for the Dew Drop Gang or the lifeguard's uniform had been for Teel—the joyful screaming, these were markers that were intended to create a sense of identity but also to send a signal to other gay people. And in doing that they were transgressing the heterosexual space of the board-walk and reshaping that space for their own purposes. Smith—who noted, "It's a wonder we didn't get into trouble"—and his friends knew exactly what they were doing and what the risks were. Their actions remind us that the repetitive circling done by heterosexual men and women, suitably dressed and behaving according to proper masculine and feminine identities, was securing the space for heterosexual encounters.[160]

Kathleen Rees provides one more example of how identity was policed on the boardwalk. In this case a group of jockeys was vacationing at the beach. "They were all small and one of them had a girl that was six feet tall and it was comical," Rees recalled. "Some of the locals in a café, they baited them and baited them, making fun of this girl."[161] A fight ensued after the jockey jumped up on a table and bit one of his adversaries. "I guess it was the only way he could defend himself," Rees said. The RCMP looked into the incident. Rees said they came knocking on her door looking for information about the jockeys and their girlfriends, who were, as was the custom in the tourism infrastructure, quite properly staying in separate cabins. The behaviour of the jockeys and their girlfriends was being policed, however, with the locals deeming it inappropriate for a woman to be dating a man smaller than herself. In that sense, the jockey was being mocked for his size. His girlfriend was being mocked for accepting someone of his size when she should have been, as per script, with someone larger and thus more masculine. No doubt her height was also a problem.

With all the focus on the boardwalk, it could easily be forgotten that Winnipeg Beach also hosted a men's-only beer parlour at the Winnipeg Beach Hotel from 1928 into the early 1960s. Shouldering its way in between the restaurants, the beach hotel was on the boardwalk/Main Street circuit. But it was very much apart from the male and female dynamic that was at the heart of that circuit. Mildred Kelly, daughter-in-law of Hannah Kelly, the proprietor, said in the winter it was a crowd of local men who kept the beer parlour busy.[162] The architecture of beer parlours had been intended to prevent raucous behaviour and excessive drinking. Patrons were seated around small tables and were not allowed to carry drinks from table to table.[163] There was no bar to carouse around—unlike the one featured in the Empress Hotel in the early years of Winnipeg Beach, before prohibition.[164] But with beer parlours stripped down to nothing but tables, men, and beer, the *Report of the Manitoba Liquor Enquiry Commission* noted in 1955 that "All in all it

The roller coaster at Winnipeg Beach, built in 1919, was the resort's most famous attraction.

may be said that Manitoba beer parlours are places where men may drink and drink and may do nothing else."[165] As Kelly recalled, the beer parlour patrons did plenty of that at the Winnipeg Beach Hotel. Winter work crews flooded in and the combination of company and alcohol would routinely lead to fights. The beer parlour was constructed as a place for men and men only, a place where men came together to be male, to hold forth on subjects of interest, or to defend their honour on the field of battle. It had nothing to do with meeting women. And indeed when the Manitoba Liquor Enquiry Commission announced its suggestions for new liquor laws in Manitoba, it went against allowing women into beer parlours[166] exactly because of the working-class male atmosphere.[167] What makes the beer parlour at Winnipeg Beach interesting for this project is how out of step that men-only nature made it to the rest of the heterosocial boardwalk facilities.

While Val Kinack and her friends would circle the boardwalk and Main Street and nip into the restaurants, they had nothing to do with the beer parlour. Kinack's earliest memories of the beer parlour were probably of the smell: "it smelled like stale beer." In fact, she said, the wafting smell of beer was enough to knock a person over. From day one, it was imprinted as a place she did not want to enter. But after she was married, it was a place that her husband did go. "When my husband's friends came down, they would go to the beer parlour. Cause that was, I guess they got away from us wives. We couldn't get at them. Directly. And frankly, we were glad to get rid of them for a while, if you want to know the truth," Kinack recalled.[168] In other words, getting rid of the men gave the women a chance to be together.

Things could have gone differently with respect to public drinking and Winnipeg Beach, and perhaps for alcohol and Manitoba as a whole. While women's beer parlours never became part of the drinking regime in Manitoba, the law did not expressly prohibit them, but rather the issue was mixing men and women together with alcohol. So it was that for a few hours in 1928, Winnipeg Beach was the home of Manitoba's only women's beer parlour. The Winnipeg Beach Hotel opened a women's beer parlour adjacent to its men's beer parlour in the spring of 1928.[169] It lasted a bare few hours before being closed down for not having obtained "the necessary license, from the commission." But because it had been located in a separate area of the hotel from the men's beer parlour, the hotel was able to keep operating its men's beer parlour unimpeded.[170] It is worth noting that it was a woman who opened the women's beer parlour. Hannah Kelly was the proprietor of the hotel and had just applied for and received a licence to run the men's beer parlour.[171]

The Dance Palace

Jessica's recollections of Winnipeg Beach at the beginning of this chapter brought together the boardwalk, the rides, the sand, and the smell of the lake—in other words, culture meeting with nature. The CPR had this experience in mind when it was building its new dance hall in 1924. The company took a direct hand in the dance hall's construction, sending its engineers to look over some of the "leading resorts in the United States with a view to incorporate all the latest ideas required in such a largely patronized resort as Winnipeg Beach is."[172] The company was careful to ensure that the new location was as close to the water as possible, feeding, again, off Winnipeg Beach's juxtaposition of the cultural and the natural. [173] And it would seem the positioning worked. A *Free Press* writer covering one of the dance hall's first evenings in 1924 certainly appreciated this link of culture and the natural. The article used gendered language to note that while jazz music played indoors, outdoors "a chaste moon filtered its soft, silvery beams through the blue twilight that rested on the bosom of the lake, and a short distance from the dancers, tiny waves reluctantly curled over the yellow sand and broke with little muffled sighs, forming an endless, diminutive sea symphony."[174] Nestor Mudry played at Winnipeg Beach as part of Leonard's

Casino Band in the summer of 1941 and danced there as a customer in the late 1930s and '40s. He recalled the appeal of Winnipeg Beach in an interview: "[The Dance Palace] was an open air place, the windows were all open. It was kind of neat dancing out there, it was almost like dancing outside.... And just the experience of going someplace else, going out of town, so to speak."[175] Or as Orest, who travelled to the dance hall in 1955 and 1956, put it, "Winnipeg Beach was summer time. A chance to get out of Winnipeg, it was something different."[176]

The interior of the Dance Palace was constructed with a wide promenade and seating area around the dance floor that offered space for strolling or viewing the "scene" for "those who, through age or indisposition, did not dance." [177] This promenade and seating area was a feature that the original dance pavilion did not have and was probably one of the latest ideas that the CPR incorporated into the new dance hall. In the 1920s and early 1930s this promenade was occupied by a diverse range of community members. Born in 1923, Agnes Walker could recall the entire family going down to the dance hall in her youth to watch the dancers. "There was a wooden railing around the dance floor that we could stand by and enjoy the music."[178] Similarly, in 1925, when May Johnson wrote to the *Free Press's* Sunshine Club about her trip to Winnipeg Beach to stay with her aunt, she included a casual mention that they stopped into the dance hall in the evenings.[179] Rounding out these experiences are the recollections of Doris Margolis, who could recall the dance hall in the 1920s and early 1930s being open to everyone, "young and old alike."[180] Margolis could even recall calling out a song request as a child—to the amusement of the dance hall patrons—and having it played. The early appearance of Margolis, who came from a Jewish family, in the dance hall also illustrates that it was an ethnic meeting point as early as the 1920s. The dance hall would continue to be a place for community events throughout its lifespan, including the baby contests and beauty contests that began in the 1930s. But the number of children and families entering the dance hall in the evening appears to have declined in the 1940s and 1950s. This suggests that throughout the first half of the twentieth century segregation practices moved from distinguishing by gender to distinguishing by different age groups.[181] The dance hall became less of a community meeting point and more an area specifically set aside for heterosexual dating for older teens and twenty-somethings, an activity that was increasingly considered off limits to the prying eyes of children.

Robert Kendall, born in 1943, remembers the dance hall being off limits in the 1950s. "I remember seeing it. But I was too young to go into it," Kendall recalled. "Big huge wooden building, sort of round at the north end of the street that ran along the waterfront. I remember hearing about the dances that were there. Parties and things. But, like I said, I was too young to go in there. So I never got to see inside it."[182] It was similar for Barry Anderson, born in 1934: "I was very interested in it, because I'm a piano player and I always liked to be near the place to hear the piano, the piano player. Usually it was a good sized orchestra that was there. Piano, bass, drums, sax, trumpets, and the place was packed. I was too young to go in but I would stand outside and listen to the music."[183] Jessica had similar recollections from her early summers at Winnipeg Beach: "We'd go downtown to the boardwalk and we'd hear the music coming from the dance hall because there were live bands and it was pretty thrilling. We could hardly wait until we were old enough to go to the dance hall." And what age did one have to be? "You know I don't think that there was any age. But it was just sort of unspoken that you didn't go in when you were young. That you had to wait until you were at least sixteen or seventeen. Maybe there was a rule, but if there was, I don't know."[184]

The dance hall thus appealed, and in some ways was limited to, people within a certain age group, primarily single people in their late teens and twenties. It provided a different scenario from something like the CPR picnic, which had held events for married and unmarried men and women but had included activities for children. Writers such as Mary Louise Adams have argued that teens, as a distinct social group, did not emerge until the 1930s.[185] Certainly at Winnipeg Beach it was the teens and those in their early twenties who came to be the focal point of the leisure zone during the period from 1920 through to the 1950s. Older people—people in their fifties and sixties—could come into the dance hall: "The odd time we had a few older people come in, you know parents, grandparents and stuff," Ina Drummond, who worked at the dance hall in the early 1950s, recalled. "I remember one time, there was an older couple and they got into one corner and they were just having the time of their lives dancing in that one corner. Everyone just sort of stayed out of their way and left them alone. They were just having a really good time." In some ways this exception proves the rule that the dance hall was for younger people in the 1940s and 1950s, given that the exceptions to that demographic were sealed in a space of their own.

The open access to the dance hall in the 1920s and 1930s reflected how dances were organized in that period of time. People paid by the dance—or, rather, by a set, which would include two or three quick songs. The length of the sets depended on the dance-hall management. If they were looking to make a bit of extra money, they would tighten up the number of sets in an hour, but typically it would be between thirteen and fourteen sets an hour, or about two-and-a-half minutes per set, with the cost set at about five cents per set.[186] It is the jitney dances that people remember from the 1930s, and it was assumed that it would be the man buying the dance ticket for himself and his partner before they headed out to the dance floor.[187] A rope would be drawn across the dance floor at the end of the set, clearing it for a new set of ticket holders to dance.[188] Such an approach meant that, while access to the dance floor was controlled, access to the promenade around the dance floor did not need to be, and people could, as Nestor Mudry recalled, "sit around and listen to the band and watch the people dancing."[189]

During the late 1930s and early 1940s, the system was in transition. Dances during the week used the jitney approach, but during the weekends when the dance hall was busier, the fences that controlled access to the dance floor would be taken down and admission would be charged for access to the dance hall itself. Throughout the 1940s and 1950s it was the latter approach that was used, which is why Lawrence Isfeld and Orest remembered people paying to go into the dance hall and either having their hands stamped or receiving a pass when they went back outside.[190] The change in system meant people were paying for the experience of being in the dance hall. It also made it a more exclusive affair, cutting out children, who would have been non-paying customers, and community people who previously might have wandered in to enjoy the scene. The change probably also reflected the fact that what was happening in the promenade area around the dance floor was as critical to the experience of being in the dance hall as what was happening on the dance floor.

The jitney dances were accepted because people were expected to change partners throughout the evening. Men buying tickets had an opening to ask for a dance, and women looking to dance were, to a degree, beholden to men who had bought tickets.[191] Etiquette books from the period show that dancers were encouraged to change partners throughout the evening. Dancing was a competitive opportunity for display, and, as Beth Bailey explains in *From Front Porch to Back Seat*, "spending all your time with the same man ... was in poor taste unless you were engaged to him."[192] Some writers have suggested this pre–World War II approach to dating may have been a competitive game that had the goal of demonstrating the individual's popularity, and that, after World War II, the scarcity of men led women to take a "going steady" approach and stick to one partner when they headed out dancing.[193] But other writers have argued, and I agree, that the post–World War II approach was not based on a scarcity of men, but rather on women seeking more control of the relationship and the potential for "more power and respect, more trust and sexual pleasure" in their relationships.[194] The changes in dating patterns also reflected the fact that men and women were becoming less regulated in how they could spend time with each other. At Winnipeg Beach's Dance Palace during the 1930s, '40s, and even into the early '50s, the casual atmosphere of swapping dance partners was a part of the evening.

Writing in 1961 and sticking tightly to the script that Bailey outlines, Dorothy Garbutt recalled her own trips to Winnipeg Beach in the summer of 1919. Typically she and her friends would travel in groups of four or six to ensure plenty of dance partners. "For, you see, we didn't go steady in those days. We had our boyfriends, to be sure (I think mine was named Frank that summer) but we usually only danced with him the first and last dance. In between times we had ourselves a ball by dancing with everyone we knew. We would have been mortally ashamed to be seen dancing with 'the guy what brung us' all evening, for it would have meant that he was stuck with us and out of gallantry was seeing to it that we weren't sitting on the sidelines as woeful wallflowers. Oh well, other times, other customs."[195] Garbutt's last words indicate that things had changed by the 1960s.

Similarly, Izzy Peltz and Mary, his future wife, travelled to the dance hall in the late 1930s with a group of friends for an evening of fun in the dance hall. Peltz said the group stayed together throughout the evening, so the scenario was probably similar to Garbutt's description.[196] Val Kinack's memories are along the same lines. She would have been going during the 1940s and can still remember the approach of having to purchase tickets for every dance. While Garbutt was heading out on the Moonlight special, Kinack and her friends were wandering over to the dance hall from their cabins or rental accommodations: "You would go with two or three other couples, depending on who was down there at the time, not everybody was there at the time. You'd all go to the dance, you'd dance with each other, you wouldn't just dance with the person you went with, you'd dance with some-body else, and there's every possibility somebody, if you're sitting on that bench on the side waiting for somebody, a complete stranger would come up and ask you to dance. And you'd probably say yes because it was so safe with all those people there."[197]

There is something fundamental in Kinack's statement that "it was so safe with all those people there." The freedom at Winnipeg Beach was based on being part of this collective experience. People might not have been un-der the surveillance of their parents, but they were under the surveillance of the crowd, which was both a limiting and an enabling factor. The crowd helped create a safe space. But the safety was also founded on an under-standing of how far people would or would not go. People could skip from dance partner to dance partner knowing that a shared understanding of sexual boundaries and limitations at the time ensured that a dance was just a dance. Thus Kinack's earlier statement, about throwing over a date when she and her friends were offered a ride by another man (her future husband, as it turned out), is not surprising. This freedom of movement also allowed Pauline Ketch, who worked with her husband at a restaurant in Winnipeg Beach, to drop over to the dance hall on her own. "I used to go to the dance hall without my husband after I was finished working and the strange men would ask me to dance and I'd dance, and one guy said, 'Do you want to go out for a walk and maybe [a drink],'" Ketch recalled. "I said, 'I don't think my husband would like it.' He dropped me like a hot potato, left me stand-ing there. My husband always came for the last waltz."[198] While the safety of the dance hall allowed Ketch to dance with strange men, there was a limit to how far this could go. The abrupt reaction of her dance partner is also a reminder that some men and women were looking for something more than just a two-minute-and-thirty-second dance.

While Kinack and other couples headed to the Dance Palace in a group, other people entered with same-sex groups of friends. Aggressive moral discourses around the behaviour of women in the first decades of the twen-tieth century claimed that a woman entering the dance hall alone might be seen as a prostitute and that female dancers could avoid this suggestion by "hunting in pairs" or entering in groups.[199] This discourse was at work in the Winnipeg Beach experience in encouraging people to head to the lei-sure area in homosocial groups. But obviously locals such as Pauline Ketch did have the freedom to enter the dance hall alone without fear of moral

*Interior of the Dance Palace. The railing around the dance floor helped control access;
a critical addition in the period when people paid by the set.*

sanction. Once inside, these groups would blend into the heterosocial experience. The promenade that offered people the chance to sit back and view the dance was also the location where the groups of people mixed and mingled and individuals asked each other to dance. Given that the Dance Palace had been built when dating and changing dance partners was the standard approach, the promenade had probably been constructed with that purpose in mind. It was the dance hall's equivalent of the boardwalk/ Main Street circuit. "We wouldn't date, at that age we couldn't afford to date. Because you'd have to pay for her to go to the dance hall," Barney Charach recalled. "You'd meet them inside the dance hall and you'd go up to them, 'Would you care to dance?' and they'd be very happy to dance with you."[200] Garth Teel was old enough to date while he was lifeguarding at Winnipeg Beach in his late teens, but he says the dance hall was a place to meet ladies and friends, not a place where he would take a date. This approach carried on at least into the 1950s. From his visits to the beach in 1955 and 1956, Orest could recall "pacing, walking around and checking out the chicks or the girls or whatever you want to call them, and then if you asked for a dance, they'd dance for you."[201]

Of course, if people wanted to succeed in this venue, they had to know how to dance. The situation was illustrated by an advertisement that ran in 1911: "WINNIPEG BEACH. Going there this summer? Can you dance? No! Take a few PRIVATE DANCING LESSONS from PROF. WILLIAM E. NORMAN (12 years experience). WINNIPEG'S LEADING TEACHER"[202] The use of Winnipeg Beach in the advertisement also shows how the resort was at the leading edge of this sort of experience. In 1911 there were few commercial entertainment venues in the city of Winnipeg and certainly nothing of the same calibre. It was a position of dominance that Winnipeg Beach had lost by mid-century, when a range of dance clubs had opened, or even in 1916, when Grand Beach's dance hall opened.[203] People took the need to know how to dance seriously.[204] "I always said to myself, and I made sure I became a pretty good dancer, because I noticed these guys always had the best looking girls and they were dancing all night," Lawrence Isfeld recalled. It would have been a lesson he took to heart while working in the dance hall as a young teenager in the early 1950s. Men who could not dance, and went with a girlfriend, were expected to find her a suitable dancing partner who could. Harry Simpson recalled going with former Blue Bomber Martin Hatch to the dance hall, around 1940. "Martin said, 'Harry, you've got to dance with my girl, I can't dance,'" Simpson recalled.[205] Presumably, women had to be good dancers too, but the interview subjects who expressed the concern most clearly were men, indicating that dance steps were one more tool in the arsenal of skills that men were supposed to have, as the pursuers.

By law nobody could drink in the dance hall. Until 1957 public drinking in Manitoba was restricted to all-male beer parlours, private members clubs, or socials.[206] This regulatory regime meant that at Winnipeg Beach public drinking was officially pushed out of the leisure zone, with the exception of the Winnipeg Beach beer parlour, where men could drink. Unofficially, of course, people did drink in and around the dance hall, and the tourism infrastructure was filled with a range of options for people looking to imbibe. Orest says it was not uncommon when he was going to Winnipeg Beach in the 1950s for men to bring a mickey of alcohol with them—"for a little bit of courage"—and mix it with some Coke and Pepsi.[207] A mickey is a pint-sized bottle that can be easily pocketed. The word *courage* provides a sense of how alcohol was being used. It was intended as a lubricant for the heterosocial experience of the dance hall. Working at the concession stand in the 1940s, Val Kinack could remember pouring the sodas: "They'd bring their own bottles and get the Coke from us if they wanted to drink at the dance hall. In a cup. They'd ask for a cup. Paper cups. But you could smell it, that's for sure."[208] There was an etiquette to the process—people would buy the mix, or maybe just a cup, but they knew enough not to mix their drinks at the concession stand. "But you knew they were. Oh sure. That was kind of a standing joke," Kinack recalled.[209] Some of these mixed drinks were probably tipped back inside the dance hall, but the assumption among the interview subjects was that most of the drinking was done outside. "It was just a steady flow [in and out of the building]," Lawrence Isfeld recalled, looking back at the early 1950s. "Cause they were running outside and drinking, they had mickeys of whiskey."[210]

The Dance Palace had never been intended as a mixed-drinking establishment. It was built in 1924, a year after Manitoba had ended prohibition by allowing the sale of alcohol through government stores, but four years before the sale of beer by the glass in beer parlours.[211] Even when beer by the glass was allowed in 1928, it was premised on the alcohol being sold to men only in men-only beer parlours. At the time, the idea of men and women drinking in public together brought forth connotations of prostitution rather than mixed-gender socialization.[212] And yet recollections from the 1940s and 1950s make it clear that alcohol was likely being consumed in the dance hall, and most certainly outside in the dark areas around it. The focus was on the men, but women could just as easily pocket a mickey.[213] While not officially allowed, the behaviour was being quietly tolerated by workers who knew exactly what their customers were doing with their requests for cups and soda pop.[214] In a sense, Winnipeg Beach was a transitional zone for alcohol as a lubricant for male and female encounters, but the practice was tucked out of sight and not part of the official face of the boardwalk and dance hall. Legally, it was not until 1957 that liquor laws changed in Manitoba to allow public mixed-gender drinking in cocktail lounges, beverage rooms, and restaurants.[215] Mariana Valverde has argued that "class, sex, and gender had to be simultaneously reorganized in relation to spirits drinking in order to make the cocktail lounge possible."[216] Mixed public drinking, once associated with prostitution, became central to the new drinking establishments that emerged after World War II. But by the late 1950s the Winnipeg Beach dance hall was serving double duty as a roller rink. Legalized public mixed drinking was never part of its experience.

People did more than just drink outside; couples would routinely head outside for time alone or simply to catch their breath. The script typically followed by moral reformers at the start of the twentieth century said that if a woman headed out of the dance hall with a man, she could face accusations of poor moral behaviour because the departure was a red flag that the couple might be going to engage in sexual acts.[217] But at Winnipeg Beach, the extended leisure zone encouraged people to go outside. All the sights and sounds of the boardwalk were available. People who did not want to take part in the dancing could while away their time on the boardwalk and continue to walk along the circuit through town.[218] For couples looking for their own space, the CPR pier, located right next to the dance hall, would have been a charming location. "Until they tore it down, if you wanted to go out with a boyfriend, or whoever, alone, you would generally go for a walk on the CPR pier because the moon was so, the stars were shining the lights were low. It was, you know, it was a romantic place to go," Val Kinack recalled.[219]

Izzy Peltz and his future wife, Mary, spent as much of their time in the dance hall as they could, "dancing and kibitzing with friends," but even they would take a break for a walk on the pier.[220] And when Agnes Walker travelled to Winnipeg Beach in the 1930s with a friend to meet a blind date—who was, as it turned out, her future husband—it was to the pier that she and her date headed after a few dances to get to know each other better.[221] Like the dance hall, the pier offered safe social space.[222] While the remembered experience is of finding privacy and being able to stare out across the water, the pier was busy throughout the evening. People found privacy by tuning out the other couples around them, and yet the couples surrounding them ensured that the pier was a safe location.

There were other more private areas that people could, and did, seek out. These areas took them away from the bright lights of the boardwalk, into the darkness, the quintessential unregulated zone.[223] Some couples, such as our spooning friends in 1906, would have headed down to the inky darkness of the beach, unlit despite the musings of the CPR about extending lights along the beachfront, for a little more privacy.[224] To the south of the boardwalk circuit they might have strolled down a lover's lane that stretched along the shore towards Stephenson's Point. It was here that Christopher Dafoe could recall seeing in the 1950s "entwined couples, labouring silently together, oblivious to all passersby" even during daylight hours, and it was here that Lawrence Isfeld could recall strolling the next morning to find beer bottles, condom wrappers, and the crushed grass where, presumably, people had bedded down for a time.[225]

The CPR Pier was an ideal spot to step out of the dance hall and catch your breath. Winnipeg Beach's second pier, the Government Pier, was located next to the harbour.

Similarly, the park area north of the dance hall was filled with trees and was not lit up at night. It was here that the RCMP, lifeguards, and a group of local residents lured the Dew Drop Gang before hanging a beating on them and chasing them out of town. It was also to this forested area around the dance hall that people would have headed to tip back their alcohol. These areas would have been appropriate choices for couples seeking space of their own. An interview subject who self-identified as Tadpole could recall a friend bragging about taking a girl outside and "doing the deed" and still being back inside to start dancing for the next set.[226] A Brandon resident, Tadpole had also had the dubious pleasure of being kicked out of the tent when he was camping with a male companion at Clear Lake in the 1930s. His companion had just brought home a date from the Clear Lake dance hall. Barry Anderson used to walk through the area around the Dance Palace on his way to and from Boundary Park. It was a shortcut that ranged along the waterfront and Prospect Drive. "But I wouldn't take that route at night," he recalled. "I would go the roadway, instead of going that way at night when there was activity. I guess my mother told me not to walk that way."[227] Other couples would have, as Mildred Kelly could recall, headed to the Winnipeg Beach Hotel for a few hours together.[228] And others would have walked along the beach with a boy, as Jessica had during one sunny afternoon, and simply talked and stared at the sky.

When Pauline Ketch headed to the dance hall without her husband and danced the evening away with strangers until her husband arrived, she was following a certain set of rules that were embedded in mid-century courtship. Dancing with strange men in the dance hall was perfectly acceptable. But the moment she was asked to go for a walk outside, she had to make her marital situation and her intentions for the evening clear to her dance partner. And he, by dropping her "like a hot potato" after she told him, made his intentions clear as well.[229] The boardwalk and the dance hall were two sides of the same coin, a place where men and women could go to be with one another.[230] Indeed, this was a place where men and women were expected to go with one another. When we push through the individual activities we see that the ritualized behaviour, the circling on the boardwalk, the walking and sitting in the promenade in the dance hall, were really about laying the grounds for encounter. Conflict showed on the boardwalk when people acted in ways that were contrary to this script, such as the Dew Drop Gang, or when they flouted the expected boundaries of masculinity by wearing red clogs or of femininity by dating a smaller man. Conflict also occurred when, like drunken men outside the dance hall, men turned to fighting to showcase their masculine prowess. The leisure zone was the focal point for such behaviour.

The evolved leisure zone described here barely existed in the earliest years of Winnipeg Beach, when the area was a focal point instead for genteel middle-class behaviour and a system of courtship that focused on distinct social groups. Indeed, dating as a system of courtship was critical to the construction of Winnipeg Beach's leisure zone. It was a system suspended between regulation and freedom. Unmarried men and women were restricted when it came to their opportunities for being together alone, but getting together in public was perfectly acceptable. The leisure zone at Winnipeg Beach was one of these public meeting points; in fact, that was its primary role, a role that was embedded in the wooden boardwalk by the countless footsteps of men and women who circled their way through the amusement area. What happened after they met in public was their own concern, but Winnipeg Beach provided the grey zones for them to seek out privacy—whether at the pier, on the beach, on a trail through the bush, or in the sudden darkness of the Moonlight train on the trip home.

Chapter Four
Remaking the Beach

Winnipeg Beach proudly marketed itself as the Coney Island of the West. It was one of hundreds of amusement parks across North America that attempted to replicate the experience of North America's most famous amusement area.[1] The numbers of people served were vastly different: Winnipeg Beach would see 40,000 people on a busy weekend; Coney Island could hit 1.5 million.[2] But their role as an interaction point for men and women—a locale for dating—was much the same. Both resorts attracted a similar youthful demographic and both had trended towards a working-class clientele. These similarities help account for their rise in the first decades of the twentieth century and steady decline after the World War II. The similarity continued until Winnipeg Beach's boardwalk and dance hall closed down in 1964, the same year that Steeplechase Park, the last of the original Coney Island amusement parks, closed its gates.[3]

Other amusement parks met a similar fate. In Manitoba, Grand Beach was taken over by the province and reopened as a provincial park in 1961. Its dance hall had burned down in 1950, and the new provincial park was shorn of any of the remaining amusement facilities, save for the spectacular beach.[4] Toronto's east-side shoreline saw a succession of amusement areas: Victoria Park, Munro Park, Kew Gardens, and finally Scarboro Park. The names still linger on Toronto's shoreline, but Scarboro Park was closed in 1925 and the amusements were quickly cleared away.[5] The beach remained, of course. The Hanlan's Point amusement area on Toronto Island was billed as Canada's most popular amusement area during its heyday at the start of the twentieth century, but it was closed in the 1930s to make way for the

Winnipeg Beach played many different roles; its space as a place for men and women to meet changed as the twentieth century moved on. But the beach's role as a place for families has remained.

Billy Bishop City Airport (known better locally as the Island airport).[6] The role of Toronto Island as an amusement area was further diminished in the 1950s and 1960s when the city began to clear out the local community to make room for an open park setting.[7] Finally, Sunnyside Amusement Park was closed and then demolished in the 1950s to make way for the Gardiner Expressway. As Mike Filey notes in his book *I Remember Sunnyside*, the "boardwalk planks were standing in the way of progress."

People did see change coming at Winnipeg Beach. The Great Depression caused people at the resort to tighten their belts, just as it did at other amusement areas in North America.[8] But tight finances also worked in Winnipeg Beach's favour because its close proximity to Winnipeg and low cost meant that it was still able to draw people in even as Manitoba's economy shuddered in the 1930s. However, the Empress Hotel burned down at the end of the summer in 1935 and was never replaced, extinguishing Winnipeg Beach's most visible link with upper-class patrons.[9] And concerns about the future of Winnipeg Beach and its popularity were being raised as early as 1939.[10] In 1951, following disruptions brought on by the 1950 Red

The Empress Hotel burned down in 1935 and was never replaced. While Winnipeg Beach carried on, the hotel's loss signalled the end of the resort's high tide and symbolically suggested the decline of the upper-middle-class presence at the resort.

River flood, there was talk that the Moonlight train would stop running, and a nostalgic story ran in the *Winnipeg Free Press* reminiscing about how popular Winnipeg Beach had once been.[11] In the mid-1950s concerns about the resort's future began to truly be felt. Winnipeg Beach resident Lawrence Isfeld could remember the boardwalk buzzing with activity when he started working there at twelve years old in 1952. But by the time he turned fifteen it had gone quiet. The transformation happened before his eyes: "All of a sudden when I was fifteen it would be like a ghost town. There was nobody there Friday night, we would open the whole boardwalk up, but unless the weather was perfect there was very few people coming.... It changed so fast.... It all happened from about 1952 to 1956, it was like it was on a fast downhill slide. I just can't remember when they stopped those Moonlight trains. I still think they were there in 1956, those Moonlights, but I think that might have been the last year."[12]

It was. The Moonlight trains were discontinued after the 1956 season. Regular passenger service ended in 1961.[13] The removal of train service was the last step in the CPR's withdrawal from Winnipeg Beach. It had already sold its cabin property in the period between 1940 and 1945, and in 1952 it sold the amusement area property and equipment to J.C. Hewitt of Beachside Attractions Limited for $45,000.[14] Beach Enterprises Limited under Harry Silverberg purchased the amusement area in 1961 for $80,000.[15] The CPR spearheaded Winnipeg Beach's creation and played a direct role in helping it transition to a centre for dating. But after the sale of the amusement area in 1952, interview subjects such as Jack London remembered the CPR stepping back: "Prior to that the railway was everything and after that it was nothing."[16] Winnipeg Beach was only valuable to the CPR if people wanted to take the train to reach it. As people began to go elsewhere and began to use cars to get there, the CPR withdrew.

The arrival of the first car in Winnipeg Beach has become part of the mythology of the resort. Former mayor W.J. Wood penned the tale in his "A Brief History of Winnipeg Beach 1901–1955": "When the first car landed in Winnipeg Beach it ran over a dog which belonged to [police magistrate] Mr. Kernested. This dog was a public nuisance, but in spite of this Mr. Kernested was quite fleet of foot and ran down the road trying to catch the car number, but it had gone beyond his reach."[17] The story is repeated in nearly every historical account of the community, including Frances Russell's *Mistehay Sakahegan, the Great Lake: The Beauty and the Treachery of Lake Winnipeg* and David Laurence Jones's *Tales of the CPR*, a book filled with anecdotes about the railway company.[18] It is hard to imagine that Wood was not indulging in a bit of myth-making. Later in his recollections, he mentions that the first car had arrived at Winnipeg Beach in 1913 with an empty gas tank and punched-out springs, hardly a vehicle capable of making a quick getaway. At the very least, the year 1913 is wrong. The first cars were arriving in Winnipeg Beach by 1910 and were already using the *Free Press* as a venue to debate the best route for getting there.[19] Yet the story is

Cars came early to Winnipeg Beach, and as more came deciding how to deal with traffic became more and more of an issue for the community.

irresistible as a premonition of how the car would change life at Winnipeg Beach.

The flexibility of the car opened new vistas for vacationers, scattering them across the province to competing resorts and taking away business that had once gone to Winnipeg Beach.[20] Yet the car was both friend and enemy. The resort became the destination of one of the first provincial highways from the city of Winnipeg, which meant that during the 1920s and 1930s it benefited from the arrival of the car. Drivers crowded the highway to Winnipeg Beach, and as rail travel declined some of the biggest challenges facing the resort—and arguments between it and the province—were on how to deal with the volume of cars coming into the community.[21] It was not until other resort regions, such as the Whiteshell, developed and became more accessible through provincial highways in the 1950s that the flexibility of the car truly began to draw people away from Winnipeg Beach.[22]

Coney Island and Blackpool encountered their own challenges from vehicular traffic. Coney Island faced increasing competition in the 1920s from a series of beaches on Long Island that became accessible to cars, although not to public transit. The impact was two-fold: car owners could go elsewhere, thus cutting business at the resort, while people who could not afford cars focused on Coney Island, increasing its reputation as a working-class resort.[23] Blackpool saw rail traffic drop from 3.2 million passengers in 1937 to 630,000 in 1966. Cars picked up those lost numbers, crowding the streets of the resort. But the real issue was "how to preserve in the era of the car a crowd culture based on what was now an obsolete urban layout centered on railway depots?"[24] The solution was to direct traffic through the city along the former rail line route and use the old depot area and marshalling yards as parking areas. The traditional pedestrian traffic flow was thus maintained.[25]

Winnipeg Beach faced similar challenges with its traffic flow and had some success in focusing parking around the downtown area. But what it was not able to replicate in the era of the car was the scheduled rhythm of the train. A busy Moonlight special would drop 1,600 people at the resort, creating a buzz of excitement at the train station that would flow down to the boardwalk and into the dance hall. Even into the early 1950s, when more people arrived at the beach by car rather than train, the train station was still the community meeting place, and the train still set the schedule for events, signalling that the beach or boardwalk was going to get busy.[26] Not long after the Moonlight special ceased running, the Dance Palace, no longer guaranteed this evening crowd, was turned into a roller rink for all ages. Thereafter it served only an occasional role as a home for dancing. For people such as Orest, for whom the train ride was a foundational part of the Winnipeg Beach experience, there was little reason to visit after 1956.[27]

In an epilogue of sorts to the train's role in Winnipeg Beach, Heather Manz took one of the last train rides to the beach, as a child with her family. She remembers it distinctly because she was able to smuggle her puppy on board the train, with the conductor being none the wiser. But the ride itself had none of the romance that had once been attached to the train: "To me it seemed that it took forever because we trundled down the track, you know like rails, slow, clack clack clack clack, not clickety clack. Clack. It was very ponderous I would call it. That's a good word, ponderous. And when we finally did reach the station, I was so glad to get off that train because those seats were made out of wood. There was no padding on it. You know, like a pew at a church."[28]

The car created a new social space. Part of what the train had offered was the ability to maintain boundaries on the way to Winnipeg Beach. Same-sex groups travelled together with the expectation of meeting members of the opposite sex within the leisure zone. Theoretically, the car could offer the same boundaries; people could travel to the resort in separate vehicles with the expectation of meeting at the resort. But the car was far more often expected to be a place where people of the opposite sex could find a little privacy of their own, which is why Barney Charach could remember people driving around asking members of the opposite sex if they wanted to go for a ride.[29] Finding that privacy was a goal not so far removed from what couples had in mind when they extinguished the lights on the Moonlight trains.

Winnipeg Beach had been created by the CPR as an excursion point and oasis of calm to which workers could retreat from the chaotic city. Courting was part of this role, with the controlled social gatherings—whether picnics that were held by a wide range of religious, ethnic, and work-based groups, or upper-middle-class "in-house" cabin gatherings—allowing men and women to mingle. This controlled social mixing underpinned the calling system of courting that existed in the first decades of the twentieth century. But roughly during the period of World War I, Winnipeg Beach transitioned into a public amusement area, the roller coaster being the signature addition in 1919. This transition happened in lockstep with a shift in courting approach; rather than courting in private, men and women began to date in public. Winnipeg Beach became one such place for dating, and while other age groups used the resort, it was the eighteen-to-thirty-year-old demographic that was the target market for the leisure zone between 1920 and the mid-1950s. Class changes were part of this transition. The move of working-class women into the workforce gave them the means to pay their way into public amusements, and the lack of available privacy at home helped encourage public courting as well.[30] Winnipeg Beach's cabin area and colourful regattas had fit within Winnipeg middle-class society, though even from the beginning the working class had been able to reach the resort to take part in special events and picnics. However, with the growth of a public amusement area to service the dating market, the resort increasingly focused on attracting a working-class crowd to the leisure zone. The tourism infrastructure adjusted, with cabins that had housed middle-class families and social events being remade into boarding houses for young working-class men and women out for an evening, or weekend, of entertainment.

Dating carried its own set of guidelines for how people were expected to behave. Men and women were expected to stay in separate accommodations at the resort—maintaining the traditional boundaries between the sexes—and meet within the public leisure zone, perhaps stealing a kiss on the front step at the end of the night.[31] Men and women would take the train to Winnipeg Beach in their respective gender groups to look for dance partners in the dance hall. Or, relying on the safety of a group, they would travel with other couples together on the train for an evening's entertainment in the dance hall or on the boardwalk. Trading partners in the dance hall was expected and part of the evening, and so it was perfectly acceptable for a married woman to dance with a stranger, provided the encounter did not continue outside the hall. The rules existed with the understanding that there were ways to circumvent them. Couples seeking more privacy might find a quiet spot on the beach. More adventurous couples might rent a room in the Winnipeg Beach Hotel, signing in as a married couple even if they were not. These off-boardwalk zones, which were often night-time zones, gave people some precious freedom in the midst of the regulatory regime around them. Winnipeg Beach was built as a place where people could follow rules and where they could break them.

Coney Island historians have argued that it focused on the youth market and that "in the 1930s, forty and sixty year olds who had visited Coney Island at the age of twenty felt little need or desire to return."[32] The young people going to Coney Island for dates had little reason to return after they had married or had children. In contrast, Blackpool, a more distant journey from major urban centres, was able to become a life-long vacation spot that people would return to year after year.[33] Winnipeg Beach fits between Coney Island and Blackpool. Families did return to it year after year to use the cabins and beach, and children would join the crowds along the boardwalk. However, as early as the 1930s, as alternative vacation spots opened in Manitoba, this crowd began to decline. The dating crowd kept going and, if anything, the community worked harder to draw it. For the people between eighteen and thirty, the draw of Winnipeg Beach was its role as a locale for heterosexual interaction. The rides, the dance hall, and the beach provided the public setting that made this role possible, but the opportunity for men and women to meet was the draw, rather than miniature golf or even the popular roller coaster. Coney Island failed as an amusement area because it failed to recruit a new generation of pleasure seekers and ceased to be the place to take a date.[34] The same is true of Winnipeg Beach.

By the mid-1950s and certainly the 1960s the network of rules established by the dating system were changing. Using English, Dutch, German, and American manners books to track changes in courting approaches, Cas Wouters has noted, "In the early 1960s, an English author sighed, 'Boy meets girl and girl meets boy in so many different ways that it would be quite impossible to enumerate them.' ... This impossibility became taken for granted and was no longer expressed after the early 1960s. However, before that time enumerating the various places and ways of meeting had been quite normal procedure."[35] The sort of gender segregation that had underpinned Winnipeg Beach was breaking down. In Manitoba, liquor laws that had kept men and women from drinking together in public— routinely circumvented at Winnipeg Beach—were changed in 1957 to allow for the creation of mixed-gender cocktail lounges. Heterosexuality, which had once been the focus of liquor regulations, was revalorized and made central to these new drinking establishments.[36] The new mixed drinking establishments were never part of the Winnipeg Beach experience, focused as it was on boardwalk, dance hall, and beach. But their importance is not in their popularity but, rather, in illustrating the changing terrain of gender relations during the 1950s.

A moral panic developed in the 1950s over the sexual behaviour of youth. This wave of concern was part of a broader effort to ensure that teenagers achieved "normal" sexuality as they moved into adulthood. [37] The panic shows itself at Winnipeg Beach in the statements of people such as Stephen Juba, who argued that dilapidated cottages were being rented to juvenile groups from Winnipeg for "wild week-end parties."[38] In 1956 the *Free Press* ran an article discussing youth drinking. In response a teenager phoned the newspaper to argue that it was underestimating the number of teens who drink. The *Free Press*, appearing to run the teen's comments verbatim, noted that, "He said mixed parties are held in Winnipeg Beach cottages every night in the summer months, 'and they don't stop at drinking.'"[39] The comments could, of course, have been hyperbole. The more interesting detail is that the *Free Press* chose to publish them and the implied threat to propriety behind them. Speculating in 1964 that Winnipeg Beach had lost its way, Christopher Dafoe recalled similar stories of "secret and, perhaps, highly questionable pleasures" taking place in the cabins.[40] To some degree the belief that Winnipeg Beach had become too "honky-tonk"—the phrase used in the 1960s as people looked back to the 1950s—was part of the moral panic. But it was not exaggeration when people such as Dafoe argued that the dating culture of Winnipeg Beach changed in the 1950s.[41] To some degree, Winnipeg Beach, which had functioned as a place for heterosexual interaction at least since World War

I, was increasingly becoming a place for sexual action. The end of dating culture can be linked to the sexual revolution of the 1950s and 1960s, when sex became the "medium of contemporary courtship."[42] Winnipeg Beach, based as it was on a series of rules designed to regulate how men and women could interact, had no particular advantage to offer a dating culture based on intimate sex acts. Indeed, with the remaining rental cabins sitting within a now family-based residential area, it had several distinct disadvantages.

These moral concerns about the beach reflected changes in the tourism infrastructure. The growth of Winnipeg Beach's public amusement area had created a concurrent growth in the number of accommodations available for the resort's patrons. Some cabins had changed into boarding houses for young singles. Other cabins were rented to vacationing groups or families. The growing affluence of the working and middle classes after World War II meant that many families were buying their own cabins at the resort. The number of people renting declined as the number of people owning grew. Winnipeg Beach's tourism infrastructure in the 1950s was increasingly owned by middle-class people using the resort as a second home and, like Izzy Peltz, commuting into Winnipeg by car.[43] They had no interest in the resort as a place for rowdy youth. This attitude was evident in the creation of the Winnipeg Beach Taxpayers Improvements Association in 1955. At the group's first meeting, which was attended by about 500 permanent and summer residents, Winnipeg lawyer and president of the new group, J. Irving Keith, stated that he "'personally' would like to see one-day and week-end transients stay away from the beach." Other people at the meeting called for more policing to prevent the "objectionable things going on around government pier."[44] The concern about sexuality is obvious, but in responding to the meeting a *Winnipeg Free Press* letter writer argued that Winnipeg Beach, the "People's Playground," was trying to create a class enclave. The writer, who referred to himself as "a transient," wrote, "Because [J. Irving Keith] and other members of the association are fortunate enough to be able to afford private cottages at the beach they would like to see the rest of us 'transients,' to use his words, deprived of even an occasional afternoon at the lake, which quite often is all the majority of us can afford." He went on to add, "'week-enders' have kept Winnipeg Beach going for many years and I don't think they'll sit back and watch it made into a private beach for a few wealthy snobs."[45] The tension with the youth culture continued, and in 1961 the town went so far as to create a curfew aimed at keeping youth under sixteen off the streets after 10:30 p.m.[46] So much for being a place for youthful high jinks.

American writers such as Bryant Simon and David Nasaw have charged changing racial dynamics in the 1950s and 1960s with bringing down the public amusement areas in the United States. They note that Atlantic City, Coney Island, and other public amusement areas in the United States were built upon the exclusion of African Americans. They were places where America's diverse ethnic groups could go to affirm their whiteness. That dynamic held the seeds of their undoing in the 1950s and 1960s as racial segregation—both official and unofficial—broke down in the United States. Atlantic City became a "black" place in the eyes of white Americans, so it was taken off the map of places they could go.[47] Certainly the same racial dynamic was not at play at Winnipeg Beach, where patrons focused on divisions between ethnic groups. Aboriginal people played the role of cultural other at the beach, but that role neither created the amusement park experience nor ended it.

But stepping beyond the racial argument, Simon and Nasaw also saw cultural changes afoot in the American context. Simon notes that when a policeman was quizzed about the decline of Atlantic City in 1970, he was quick to say it had become filled with African Americans, homosexuals, and hippies.[48] And indeed, we see the same concerns about "sex parties" and "orgies" popping up at Atlantic City's motels as we do at Winnipeg Beach's cabins, which suggests that a changing moral order was happening before people's eyes—or at least just out of sight—and that they did not like it.[49] Meanwhile, when Nasaw notes that America's urban movie houses were undergoing their own decline in the 1950s he points to the increased racial mixing taking place in the theatres as one of the concerns but goes on to note that fears surrounding youthful sexuality were also at work.[50] This constant reference to sex—and concern about whether people were having it or not—suggests how important cultural changes were in shifting the terrain of urban landscapes.[51] We can see concerns about the sexual revolution of the 1950s and 1960s at work in Winnipeg Beach; the flip side was that if people were being pushed out of Winnipeg Beach because of these concerns they could and did go elsewhere.

While middle-class cabin owners were rejecting Winnipeg Beach's leisure zone in the 1950s, middle-class people elsewhere were being drawn to new types of public amusement areas that were built around two separate, though linked, appeals: first, "child-like innocence captured in a commercialized fantasy world that culminated in Disney," and second, "nostalgia for imagined older versions of community grounded in craft and manual skill, technologies using steam and water, and the visible proximity of nature as seen at Beamish," a British heritage park.[52] Middle-class families set the tone for these amusement areas, and as affluence grew, and family vacations became more possible, these areas became child focused. Disneyland allowed adults to thrive vicariously through the child experience, and Beamish enabled the child to be the recipient of the heritage experience.[53] In the 1950s Disney was able to tap into the same cross-class experience that Coney Island had in 1900, creating a true "mass" culture experience.[54]

There were efforts to attract a child-centred market to Winnipeg Beach. Advertisements in the 1950s from Beach Attractions Limited and the CPR included the traditional dancers and couples—hallmarks of the resort's role as a heterosexual meeting place—but others focused on the amusement park, kids, and an appeal to the "whole family." The town of Winnipeg Beach focused its advertising on attracting families.[55] Of course, children did have value to the amusement area, even if they did not to the railway. It is not coincidental that this shift in marketing came at the same time that Disneyland was being created in Anaheim. With Disneyland, Walt Disney created a fantasy land that was not tied to a natural "sacred place" but instead relied on creating a controlled commercial fantasy land as a childhood experience.[56] Control, in the United States, once again included attempts to keep African American patrons out of the scene. Disney himself was opposed to the spirit of resorts such as Coney Island, which was, like Winnipeg Beach, a place for men and women to meet. Disneyland targeted the affluent middle-class families of the 1950s and fell in line with the cultural conservatism of that period. Winnipeg Beach's family-focused advertisements make it clear that the amusement area was also trying to recreate its market, or trying to appeal to two different markets at the same time.

But Winnipeg Beach was never going to be Disneyland; the climate restricts business to the summer months, and the resort would have needed to recreate an amusement area that had been allowed to deteriorate since the CPR had ceased pumping money into it (though, to his credit, Harry Silverberg had put about $30,000 into the resort after taking it over in 1961).[57] Disneyland had an entertainment empire behind it that could create not only a theme park but also the very fantasies that that theme park was attempting to emulate.[58] Most significantly, Disneyland was created on "virgin" territory in an Anaheim orange grove. Winnipeg Beach could not recreate itself from scratch in the milieu of the 1950s. Its role and reputation as a heterosexual meeting place was too firmly embedded. And it does not seem that the boardwalk owners ever seriously tried, given that advertisements in 1962, such as the "Where's My Doll?" advertisement, still focused on men searching for women amongst the rides and games of the boardwalk.[59]

By the late 1950s and early 1960s, the eighteen-to-thirty age group that had formerly supported the leisure zone was going elsewhere to meet the opposite sex. Ina Drummond and Barry Anderson, who had spent their youth at Winnipeg Beach, never used it as a place to go on a date.[60] Orest, who had caught the last of the Moonlight trains in 1955 and 1956, also began going elsewhere. "It was towards the end," Orest said of his trips to Winnipeg Beach. "1957-1958 was almost the end."[61] After that he joined the Badminton Club in Winnipeg. It had traditionally been a white Anglo-Saxon Protestant establishment, but those boundaries were coming down and Orest was the fourth person of Ukrainian descent to become a member.[62] The spaces where different ethnic groups in Manitoba could come together were rapidly expanding after 1950. Orest also began going to the Whiteshell region with friends: "We used to go for the May the 24th weekend and the ice would be just out of the water and for a couple of years in a row after a night of great revelry and debauch, I would jump into the lake."[63] Unlike Winnipeg Beach there was no dance, no train, and no boardwalk: "It was strictly a couple of cases of beer, barbecues, and you could take a girl with you if you wanted or there were girls coming," Orest recalled.[64] The sort of rules of behaviour that had chased men and women into separate cabins during the 1920s and 1930s at Winnipeg Beach did not apply by the time Orest was heading to the Whiteshell.

Teenagers, drawn primarily from the local cabin area, still frequented the leisure zone in the early 1960s. In about 1961 Lawrence Cherniack penned a teenager's view of life in Winnipeg Beach. It is aggressive and decidedly masculine, but it still follows the familiar routine: "Our circuit is simple: Along the Main Street, then along the boardwalk; stopping whenever we please. Occasionally we drive around town, looking at the girls and assuming patronizing expressions.... The older girls walk in pairs around

The message on the back of this postcard noted: "Here we are and it's lovely." The image shows a family setting at Winnipeg Beach in 1912. The province of Manitoba would work to recreate that setting when it redeveloped the waterfront in the 1960s.

the downtown area, waiting to be picked up."[65] Aspects of his description differ from those of earlier decades. While they walk the boardwalk circuit, most of the teens congregate in the penny arcades, "where a row of cars parked in front offers convenient seats."[66] Cherniack adds, "No one is using any of the rides.... All the games, like penny toss and hit the balloon are closed."[67] The boardwalk circuit is still there, and its lingering social construction as a heterosexual encounter point is clearly what Cherniack and the other teens are drawn to. But they are just going through the motions. The boardwalk had thrived because the lights, games, and rides had provided a public cloak for the sort of heterosexual cruising that Cherniack and his friends engage in. But in this particular instance, the games of chance are silent and the rides are vacant, leaving the role of the boardwalk laid bare. To Cherniack and the others, it hardly mattered. They were as likely to meet a girl driving around town, playing a game in the arcade, or in any one of "so many different ways that it would be quite impossible to enumerate them."[68] They did not need Winnipeg Beach, but they went there because the steady drumbeat of feet on the boardwalk over the years had left a mark on the social space of the resort. They went because it was the thing to do.

Throughout the discussions of the 1950s and 1960s, the lake continued to serve its role as the natural contrast to the resort's cultural attractions.

Frances Russell's view on Lake Winnipeg's "inscrutable capriciousness and awesome power,"[69] written at the beginning of the twenty-first century, fits in neatly with Gabrielle Roy's portrayal of the lake as a "dark mass that heaved and growled dully," published in 1966.[70] Yet, there were physical changes at Winnipeg Beach that diminished its attractiveness during the period when the beach was becoming the resort's only draw. The wide beach that people saw in the first decades of the twentieth century was substantially swept away in the 1950s. Alarm about the beach's condition was raised in 1955 when Winnipeg Beach property owners asked that the lake be lowered or that a breakwater be created to protect the beach.[71] It was not until 1958 that the *Winnipeg Tribune* announced that water levels were falling in Lake Winnipeg, allowing for the revival of Winnipeg Beach. The article in question mentions, "the 'new look' at Lake Winnipeg beaches, doubled in size this year due to falling water levels after seven years of high water and merciless pounding by waves, has elated resort owners who look forward to increased tourist business."[72]

A look at the Lake Winnipeg records between 1913 and 2000 indicates that for the majority of the period between 1913 and 1945 water levels were substantially below the ninety-year average of 713.41 feet above seawater. With the exception of a few brief years in the 1910s and 1920s, Lake Winnipeg was anywhere between a foot to three feet below its average during the period from 1913 to about 1944. The earlier part of this century witnessed a drier period for the lake, with reduced inflows of water.[73] Water levels began trending upwards after 1944; with the exception of 1953 and brief periods in the late 1950s and the early 1960s, the lake was often a foot or two above average during this period, and at times three or four feet higher. To look at the extremes, water levels on Lake Winnipeg were over seven feet higher in 1951 compared to 1944.[74] The beautiful crescent of sand people frolicked on in the 1920s and 30s was underwater in the 1950s, '60s and '70s, a change that pictures illustrate and interview subjects could recall clearly.[75] "The beach got narrower and narrower, that's all I can remember, because the land was just hanging on for dear life," Heather Manz recalled.[76]

The Canadian National Railway's Grand Beach was appropriated by the provincial government as Manitoba's first provincial park. But it had only seen limited commercial and almost no residential development.[77] Winnipeg Beach's fate was debated far longer, with the former boardwalk and picnic area being taken over by the province only in 1967. The challenge for Winnipeg Beach was that it was seen as a community rather than a resort. So when the then minister of mines and natural resources, Sterling Lyon, was quizzed about its fate after the amusement area had closed in 1964, he saw little likelihood the province would get involved. He noted, "Winnipeg Beach ... is primarily a residential area. It is not a provincial park like Grand Beach and is not likely to ever be."[78] There were still rental cabins at Winnipeg Beach, but many of the traditional links that had bound the community to the leisure zone, whether through the provision of accommodations or supplies, had passed by this time. Now, there was merely a beach that sat next to a town. But despite Lyon's scepticism, the province was almost immediately involved in negotiations to purchase the leisure zone. In a letter dated 1 February 1965, Winnipeg Beach mayor Lawrence Tapper requested that the province acquire the boardwalk area. He went on to suggest that the boardwalk amusement should be razed, but that a new updated amusement area could be built south of the commercial district. Other suggestions included a new pier (the CPR's pier had been removed in the early 1950s) and the future development of a trailer camp on the south end of the town.[79] The province was interested, but purchasing the land still took another two years as the parties involved dickered over the price. Silverberg thought he should receive $250,000 for the property; the province was prepared to offer $125,000. The two sides were deadlocked until Silverberg passed away. After that his estate was prepared to accept the offer of $123,537.50 ($125,000, less a small amount set aside to pay for back taxes), and the deal went ahead on 15 February 1967.[80] As part of the redevelopment project the province also purchased or leased land south of the town—including a piece of land that was still held by the CPR—and created a small provincial park with space for picnics, swimming, and parking.

Throughout the negotiations for the land and redevelopment of Winnipeg Beach, there was never any serious suggestion that the boardwalk amusements would remain standing.[81] And only briefly did the province consider keeping the dance hall as a site for future recreation.[82] More often, in discussions among stakeholders and in the general public, the amusement area was described as an "eyesore." Interviewed about the area in 1965, Winnipeg Beach councillor Bill McGregor stated, "The boardwalk is badly rundown, and it wouldn't be much of an attraction even if it was opened. The amusement area was all right in the 1920s but it is out of date now."[83] It was more than the physical condition of the amusement area

Winnipeg Beach in 1912. Note the width of the beach in this image. That shoreline would be greatly diminished by the 1950s.

that was at issue. Discussions around revitalizing Winnipeg Beach focused directly on removing the cultural artifacts represented by the boardwalk amusements and returning the "natural" beauty of the beach. In 1964, an editorial in the *Free Press* saluted the fact that the amusement area was shutting down, arguing that it had become a "blight on the town," and not just because it was rundown:

> While it attracted tourists and weekenders to the town, it did not always attract the most desirable visitors. Too often those who came to take advantage of what the boardwalk had to offer came to raise Cain at the expense of year-round residents and cottagers. Often, of course, those who came to seek pleasure by the lake were families who could not afford cottages of their own and had to be content with day trips. More often, however, visitors of this sort were a small minority. The influx of thrillseekers and those up to no good had for years created a problem for the police and the residents of the town.[84]

The editorial went on to argue that "the town has many natural advantages" and should acquire the "rundown boardwalk with the aim of restoring the area to a natural setting for bathers," and that "the destruction of the roller coaster, too, would open up the south end of the town, an area of pleasant beaches and woods, to cottagers."[85] In presenting his views in 1965 on how the resort should be redeveloped, Christopher Dafoe tapped similar themes: "The boardwalk, to be sure, is a dreadful eyesore and it would be to the town's benefit if it were demolished. Beyond the boardwalk, however, is one of the finest bathing beaches in the province, and to the south, beyond the ancient roller coaster, is an area of pleasing woodland. The area in point of fact, has natural advantages that would easily bear looking into."[86] Similarly, in a letter to Manitoba premier Duff Roblin in response to Tapper's request for assistance, minister of education G. Johnson outlined his concern that the Winnipeg Beach areas could "sink into a slum area" and that "the large old hall is going to burn down some night and threaten the whole village. I have been waiting for this to happen, honestly feeling I should probably go down there myself and put a match to it! It would remove half our problems."[87] Like the others, Johnson recommended trying to recoup the "natural setting" of the beach.

In the end this is exactly the approach that would be taken towards Winnipeg Beach. The amusement area was razed in 1967. Gabrielle Roy's Christine and Monsieur Saint-Hilaire had voiced their own complaints about the clutter of cultural artifacts blocking their view of the lake. Coincidentally, or not, *The Road Past Altamont* was published just as this debate was going on around Winnipeg Beach. Not everyone was in favour of the razing. Bob Noble, who wrote a regular column in the *Free Press* titled "Do You Remember?" and had been a frequent visitor to the amusement area in the past, referred to the process as "tearing pieces out of Manitoba's heart."[88]

In an article entitled "Reclaiming Winnipeg Beach," *Free Press* writer Tom Saunders discussed the plans for redevelopment at the resort. He acknowledged that the resort had played a particular role for people in the 1920s and 1930s: "If there was a honky-tonk atmosphere about the beach in those days, it was an atmosphere that thousands of Winnipeggers didn't seem to mind. The boys came to see the girls and the girls came to meet, and dance with the boys. And all day long the Beach would be crowded with families and young fry swimming and sun-bathing and playing in the

*Winnipeg Beach in 1955. Rising water levels in the last half of the twentieth century
meant that much of the resort's beautiful shoreline was damaged or washed away.*

park."[89] Saunders also argued that as competition drew people elsewhere,
the "Beach became more honky-tonk and less attractive to many.... Yet the
Winnipeg Beach area is still one of the best natural holiday spots in the
province. If it has been marred, it has been marred by the incursions of
man. But it is only its man-made assets which have deteriorated; its natural
assets are still there waiting to be reclaimed."[90] Saunders went on to say:

> Those who have memories of the old Beach must not, of course,
> assume that the new Beach will be the old Beach restored. Our
> memories are what they are, and must remain what they are. The
> new Winnipeg Beach will be a new Beach for a new day and a new
> generation. But that is the way with more things than beaches.
> When the demolition crews are through this summer the park
> which attracted so many will be one with our memories—a thing
> of the past. But, in the course of time, a new Winnipeg Beach will
> be there—for other experiences and other memories.[91]

Similar progress narratives accompanied the demolition of other public amusement areas. "Nothing can be permitted to hold up progress," an editorial intoned as the Sunnyside Amusement Park was being bulldozed in Toronto to make room for the Gardiner Expressway.[92] On Toronto Island the entertainment and residential areas were labelled slums before being taken over by Toronto's Metro-Park system and bulldozed to make way for a new public park area.[93] Bulldozers rolled across sections of Atlantic City to make room for everything from roads and parking lots to housing developments—which never came—and casinos.[94] Meanwhile, at Coney Island public housing slowly marched towards the shoreline until only a husk of the former amusement area remained. This scenario fit with the post-1945 growth of what some writers have termed "high modernity," defined as a "belief in the ongoing advance of science and technology and their combined power to deliver social benefit."[95] The belief showed itself in the hydroelectric projects in British Columbia and Manitoba, but it also can be seen in urban projects that bulldozed housing to make way for expressways or redevelopment. At Winnipeg Beach we can see this belief in the demolition of the amusement area to make way for a controlled, managed natural setting; nature could be supplied as just one more resource for the population.

The goal at Winnipeg Beach was to tear out the amusement area that had become associated with youthful initiatives and indiscretions and replace it with a setting "aimed at recapturing a late 19th century park atmosphere for adults and children to enjoy together."[96] In some ways the new Winnipeg Beach was intended to capture the child-friendly market that Walt Disney was hoping to create in his theme park, albeit by removing the amusement area almost entirely. It was still a place for men and women to mingle, provided they visited together under the safe and controlled rubric of family. In many ways, Winnipeg Beach and similar amusement areas that were demolished and reopened as "natural settings" were coming full circle, back to the seaside areas and romantic park settings that had entranced the genteel middle class at the end of the nineteenth century. It even seemed that the same effort to control moral behaviour that had inspired those middle-class reformers was at work once again in the language of the 1960s.[97]

Winnipeg Beach's former role as a meeting place for young single men and women, which had been in steady decline anyway, was removed as

Winnipeg Beach had thrived as a location where men and women could meet. The expectation was that certain rules of conduct would be followed when people came to the resort. By the late 1960s the rules for how men and women could be together had changed.

neatly as the boardwalk. The businesses on Main Street stayed as the independent side of the former boardwalk–Main Street loop. But the only piece of the old CPR amusement area that was maintained was the water tower. A 1969 *Free Press* article noted, "With a first class restaurant and terrace proposed to be built near its base, and dominating the fine bathing beaches soon to be filled with happy families, the old water tower is destined to become the symbol of the new Winnipeg Beach."[98]

When Jessica and her husband drove to Winnipeg Beach sometime after it had been "reclaimed," to borrow the term from Saunders's article, she found little familiar. The old cabins she and her family once stayed in had been upgraded or replaced with permanent homes. The rides were gone and the piers were gone. She phoned a cousin after the trip and said, "You will never know Winnipeg Beach."[99] No doubt, many people who went to Winnipeg Beach in the 1920s and 1930s would not have recognized the version that emerged after 1967. And why would they? Winnipeg Beach had been an experience. It had been a place where men and women might mix and mingle in a controlled setting that conformed to the gender restrictions of the time, even while providing opportunities to press against the limits of how men and women were supposed to behave. Physical form reflected social construction: the amusement area and dance hall provided a public place for men and women to meet; the tourism infrastructure allowed them to reflect the moral restrictions of the time by retreating to same-sex and often monitored accommodations; the rail link provided a safe route to the beach, but also a precious opportunity to find a secure island of privacy in the darkness that might emerge when rowdy passengers flipped off the lights. All of this was predicated on the notion of the beach as some place outside the city limits, a liminal point pressed up against the natural setting of the lake—a natural setting that was consciously linked to romance by writers of the time and by the CPR, which constructed a ride to Winnipeg Beach on the Moonlight special as a romantic experience.

By the 1960s Winnipeg Beach was floundering in its role as a locale for dating. The end of the Moonlight specials in 1956 meant there was no longer a focused crowd for the boardwalk amusements. It also meant there was no longer a romantic entrance to (and departure from) the beach. Families bought up much of the tourism infrastructure that had serviced the dating crowd, upgrading the cabins or building permanent homes. And the baby boom and increasing middle-class wealth of the 1950s ensured that there were plenty of families to fill the tourism infrastructure, leaving it out of sync with an amusement area that was still chasing young men and women. But, of course, with the automobile opening new areas of the province and social restrictions on where men and women could be together declining, the number of men and women who wanted to use Winnipeg Beach's amusement area as a dating location was in decline anyway.

A look at Winnipeg Beach in 1979, shorn of its boardwalk amusement area.

As the discussion around Winnipeg Beach's transformation in 1967 indicates, there was a conscious effort to recast the beach as a place for families, and not as a place for men and women to mingle. Indeed, the natural setting that the CPR and others had tied to romance was now portrayed as a proper place for "happy families," a discourse that would have fit nicely with turn-of-the-century portrayals of Winnipeg Beach as a proper place for tired workers and their families. This recasting of Winnipeg Beach, which reflected a moral panic in the 1950s and 1960s about sexual behaviour, reminds us that Winnipeg Beach did not merely fail to attract the next generation of young people, as Coney Island failed to do, but consciously asked them not to come.

Epilogue

Today the old and the new Winnipeg Beach co-exist. The resort has become a bedroom community for Winnipeg, with many people choosing to retire at the beach in cabins that have been upgraded or rebuilt. After facing signs of decline in the 1970s, the town has rebounded and is growing. The former CPR amusement area is readily used for picnics on summer weekends by a wide range of people of different ethnic and class backgrounds. Work on the trailer park that the town had suggested be placed south of town was underway in 2010, albeit more than forty years after the idea had been suggested. Playland still pulls in youngsters on Main Street, but as intended Winnipeg Beach is no longer the go-to destination for youth; that role has passed to Grand Beach on the other side of the lake, where young men and women still flirt with one another on the beach, or to Gimli. And yet the images and symbols of the boardwalk and the train are sprinkled throughout Winnipeg Beach, maintaining a constant link to its past. Its role as a meeting place for young men and women was briefly revived when it provided the setting for the television show Falcon Beach, which ran from 2005 to 2007. The boardwalk itself was rebuilt in the 1990s. But now, rather than weaving through games of chance and rides, the boardwalk meanders through the park-like setting and along the beach. As part of its rebuilding of the boardwalk, the town of Winnipeg Beach offered people the opportunity to buy a plank and inscribe their name and a brief message in it. Doris Margolis's parents' names are on the boardwalk, along with those of many of the other people interviewed for this book.

The memories of the people who once circled along the board-walk in Winnipeg Beach have been embedded into the resort's new boardwalk.

It is perhaps appropriate that the people who spent so much time walking the boardwalk and creating the resort's atmosphere during its heyday have provided the planks for the new boardwalk. Their memories have become the boardwalk.

Notes

INTRODUCTION

1 Mikhail Bakhtin, *Rabelais and His World* (Bloomington: Indiana University Press, 1984), 7–10.

2 Gary S. Cross and John K. Walton, *The Playful Crowd: Pleasure Places in the Twentieth Century* (New York: Columbia University Press, 2005), 61.

3 Ibid., 7.

4 Ibid., 62.

5 David Nasaw, *Going Out: The Rise and Fall of Public Amusements* (Cambridge: Harvard University Press, 1999), 85.

6 John F. Kasson, *Amusing the Million: Coney Island at the Turn of the Century* (New York: Hill and Wang, 1978), 23–26.

7 Kathy Peiss, *Cheap Amusements: Working Women and Leisure in Turn-of-the-Century New York* (Philadelphia: Temple University Press, 1986), 124.

8 Glenn Cochrane and Jean Cochrane, *The Beach: An Illustrated History from the Lake to Kingston Road* (Toronto: ECW Press, 2009), 8, 19, 20. Barbaranne Boyer, *The Boardwalk Album: Memories of The Beach* (Erin, ON: Boston Mills Press, 1985), 21.

9 Robert McDonald, "'Holy Retreat' or 'Practical Breathing Spot'?: Class Perceptions of Vancouver's Stanley Park, 1910–1913," *Canadian Historical Review* 65, 2 (1984): 135, 151, 153.

10 Patricia Jasen, *Wild Things: Nature, Culture, and Tourism in Ontario 1790–1914* (Toronto: University of Toronto Press, 1995), 11. Kasson, *Amusing the Million*, 4–6.

11 Kasson, *Amusing the Million*, 4.

12 Ibid., 8.

13 Ibid., 26.

14 Peiss, *Cheap Amusements*, 137.

15 Kasson, *Amusing the Million*, 4.

16 Royden Loewen and Gerald Friesen, *Immigrants in Prairie Cities: Ethnic Diversity in Twentieth Century Canada* (Toronto: University of Toronto Press, 2009), 4–13.

17 "The History of Winnipeg Beach" oral history project, The Boundary Creek District Development, Doris Margolis C2121 interview, 5 December 1990, with D. Harrison and D. Carpenter, Archives of Manitoba.

18 "The History of Winnipeg Beach" oral history project, The Boundary Creek District Development, Mildred Kelly C2114 interview, 18 July 1990, with D. Harrison and D. Carpenter, Archives of Manitoba.

19 Loewen and Friesen, *Immigrants in Prairie Cities*, 4.

20 Nasaw, *Going Out*, 47.

21 Bryant Simon, *Boardwalk of Dreams: Atlantic City and the Fate of Urban America* (New York: Oxford University Press, 2004), 13, 24.

22 Nasaw, *Going Out*, 238. Simon, *Boardwalk of Dreams*, 21. Eric Avila, *Popular Culture in the Age of White Flight: Fear and Fantasy in Suburban Los Angeles* (Berkeley: University of California Press, 2006), 16.

23 Russell David Field, "A Night at the Garden(s): A History of Professional Hockey Spectatorship in the 1920s and 1930s" (PhD diss., University of Toronto, 2008), 104, 207.

24 Sally Gibson, *More Than an Island: A History of the Toronto Island* (Toronto: Irwin Publishing, 1984), 88.

25 Field, "A Night at the Garden(s)," 207.

26 There is no record of blackface entertainment in the written record of Winnipeg Beach that I have examined, and it was not mentioned during interviews. But I would be hesitant to say that it never happened at the resort.

27 Jim Blanchard, *Winnipeg 1912* (Winnipeg: University of Manitoba Press, 2005), 13–16.

28 Lawrence Isfeld, interview with the author, 5 December 2007. Garth Teel, interview with the author, 5 January 2008.

29 Sherene H. Razack sums up the process of linking place and race in her introduction to *Race, Space, and the Law: Unmapping a White Settler Society* (Toronto: Between the Lines, 2002), 1-20.

30 Julia Roberts, *In Mixed Company: Taverns and Public Life in Upper Canada* (Vancouver: University of British Columbia Press, 2009), 104–109.

31 Kasson, *Amusing the Million*, 34.

32 Peiss, *Cheap Amusements*, 40.

33 Ibid., 4–5.

34 Craig Heron, *Booze: A Distilled History* (Toronto: Between the Lines, 2003), 106, 113.

35 Beth Bailey, *From Front Porch to Back Seat* (Baltimore: The Johns Hopkins University Press, 1988), 13.

36 Angela J. Latham, "Packaging Woman: The Concurrent Rise of Beauty Pageants, Public Bathing, and Other Performances of Female 'Nudity,'" *Journal of Popular Culture* 29, 3 (1995), 150. Carolyn Strange, *Toronto's Girl Problem: The Perils and Pleasures of the City, 1880–1930* (Toronto: University of Toronto Press, 1995), 3, 5, 10. Mariana Valverde, *The Age of Light, Soap, and Water: Moral Reform in English Canada, 1885–1925* (Toronto: McClelland and Stewart, 1991), 99.

37 Bailey, *From Front Porch to Back Seat*, 4, 18.

38 Ibid., 5, 57. Peiss, *Cheap Amusements*, 4, 35, 114, 186. Eva Illouz, *Consuming the Romantic Utopia: Love and the Cultural Contradictions of Capitalism* (Los Angeles: University of California Press, 1997), 67.

39 "May 24th Dancing at the Beach," *Manitoba Free Press*, 21 May 1920, 18. "Winnipeg Beach Notes," *Manitoba Free Press*, 13 July 1906, 8. "Canadian Pacific" Advertisement, *Manitoba Free Press*, 20 June 1910, 3.

40 Blanchard, *Winnipeg 1912*, 131–134.

41 Bailey, *From Front Porch to Back Seat*, 101.

42 Strange, *Toronto's Girl Problem*, 10.

43 Ibid., 3, 5, 10. Valverde, *Age of Light*, 99.

44 Illouz, *Consuming*, 56.

45 Annette Pritchard and Nigel J. Morgan, "Privileging the Male Gaze: Gendered Tourism Landscapes," *Annals of Tourism Research* 27, 4 (2000): 885. To quote Annette Pritchard and Nigel Morgan, "Tourism sites, attractions, landmarks, destinations, and landscapes are seen as spaces through which 'power, identity, meaning and behaviour are constructed, negotiated, and renegotiated according to sociocultural dynamics.' Gender is critical to this construction, and spaces and places are 'both shaped by, and a shaper of, gender in a gender-space dialectic.'" Pritchard and Morgan are quoting C. Aitchison and C. Reeves, "1998 Gendered (Bed) Spaces: The Culture and Commerce of Women only Tourism," in *Gender, Space and Identity: Leisure, Culture and Commerce*, ed. C. Aitchison and F. Jordan (Brighton: Leisure Studies Association, 1998), 51.

46 David Bell and Gill Valentine, *Mapping Desire: Geographies of Sexualities* (Routledge: New York, 1995), 18.

47 Bailey, *From Front Porch to Back Seat*, 3, 7, 13.

48 Ibid., 141.

49 Ibid., 141.

50 Strange, *Toronto's Girl Problem*, 14. Valverde, *Age of Light*, 130.

51 "Sandy Hook is on the Market," *Manitoba Free Press*, 27 April 1912, 20.

52 John Fiske, "Surfalism and Sandiotics: The Beach in Oz Culture," *Australian Journal of Cultural Studies* 1, 2 (1983): 120.

53 Cross and Walton, *Playful Crowd*, 40.

54 Bryan Palmer, *Cultures of Darkness: Night Travels in the Histories of Transgressions* (New York: Monthly Review Press, 2000), 19.

55 David Churchill, "Mother Goose's Map: Tabloid Geographies and Gay Male Experience in 1950s Toronto," *Journal of Urban History* 30, 6 (2004): 829. But see also Anthony Giddens, "Time, Space and Regionalisation," in *Social Relations and Spatial Structures*, ed. Derek Gregory and John Urry (London: MacMillan Publishers, 1985), 271–272. Winnipeg Beach was a *locale*, to borrow a term from Giddens. Winnipeg Beach and other spaces like it are "relational spaces determined by the activities that [happen] within their oblique boundaries." Churchill, 829.

56 Giddens, "Time, Space and Regionalisation," 274–275.

57 Bell and Valentine have argued that the street has been created as heterosexual, heterosexist, and heteronormative. We need to consider that act of creation and how it is an active process. See Bell and Valentine, *Mapping Desire*, 18.

58 Karen Dubinsky, *The Second Greatest Disappointment: Honeymooning and Tourism at Niagara Falls* (Toronto: Between The Lines, 1999), 13.

59 Strange, *Toronto's Girl Problem*, 16.

60 John C. Lehr, H. John Selwood, and Eileen Badiuk, "Ethnicity, Religion, and Class as Elements in the Evolution of Lake Winnipeg Resorts," *The Canadian Geographer* 35, 1 (1991): 52.

61 Bailey, *From Front Porch to Back Seat*, 78.

62 Mary Louise Adams, *The Trouble with Normal: Postwar Youth and the Making of Heterosexuality* (Toronto: University of Toronto Press, 1997), 56.

63 Cross and Walton, *Playful Crowd*, 242.

64 Jon Binnie, "Trading Places: Consumption, Sexuality and the Production of Queer Space," in *Mapping Desire: Geographies of Sexualities*, ed. Bell and Valentine, 187. I borrow the term *safe space* from Binnie. While his focus is on gay men, I think this notion of creating or performing one's identity applies to heterosexual men and women as well, even if the terrain on which they performed had very different connotations.

65 Frances Russell, *Mistehay Sakahegan the Great Lake: The Beauty and the Treachery of Lake Winnipeg* (Winnipeg: Heartland, 2004), 137.

66 Mike Filey, *I Remember Sunnyside: The Rise and Fall of a Magical Era* (Toronto: Dundurn Group, 1996), 80.

CHAPTER 1

1 Wolfgang Schivelbusch, *The Railway Journey: The Industrialization of Time and Space* (Berkeley: University of California Press, 1986), 38.

2 W.J. Wood, "A Brief History of Winnipeg Beach 1901–1955." Unpublished manuscript. Hudson's Bay Company Archives, Winnipeg Beach Vertical File, 1.

3 Gerald Friesen, *The Canadian Prairies: A History* (Toronto: University of Toronto Press, 1987), 39.

4 Gerald Friesen as quoted in Russell, *Misteshay Sakahegan*, 57.

5 Ibid., 77.

6 Ryan C. Eyford, "Quarantined within a New Colonial Order: The 1876–1877 Lake Winnipeg Smallpox Epidemic," *Journal of the Canadian Historical Association / Revue de la Société historique du Canada* 17, 1 (2006): 77, 78.

7 "Winnipeg Soon to Have New Resort," *Morning Telegram*, 1 June 1901, 9, 13.

8 Renisa Mawani, "Imperial Legacies (Post)Colonial Identities: Law, Space and the Making of Stanley Park, 1859–2001," *Law Text Culture* 7 (2003): 106. Sherene H. Razack, *Race, Space, and the Law: Unmapping a White Settler Society* (Toronto: Between the Lines, 2002), 1, 3.

9 Donald Urquhart Western Land Grants (1870-1930), Volume: 96 Folio: 511 Microfilm reel number: C-6012, Library and Archives Canada. http://www.collectionscanada.gc.ca/databases/western-land-grants/001007 - 119.02-e.

php?sisn_id_nbr=502462&page_sequence_nbr=1&t=1&PHPSESSID=gcig4vku
u9ngd5botdvclmei37 (accessed 9 November 2010).

10   Wood, "Brief History of Winnipeg Beach," 2.

11   "At Lake of Killarney and Winnipeg Beach," *Manitoba Free Press Magazine Section*, 22 June 1907, vol. 34, no. 302.

12   Blanchard, *Winnipeg 1912*, 94.

13   "Winnipeg Beach," *Manitoba Free Press*, 26 November 1910, 6.

14   Lehr, Selwood, and Badiuk, "Ethnicity, Religion, and Class," 48. James Walvin, *Leisure and Society 1830–1950* (London: Longman Group, 1978), 69.

15   Walvin, *Leisure and Society*, 71. Robert E. Snow and David E. Wright, "Coney Island: A Case Study in Popular Culture and Technical Change," *Journal of Popular Culture* 9, 4: 962.

16   Walvin, *Leisure and Society*, 69.

17   E.J. Hart, *The Selling of Canada: The CPR and the Beginnings of Canadian Tourism* (Banff, AB: Altitude Publishing, 1983), 41.

18   Walvin, *Leisure and Society*, 72.

19   Ibid., 71. Snow and Wright, "Coney Island," 963.

20   Cross and Walton, *Playful Crowd*, 32. Nasaw, *Going Out*, 80.

21   Don Aiken and Chris Thain, *It Happened in Manitoba: Stories of the Red River Province* (Calgary: Fifth House, 2004), 159.

22   Lehr, Selwood, and Badiuk, "Ethnicity, Religion, and Class," 48.

23   Ibid., 48.

24   "Trip to Lake Winnipeg," *Morning Telegram*, 27 August 1900, 5.

25   *Minnedosa Tribune*, 26 April 1900, 2. "Selkirk," *Morning Telegram*, 14 May 1900, 8.

26   Cross and Walton, *Playful Crowd*, 12.

27   "Winnipeg Soon to Have New Resort," 9, 13.

28   Kasson, *Amusing the Million*, 8.

29   "Newest Summer Resort," *Manitoba Morning Free Press*, 3 November 1902, 5.

30   "Selkirk Line Completed," *Manitoba Free Press*, 8 September 1902, 5. (See also "Local Notes," *Manitoba Free Press*, 10 June 1902, 9 for expectations about Winnipeg Beach's popularity.)

31   Blanchard, *Winnipeg 1912*, 7, 9. Daniel Hiebert, "Class, Ethnicity and Residential Structure: The Social Geography of Winnipeg, 1901–1921," *Journal of Historical Geography* 17, 1 (1991): 64, 67.

32   Kurt Korneski, "Minnie J.B. Campbell, Reform and Empire," in *Prairie Metropolis: New Essays on Winnipeg Social History,* ed. Esyllt Jones and Gerald Friesen (Winnipeg: University of Manitoba Press, 2009), 33.

33   Cross and Walton, *Playful Crowd*, 119–120.

34   "Speaks Well of Winnipeg," *Morning Telegram*, 22 April 1901, 2.

35   "Newest Summer Resort," 5. "Winnipeg Soon to Have New Resort," 9, 13. "Train Service to Winnipeg Beach," *Morning Telegram*, 21 May 1903, 2.

36   Bryan Palmer, *A Culture in Conflict: Skilled Workers and Industrial Capitalism in Hamilton, Ontario, 1860–1914* (Montreal: McGill-Queen's University Press, 1979), 52, 58.

37 Loewen and Friesen, *Immigrants in Prairie Cities*, 13, 18.

38 Kasson, *Amusing the Million*, 8.

39 "What To Do on Civic Holiday: The Attractions are Many and Varied – Thirteen Trains to the Beach," *Manitoba Free Press*, 16 August 1906, 16.

40 "About 15,000 People Taken On Winnipeg Beach Trains," *Manitoba Free Press*, 2 July 1920, 3.

41 Russell, *Mistehay Sakahegan*, 122.

42 "Winnipeg Celebrates Holiday at Beaches," *Manitoba Free Press*, 2 July 1925, 4.

43 Russell, *Mistehay Sakahegan*, 122.

44 "Horace Waters Killed in Wreck," *Manitoba Free Press*, 22 August 1906, 2.

45 "Winnipeg Beach Trains Collide," *Manitoba Free Press*, 21 August 1906, 1.

46 "Engineer Maneally Killed in Run-Off, *Manitoba Free Press*, 20 August 1907, 1.

47 Cross and Walton, *Playful Crowd*, 7.

48 Peiss, *Cheap Amusements*, 13, 27.

49 And here I mean a boundary zone in the sense that Loewen and Friesen have suggested, Loewen and Friesen, *Immigrants in Prairie Cities*, 35, 42.

50 Lehr, Selwood, and Badiuk, "Ethnicity, Religion, and Class," 49.

51 Wood, "Brief History of Winnipeg Beach," 6.

52 Letter from W. Whyte, second vice president, to Sir Thomas G. Shaughnessy, president, 9 June 1908, 1, Canadian Pacific Railway Archives.

53 Ibid., 3.

54 Canadian Pacific Railway Company Telegram, from W. Whyte, second vice president, to Sir Thomas G. Shaughnessy, president, 16 June 1908, Canadian Pacific Archives.

55 *Manitoba Free Press*, 22 May 1907, 12.

56 Lehr, Selwood, and Badiuk, "Ethnicity, Religion, and Class," 50–51.

57 Empress advertisement, *Manitoba Free Press*, 27 May 1910, 9. "C.P.R. Appealing: Hearing Started in Empress Hotel Arbitration Case," *Manitoba Free Press*, 30 October 1915, 10. "Winnipeg Beach Hotel Case Again: C.P.R. vs. Windebank Before the Supreme Court at Ottawa—Buck's Appeal," *Manitoba Free Press*, 24 February 1917, 2.

58 "Beach Attractions Limited," *Manitoba Free Press*, 21 May 1915, 5.

59 Dr. Paul Adams, interview with the author, 21 December 2007.

60 Wood, "Brief History of Winnipeg Beach," 4. "Winnipeg Soon to Have New Resort," 9, 13.

61 *Manitoba Free Press*, 1 July 1905, 5.

62 "Complaints from Beach Residents," *Manitoba Free Press*, 10 July 1911, 15.

63 Gabrielle Roy, *The Road Past Altamont* (Toronto: McClelland and Stewart, 1989), 62.

64 Bob Noble, "Do You Remember?" *Winnipeg Free Press TV-Radio*, 4 August 1962, 5.

65 Nasaw, *Going Out*, 116.

66 Kasson, *Amusing the Million*, 8.

67 Cross and Walton, *Playful Crowd*, 112.

68 Pritchard and Morgan, "Privileging the Male Gaze," 889. Cross and Walton, *Playful Crowd*, 72–73.

69 "May 24th Dancing at the Beach," *Manitoba Free Press*, 21 May 1920, 18.

70 "Where Manitoba Plays," *Winnipeg Free Press*, 8 July 1938, 4.

71 "Changes in CPR Timetables," *Manitoba Free Press*, 10 August, 1908, 8.

72 Russell, *Mistehay Sakahegan*, 122. "The History of Winnipeg Beach" oral history project, The Boundary Creek District Development, Victor Martin C2123 Interview, Date NA 1991, with D. Harrison and D. Carpenter, Archives of Manitoba.

73 Schivelbusch, *Railway Journey*, 38, 64, 193.

74 "Winnipeg Soon to Have New Resort," 9, 13.

75 Cross and Walton, *Playful Crowd*, 11, 14, 240.

76 Dubinsky, *The Second Greatest Disappointment*, 56.

77 "Many Excursions to Winnipeg Beach," *Manitoba Free Press*, 15 May 1913, 2.

78 "The Caterers' Picnic," *Manitoba Free Press*, 24 August 1904, 3.

79 "Caterers' Picnic," *Winnipeg Free Press*, 6 July 1962, 14.

80 "Canadian Pacific Employees Picnic," *Manitoba Free Press*, 17 July 1911, 9.

81 Ibid., 9.

82 Lawrence Isfeld interview.

83 Jasen, *Wild Things*, 128.

84 Nestor Mudry, interview with the author, 12 December 2007.

85 Ibid.

86 Ibid.

87 Peiss, *Cheap Amusements*, 137. Bill Freeman, *A Magical Place: Toronto Island and its People* (Toronto: James Lorimer and Company, 1999), 46.

88 "Winnipeg Beach," *Manitoba Free Press*, Saturday, 17 May 1913, 13.

89 Lehr, Selwood, and Badiuk, "Ethnicity, Religion, and Class," 48.

90 Winnipeg Beach, Matlock Beach advertisements, *Manitoba Free Press*, 17 May 1913, 13.

91 Orvar Lofgren, *On Holiday: A History of Vacationing* (Los Angeles: University of California Press, 1999), 135–136.

92 Ina Drummond, interview with the author, 18 December 2007.

93 Ina Drummond interview.

94 Jessica, interview with the author, 29 November 2007. Orest, interview with the author, 5 December 2007.

95 "Notice," *Winnipeg Free Press*, 3 November 1944, 4. "Beach Residents Will Have Trouble Finding City Homes," *Winnipeg Free Press*, 26 August 1946, 1.

96 Freeman, *Magical Place*, 42.

97 Dolores Hayden, *Redesigning the American Dream: The Future of Housing, Work, and Family Life* (New York: W.W. Norton, 2002), 58–59. American writers have been particularly interested in how race has played out in the suburbs; see for example Lizabeth Cohen, *A Consumers' Republic: The Politics of Mass Consumption in Postwar America* (New York: Vintage Books, 2003).

98 Howard Dundas, *Wrinkled Arrows: Good Old Days in Winnipeg* (Winnipeg: Queenston House, 1980), 93.

99 Ibid., 91.

100 Ibid., 93.

101 "Winnipeg Beach Notes," *Manitoba Free Press*, 13 July 1906, 8. CPR advertisement, *Manitoba Free Press*, 20 June 1910, 3.

102 "Dancing Every Evening at Winnipeg Beach" CPR advertisement, *Manitoba Free Press*, 22 June 1917, 7. Illouz, *Consuming*, 67.

103 Victoria Day advertisement, *Manitoba Free Press*, 21 May 21 1920, 18. "Dancing Every Evening at Winnipeg Beach" CPR advertisement, *Manitoba Free Press*, 22 June 1917, 7.

104 Dubinsky, *Second Greatest Disappointment*, 155.

105 Dundas, *Wrinkled Arrows*, 93–94.

106 Ibid., 95–96.

107 "Winnipeg Beach," *Manitoba Free Press*, 12 July 1910, 3.

108 Dundas, *Wrinkled Arrows*, 96.

109 Ibid., 96.

110 Ibid., 96.

111 Palmer, *Cultures of Darkness*, 19.

112 Bailey, *From Front Porch to Back Seat*, 87.

113 Dundas, *Wrinkled Arrows*, 96–97.

114 Peiss, *Cheap Amusements*, 61. Strange, *Toronto's Girl Problem*, 112.

115 "A Child's Dream: Life in The Alex," *Winnipeg Free Press Leisure Magazine*, 13 May 1967, 6.

116 Dundas, *Wrinkled Arrows*, 97.

117 Bailey, *From Front Porch to Back Seat*, 87.

118 Strange, *Toronto's Girl Problem*, 17, 59, 119, 120, 123.

119 Helen Sigurdur letter. Dorothy Lynch letter. Agnes Walker letter. The letters were solicited for the Dance Hall Film Project. Vienna Badiuk, *Dance Hall Film Project* (Winnipeg: Manitoba Culture, Heritage and Citizenship, Heritage Grants Program, 1999).

120 Dorothy Lynch letter, *Dance Hall Film Project*.

121 Val Kinack, interview with the author, 16 January 2008.

122 Orest interview.

123 Myrna Charach, interview with the author, 8 December 2007.

124 Peiss, *Cheap Amusements*, 105.

125 Izzy Peltz, interview with the author, 15 December 2007.

126 Valverde, *Age of Light*, 92.

127 Ina Drummond interview. Orest interview.

128 Graeme H. Patterson, *History and Communications: Harold Innis, Marshall McLuhan, the Interpretation of History* (Toronto: University of Toronto Press, 1990), 166.

129 Orest interview.

130 Izzy Peltz interview.
131 "The History of Winnipeg Beach" oral history project, Victor Martin C2123 interview.
132 Nestor Mudry interview.
133 Dr. Paul Adams interview.
134 Jessica interview.
135 Val Kinack interview.
136 Myrna Charach interview.
137 "Fancy Free," *Winnipeg Free Press Special Features*, 3 June 1961, 22.
138 "Putting out Train Lights Brings Fine for 2 Youths," *Winnipeg Free Press*, 28 June 1946, 1.
139 "Warns Romeos," *Lethbridge Herald*, 10 August 1946, 1.
140 "Young Hooligans on Beach Trains Get Warning," *Winnipeg Free Press*, 15 July 1950, 1.
141 Susan, interview with the author, 11 December 2007. Orest interview. Jessica interview.
142 Manitoba Gay/Lesbian Oral History Project, David B. C1864 interview, 7 June 1990, with David Theodore, Archives of Manitoba.
143 Dubinsky, *Second Greatest Disappointment*, 168.
144 Manitoba Gay/Lesbian Oral History Project, David B. C1864 interview.
145 Val Werier, "In the Evening There is No Longer a Moonlight," *Winnipeg Tribune*, 7 August 1965.
146 Jessica interview.
147 Retired CN employee, interview with the author, 27 November 2007.
148 Winnipeg Beach 15 c1908 N13282 picture, Archives of Manitoba.
149 Lawrence Isfeld interview.
150 Garth Teel, interview with the author, 5 January 2008. Barry Anderson, interview with the author, 10 December 2007. Barney Charach, interview with the author, 8 December 2007.
151 Bob Noble, "Remember the 'Moonlight' to Winnipeg Beach," *Winnipeg Free Press*, 20 June 1964, 21.
152 "Watching for People Selling Return Stubs," *Manitoba Free Press*, 7 August 1918, 4.
153 Barney Charach interview.
154 Jean Tullett Read, "Bath-House Harry and Tales of Grand Beach," in *Through the Window of a Train: A Canadian Railway Anthology*, ed. Barbara Lange (Nepean, ON: Borealis Press, 2010), 240.
155 Val Kinack interview.
156 "Winnipeg Beach," *Manitoba Free Press*, 15 June 1909, 10. "Trip to the Beach," *Manitoba Free Press Automobile Section*, 6 August 1910.
157 "Lady Wins Gold Medal," *Manitoba Free Press*, 20 July 1914, 22.
158 "Winnipeg Celebrates Holiday at Beaches," *Manitoba Free Press*, 2 July 1925, 4.
159 "Where Manitoba Plays," *Winnipeg Free Press*, 8 July 8 1938, 4.

160 Richard Harris, *Creeping Conformity: How Canada Became Suburban, 1900–1960* (Toronto: University of Toronto Press, 2004), 162.

161 Mimi Sheller and John Urry, "The City and the Car," *International Journal of Urban and Regional Research* 24, 4 (2000): 745, 746.

162 Russell, *Mistehay Sakahegan*, 137. Eddy Walker, "Winnipeg Beach," *Winnipeg Free Press*, 11 June 1960, 10.

163 Nestor Mudry interview.

164 "Irene and Billy Safe at the Beach," *Winnipeg Free Press*, 21 August 1944, 1. "7-year-old Does Disappearing Act," *Winnipeg Free Press*, 23 September 1944, 1. In the latter article, Irene Feasey had just stowed away on the SS *Keenora*.

165 Lofgren, *On Holiday*, 63.

166 "Record Crowds Go to Beach," *The Winnipeg Evening Tribune*, 12 August 1940, 2. "One 'Moonlight' Only Saturday," *The Winnipeg Evening Tribune*, 10 July 1943, 12.

167 Christopher Dafoe, "On the 'Broadwalk': Ghosts in the Penny Arcade," *Winnipeg Free Press*, 10 October 1964, 31.

168 Orest interview.

CHAPTER 2

1   "Winnipeg Beach 'The People's Playground,'" *Manitoba Free Press*, 11 August 1923, 6.

2   "Newest Summer Resort," *Manitoba Free Press*, 3 November 1902, 5.

3   "Boom at Gimli," *Manitoba Free Press*, 6 April 1905, 9. Hiebert, "Class, Ethnicity and Residential Structure," 57.

4   "Newest Summer Resort," 5. "Notice, Winnipeg Beach Property," *Manitoba Free Press*, 7 May 1910, 7. "Winnipeg Beach," *Morning Telegram*, 17 January 1905, 2.

5   "The Proposed License at Winnipeg Beach," *Manitoba Free Press*, 22 May 1907, 12.

6   Wood, "Brief History of Winnipeg Beach," 3.

7   Joan Bowman, "The Recreational Function and Related Problems of the Winnipeg Beach-Sandy Hook Section of the Lake Winnipeg Shoreline" (master's thesis, University of Manitoba, 1966), 23.

8   Wood, "Brief History of Winnipeg Beach," 3.

9   "Summer Residents Barred," *Manitoba Free Press*, 9 December 1909, 2. "Government Tries to Rush Session," *Manitoba Free Press*, 16 February 1910, 8. "Can Have Mayor," *Manitoba Free Press,* 24 February 1910, 10.

10 "Winnipeg Beach the People's Playground: Twentieth Anniversary of Western Canada's Greatest Resort Displays Marvelous Growth," *Manitoba Free Press*, 11 August 1923, 6. Bowman, "The Recreational Function," 36–37.

11 Inter-departmental memorandum, from W.W. Danyluk, director of parks, to Mr. Guy E. Moore, deputy minister, dated 20 April 1967, Archives of Manitoba, Q026770, 206.11.

12 "Charging Railway Fare Between the Beaches," *Winnipeg Free Press*, 31 July 1937, 25.

13   Walvin, *Leisure and Society*, 72.

14   Valverde, *Age of Light*, 130, 17.

15   Ibid., 130.

16   "In the Swim at Winnipeg Beach," *Manitoba Free Press*, 4 July 1919, 6.

17   *Manitoba Free Press*, 27 April 1912, 20. See also Blanchard, *Winnipeg 1912*, 162.

18   Russell, *Mistehay Sakahegan*, 136. "Patients of Red Cross Home are Grateful," *Manitoba Free Press*, 21 July 1920, 9.

19   "Days of Delight: Bronzed and Happy, Cadets Find Camp Life Big Success," *Winnipeg Free Press*, 11 July 1942, 21.

20   Myrna Charach, interview with the author, 8 December 2007.

21   Val Kinack, interview with the author, 16 January 2008.

22   Christopher Rutty, "The Middle Class Plague: Epidemic Polio and the Canadian State 1936–1937," *Canadian Bulletin of Medical History* 13 (1996): 280.

23   Bailey, *From Front Porch to Back Seat*, 7.

24   Blanchard, *Winnipeg 1912*, 164–165.

25   "Winnipeg Beach," *Manitoba Free Press*, 20 August 1906.

26   Blanchard, *Winnipeg 1912*, 26–27, 37–38. Bailey, *From Front Porch to Back Seat*, 15.

27   "City and General," *Manitoba Free Press*, 22 August 1904, 14.

28   "Winnipeg Beach Notes," *Manitoba Free Press*, 4 July 1905, 9.

29   Bailey, *From Front Porch to Back Seat*, 15.

30   "Personal and Social," *Manitoba Free Press*, 18 May 1915, 3.

31   "Winnipeg Beach," *Manitoba Free Press*, 30 June 1906, 9.

32   "Winnipeg Beach," *Manitoba Free Press*, 12 July 1910, 3.

33   "A Pretty Summer Home," *Manitoba Free Press*, 18 July 1906, 13.

34   "Winnipeg Beach," *Manitoba Free Press*, 22 June 1912.

35   "Winnipeg Beach," *Manitoba Free Press*, 12 July 1910, 3.

36   Heron, *Booze*, 37, 112.

37   Blanchard, *Winnipeg 1912*, 162.

38   Lehr, Selwood, and Badiuk, "Ethnicity, Religion, and Class," 31.

39   Ibid., 53.

40   Ibid., 54–55.

41   *Manitoba Free Press*, 6 April 1911, 13. Capitals in original. See also, "Winnipeg Beach: The 'Coney Island' of the West," *Manitoba Free Press*, 10 May 1911, 3.

42   Lawrence Isfeld, interview with the author, 5 December 2007.

43   Izzy Peltz, interview with the author, 15 December 2007.

44   Garth Teel, interview with the author, 5 January 2008. Barney Charach, interview with the author, 8 December 2007.

45   "The History of Winnipeg Beach" oral history project, The Boundary Creek District Development, W.J. (Lil) Teel C2135 interview, 5 September 1990, with D. Harrison and D. Carpenter, Archives of Manitoba.

46   Ibid.

47 "The History of Winnipeg Beach" oral history project, The Boundary Creek District Development, Mildred Kelly C2114 interview, 18 July 1990, with D. Harrison and D. Carpenter, Archives of Manitoba.

48 "The History of Winnipeg Beach" oral history project, The Boundary Creek District Development, Doris Margolis C2121 interview, 5 December 1990, with D. Harrison and D. Carpenter, Archives of Manitoba. Margolis was collecting her experiences for a book, and her narrative reflects this.

49 Ibid.

50 Ibid.

51 Ibid.

52 Olive Sielski, interview with the author, 5 January 2008. Val Kinack interview. Lawrence Isfeld interview.

53 Russell, *Mistehay Sakahegan*, 128. Dubinsky, *The Second Greatest Disappointment*, 204.

54 "The History of Winnipeg Beach" oral history project, W.J. (Lil) Teel C2135 interview.

55 Ibid.

56 Garth Teel interview.

57 Ibid.

58 "The History of Winnipeg Beach" oral history project, The Boundary Creek District Development, Jack London C2119 interview, 22 May 1990, with D. Harrison and D. Carpenter, Archives of Manitoba.

59 "The History of Winnipeg Beach" oral history project, W.J. (Lil) Teel C2135 interview.

60 Lofgren, *On Holiday*, 125.

61 Dafoe, "On the 'Broadwalk,'" 31.

62 Garth Teel interview.

63 Allan Levine, *Coming of Age: A History of the Jewish People of Manitoba* (Winnipeg: Jewish Heritage Centre of Western Canada and Heartland Associates, 2009).

64 Gibson, *More Than an Island*, 190. Cochrane and Cochrane, *The Beach*, 28.

65 Michael Immerso, *Coney Island: The People's Playground* (Rutgers, NJ: Rutgers University Press, 2002), 152–153, 167. Cross and Walton, *Playful Crowd*, 60.

66 "Man Charged in Beach Incident," *Winnipeg Free Press*, 8 July 1963, 3. "Denies Anti-Semitic Signs on Car," *Winnipeg Free Press*, 9 July 1963, 1. "Man Fined For Beach Incident," *Winnipeg Free Press*, 5 August 1963, 19.

67 "More Police at Beach," *Winnipeg Free Press*, 19 July 1963, 1. "RCMP Patrol to the Beach," *Winnipeg Tribune*, 19 July 1963, 13.

68 "The History of Winnipeg Beach" oral history project, The Boundary Creek District Development, Kathleen Rees (née Neilson) C2130 interview, 22 May 1990, with D. Carpenter, Archives of Manitoba.

69 "The History of Winnipeg Beach" oral history project, Jack London C2119 interview.

70 Harris, *Creeping Conformity*, 89.

71   Izzy Peltz interview.

72   Ibid.

73   "The History of Winnipeg Beach" oral history project, Mildred Kelly C2114 interview.

74   "A Day with a Camera at Winnipeg Beach," Winnipeg Beach 13, 22 July 1907, Archives of Manitoba.

75   "Beach Charges are Dismissed," *Manitoba Free Press*, 2 September 1914, 16.

76   Dubinsky, *Second Greatest Disappointment*, 118.

77   Val Kinack interview.

78   Lawrence Isfeld interview.

79   Dubinsky, *Second Greatest Disappointment*, 131, 133, 134.

80   Gary S. Cross, *Worktowners at Blackpool: Mass-Observation and Popular Leisure in the 1930s* (New York: Routledge, 1990), 1, 63.

81   Cross and Walton, *Playful Crowd*, 17. Lofgren, *On Holiday*, 128.

82   "The History of Winnipeg Beach" oral history project, Mildred Kelly C2114 interview. *Manitoba Free Press*, 8 July 1920, 19.

83   *Manitoba Free Press*, 27 May 1920, 25. *Manitoba Free Press*, 11 June 1918, 14. *Manitoba Free Press*, 19 July 1929, 24.

84   Ruth A. Frager and Carmela Patrias, *Discounted Labour: Women Workers in Canada, 1870–1939* (Toronto: University of Toronto Press, 2005), 32.

85   "The History of Winnipeg Beach" oral history project, W.J. (Lil) Teel C2135 interview.

86   "The History of Winnipeg Beach" oral history project, The Boundary Creek District Development, Harry Simpson C2133 interview, 24 October 1990, with D. Harrison and D. Carpenter, Archives of Manitoba.

87   Cross, *Worktowners at Blackpool*, 190.

88   Dubinsky, *Second Greatest Disappointment*, 134.

89   "The History of Winnipeg Beach" oral history project, W.J. (Lil) Teel C2135 interview.

90   Ibid.

91   "The History of Winnipeg Beach" oral history project, Doris Margolis C2121 interview.

92   Ibid.

93   Robert A. Campbell, *Sit Down and Drink Your Beer: Regulating Vancouver's Beer Parlours, 1925–1954* (Toronto: University of Toronto Press, 2001), 75–76. David Churchill, "Mother Goose's Map," 826–852.

94   Manitoba Gay/Lesbian Oral History Project, Gerry C1883 interview, 26 July 1990, with David Theodore, Archives of Manitoba.

95   Ibid.

96   Manitoba Gay/Lesbian Oral History Project, George M. Smith C1869 interview, 25 June 1990, with David Theodore, Archives of Manitoba.

97   "Winnipeg Beach and Gimli," *Winnipeg Free Press*, 14 August 1941, 17.

98   Nestor Mudry, interview with the author, 12 December 2007.

99 "The History of Winnipeg Beach" oral history project, Mildred Kelly C2114 interview.

100 Ibid.

101 Russell, *Mistehay Sakahegan*, 124.

102 Heron, *Booze*, 37, 112.

103 *Manitoba Free Press*, 18 July 1905, 20.

104 "Conditions at Winnipeg Beach," *Manitoba Free Press*, 25 July 1914, 13.

105 "Beach Charges are Dismissed: Cases against Windebank and Counter-Charge against Savage Fall Through," *Manitoba Free Press*, 2 September 1914, 16.

106 Ibid.

107 "Congregation Supports Student," *Manitoba Free Press*, 16 August 1914, 18.

108 "Beach Charges are Dismissed," 16.

109 "Weed out Booze Joints of City," *Manitoba Free Press*, 21 May 1915, 5.

110 CPR Appealing: Hearing Started in Empress Hotel Arbitration Case," *Manitoba Free Press*, 30 October 1915, 10.

111 "Military funeral for late Maj. Windebank," *Manitoba Free Press*, 5 January, 1925, 1.

112 Heron, *Booze*, 270.

113 The Report of the Manitoba Liquor Enquiry Commission, 49, 55, 73, 216, 226. "On Guard Manitoba! It All Began in a Glass of Beer," *The Winnipeg Tribune*, 19 September 1956, 1. Heron, 37, 112.

114 "Winnipeg Beach Woman Acquitted of Charge," *Manitoba Free Press*, 9 September 1927, 6.

115 Ibid, 6.

116 "City and District," *Manitoba Free Press*, 28 July 1927, 6.

117 *Manitoba Free Press*, 18 August 1927, 2.

118 "Woman is Convicted of Illegal Liquor Sale," *Manitoba Free Press*, 9 September 1927, 20.

119 "The History of Winnipeg Beach" oral history project, W.J. (Lil) Teel C2135 interview.

120 "City and District," *Manitoba Free Press*, 23 August 1924, 2.

121 "The History of Winnipeg Beach" oral history project, W.J. (Lil) Teel C2135 interview.

122 "The History of Winnipeg Beach" oral history project, Kathleen Rees (née Neilson) C2130 interview.

123 Isfeld interview.

124 Isfeld interview. Heron, *Booze*, 252.

125 "The History of Winnipeg Beach" oral history project, W.J. (Lil) Teel C2135 interview.

126 "The History of Winnipeg Beach" oral history project, Mildred Kelly C2114 interview.

127 Ibid.

128 "Two Pay Fines on Liquor Counts," *Winnipeg Free Press*, 17 August 1946, 6. "$200 Homebrew Fine," *Winnipeg Free Press*, 23 February 1951, 11. "Beach Cabbie Fined For Liquor Sale," *Winnipeg Free Press*, 18 July 1963, 16.

129 Heron, *Booze*, 293.

130 Frager and Patrias, *Discounted Labour*, 32.

131 "At the Beach: Winnipeg Beach," *Manitoba Free Press*, 19 July 1910, 16.

132 "The History of Winnipeg Beach" oral history project, W.J. (Lil) Teel C2135 interview.

133 Isfeld interview.

134 "The History of Winnipeg Beach" oral history project, The Boundary Creek District Development, John Reykdal Thedrikson, R. C2131 interview, Date NA 1990/91, with D. Harrison and D. Carpenter, Archives of Manitoba interview.

135 Olive Sielski interview.

136 Ibid.

137 Ibid.

138 "One 'Moonlight' Only Saturday," *The Winnipeg Evening Tribune*, 10 July 1943, 12.

139 Olive Sielski interview.

140 Ibid.

141 Ibid.

142 Ibid.

143 Ibid.

144 "The History of Winnipeg Beach" oral history project, Doris Margolis C2121 interview.

145 "Cutting Ice, Winnipeg Beach," Foote 2436 N3058 16 January 1924, Archives of Manitoba.

146 Val Kinack interview.

147 Bowman, "The Recreational Function," 26–27.

148 "The History of Winnipeg Beach" oral history project, Jack London C2118 interview.

149 Ibid.

150 Ibid.

151 "Alliance Wants Quiet Sunday at Beaches," *Winnipeg Free Press*, 21 February 1952, 11.

152 *Manitoba Free Press*, 18 July 1905, 20.

153 "Sunday Trains' Bill Passes Through House," *Manitoba Free Press*, 13 February 1923, 4.

154 "The History of Winnipeg Beach" oral history project, Jack London C2118 interview.

155 Lawrence Isfeld interview.

156 Owen Clark, *Musical Ghosts: Manitoba's Jazz and Dance Bands 1914–1966* (Winnipeg: Clark Productions, 2007), 53.

157 Ina Drummond, interview with the author, 18 December 2007.

158 "The History of Winnipeg Beach" oral history project, The Boundary Creek District Development, Bill McIntosh C2124 interview, 17 April 1991, with D. Harrison and D. Carpenter, Archives of Manitoba interview.

159 Ina Drummond interview.

160 Ibid.

161 Val Kinack interview.

162 "Prime Favourites," *Winnipeg Free Press*, 15 July 1939, 38. "Holiday Haven" and "Beach Resorts are Within Easy Reach," *Winnipeg Free Press*, 21 June 1941, 12.

163 "Winnipeg Beach Progress Reviewed," *Winnipeg Free Press*, 25 January 1941, 18.

164 "The Mayor and Council," *Winnipeg Free Press*, 11 July 1942, 15.

165 Val Kinack interview.

166 "The History of Winnipeg Beach" oral history project, Kathleen Rees (née Neilson) C2130 interview.

167 "The History of Winnipeg Beach" oral history project, Doris Margolis C2121 interview.

168 Dafoe, "On the 'Broadwalk,'" 31.

169 "Premier Plans First Hand Look at Winnipeg Beach," *Winnipeg Free Press*, 22 July 1955, 2.

170 "Letters to the Editor: Beach Cabins," *Winnipeg Free Press*, 28 July 1955, 28.

171 Dafoe, "On the 'Broadwalk,'" 31.

172 Adams, *Trouble with Normal*, 56.

173 Gibson, *More Than an Island*, 261. Mary Louise Adams, "Almost Anything Can Happen: A Search for Sexual Discourse in the Urban Spaces of 1940s Toronto," in "Moral Regulation," special issue of *The Canadian Journal of Sociology/Cahiers canadiens de sociologie* 19, 2 (1994): 223.

174 "For Rent," *Winnipeg Free Press*, 18 January 1962, 37. "Boardwalk," *Winnipeg Free Press*, 5 May 1964, 41.

175 "Beach Delegation Given Inspection Tour Promise," *Winnipeg Tribune*, 22 July 1955, 4.

CHAPTER 3

1   Cross and Walton, *Playful Crowd*, 7.

2   Jessica, interview with the author, 29 November 2007.

3   Kasson, *Amusing the Million*, 44.

4   Latham, "Packaging Woman," 149.

5   Bailey, *From Front Porch to Back Seat*, 141.

6   Nasaw, *Going Out*, 111. (But see also Walvin, *Leisure and*, 161.)

7   Nasaw, *Going Out*, 116.

8   Dorothy Garbutt, "Fancy Free: Happy Times at the Old Winnipeg Beach," *Winnipeg Free Press*, 3 June 1961, 22.

9   Kasson, *Amusing the Million*, 4–6.

10 Palmer, *Cultures of Darkness*, 19.

11 Christopher Dafoe, "On Manitoba's Inland Seas: The Lake Winnipeg/Lake Manitoba Region," in *The Lake: An Illustrated History of Manitoba's Cottage Country*, ed. Jake MacDonald (Winnipeg: Great Plains Publications, 2000), 33, 36.

12 Russell, *Mistehay Sakahegan the Great Lake*, 16.

13 Fiske, "Surfalism and Sandiotics," 120.

14 Ibid., 121–122.

15 Roy, *Road Past Altamont,* 63–64.

16 Fiske, "Surfalism and Sandiotics," 122.

17 "Winnipeg Beach," *Manitoba Free Press,* 1 July 1, 1905, 5.

18 "At Lake of Killarney and Winnipeg Beach," *Manitoba Free Press Magazine Section,* 11 June 1907, 1.

19 Wendy Mitchinson, *Giving Birth in Canada: 1900–1950* (Toronto: University of Toronto Press, 2002), 160–161

20 Jasen, *Wild Things,* 16, 43, 50, 82.

21 Mawani, "Imperial Legacies (Post)Colonial Identities," 113, 125.

22 "Motor Parties Swell Train Crowds at Winnipeg Beach," *Manitoba Free Press,* 2 July 1924, 6.

23 Bess Kaplan, *Corner Store* (Winnipeg: Queenston House, 1975), 198.

24 Roy, *Road Past Altamont,* 65.

25 Fiske, "Surfalism and Sandiotics," 123.

26 "The History of Winnipeg Beach" oral history project, The Boundary Creek District Development, Victor Martin C2123 Interview, Date NA, 1991, with D. Harrison and D. Carpenter, Archives of Manitoba.

27 "The History of Winnipeg Beach" oral history project, R. Thedrikson (née Raykdal) C2131 interview, 1990-1991, with D. Harrison and D. Carpenter, Archives of Manitoba.

28 Kaplan, *Corner Store,* 196.

29 "The History of Winnipeg Beach" oral history project, R. Thedrikson (née Raykdal) C2131 interview.

30 Lofgren, *On Holiday,* 223.

31 From Jessie to Miss J. Mulholland, 01 September, 1930, Prairie Postcards PC002307, Alberta Collection.

32 Kasson, *Amusing the Million,* 6.

33 "Winnipeg Beach," *Manitoba Free Press,* 1 July 1905, 5. "Anglican Picnic," *Manitoba Free Press,* 27 June 1904, 14. Note pictures.

34 "Boston Baths," *Morning Telegram,* 6 August 1901, 4.

35 Gibson, *More Than an Island,* 92.

36 "Eaton's Midsummer Sale," *Manitoba Free Press,* 25 July 1911, 12.

37 "Must Have Bathing Suits," *Manitoba Free Press,* 5 June 1912, 3.

38 Garth Teel, interview with the author, 5 January 2008.

39 Immerso, *Coney Island,* 158.

40 Latham, "Packaging Woman," 151. Ian Jobling and John A. Lucas, "Troubled Waters: Fanny Durack's 1919 Swimming Tour of America amid Transnational Amateur Athletic Prudery and Bureaucracy," *OLYMPKA: The International Journal of Olympic Studies* 4 (1995): 94.

41 Jobling and Lucas, "Troubled Waters," 95.

42 Ibid., 95.

43 Ibid., 96.

44 "Winnipeg Beach," *Manitoba Free Press*, 16 July 1910, 10.

45 "Water Baby Instructor Shy as to Achievements but Hates to Stop Work," *Winnipeg Free Press*, 11 November 1933, 11.

46 Latham, "Packaging Woman," 151, 152.

47 Immerso, *Coney Island*, 158.

48 *Winnipeg Free Press*, 21 June 1941, 12.

49 Immerso, *Coney Island*, 158.

50 "'Bathing Suits All What You Get Used To,' Say Beach Police Officers," *Winnipeg Free Press*, 25 June 1932, 18. See "Eaton's Daily Store News," *Winnipeg Free Press*, 28 July 1937, 19, for a look at a zipper-top bathing suit.

51 "'Bathing Suits All What You Get Used To,'" 18.

52 Ibid., 18.

53 "Morals and Geography," *Winnipeg Free Press Editorial Section*, 2 July 1932, editorial page.

54 Cross and Walton, *Playful Crowd*, 139.

55 "The History of Winnipeg Beach" oral history project, The Boundary Creek District Development, Pauline Ketch C2116 interview, 1 June 1991, with D. Harrison and D. Carpenter, Archives of Manitoba.

56 "Beach Bathers Must Wear More Clothes," *Winnipeg Free Press*, 8 July 1943, 7.

57 "Queer Edict," *Winnipeg Free Press*, 12 July 1943, editorial page.

58 "Appreciates Letters in the Free Press," *Winnipeg Free Press*, 24 July 1943, 18.

59 Fred Williams, "On this Date," *Lethbridge Herald*, 22 June 1936, 4.

60 Latham, "Packaging Woman," 162.

61 Ibid., 165.

62 Peiss, *Cheap Amusements*, 186.

63 "Water Babies," *Winnipeg Free Press*, 3 August 1950, 1.

64 Orest, interview with the author, 5 December 2007.

65 Jessica interview.

66 "Winnipeg Girl is Winner of Beach Beauty Contest," *Winnipeg Free Press*, 18 July 1935, 1. "Wins Beauty Contest," *Winnipeg Free Press*, 26 July 1954, 1. "Beauties Pack Beach for Caterers' Picnic," *Winnipeg Free Press*, 3 August 1950, 1. "Storm's no Picnic," *Winnipeg Free Press*, 19 July 1962, 1. "Mother of Three Tops in Glamor," *Winnipeg Free Press*, 23 July 1964, 1. "Donna Sutton, 16, Wins Beauty Contest," *Winnipeg Free Press*, 26 August 1949, 1. "Beauty Contest at Winnipeg Beach Draws 125 Entries," *Winnipeg Free Press*, 20 July 1939, 4. "Eileen Jacobson is Beach Beauty," *Winnipeg Free Press*, 23 August 1946, 7. "Beauty Contest Held at Winnipeg Beach," *Winnipeg Free Press*, 20 August 1948, 5. "Norma Snider Made Champion at Winnipeg Beach," *Winnipeg Free Press*, 23 July 1937, 20. "Bathing Beauty Contest Attracts 100 Contestants," *Winnipeg Free Press*, 21 July 1934, 6. "Bathing Beauty Contest —Infant Style—At Beach," *Winnipeg Free Press*, 14 July 1949, 1. "Youngest Entries Win Special Prizes in Baby Contest," *Winnipeg Free Press*, 10 July 1947, 13. "Annual Baby Contest Held at Winnipeg Beach," *Winnipeg Free Press*, 15 August 1944, 19. "Baby Knight Wins Contest at Winnipeg Beach," *Winnipeg Free Press*, 24 August 1943, 9.

67   Palmer, *Cultures of Darkness*, 19.

68   "Winnipeg Beach," *Manitoba Free Press*, 4 July 1906, 6, 8.

69   Ibid., 6, 8.

70   "Improvements at Winnipeg Beach," *Manitoba Free Press*, 23 July 1906, 2.

71   Nasaw, *Going Out*, 6. Adams, "Almost Anything Can Happen," 228.

72   "The History of Winnipeg Beach" oral history project, The Boundary Creek District Development, Bill McIntosh C2124 interview, 17 April 1991, with D. Harrison and D. Carpenter, Archives of Manitoba interview.

73   "The History of Winnipeg Beach" oral history project, The Boundary Creek District Development, Trish Jones C2113 interview, Date NA 1990/91, with D. Harrison and D. Carpenter, Archives of Manitoba.

74   Jessica interview.

75   Ibid.

76   Ibid. Barney Charach, interview with the author, 8 December 2007.

77   "The History of Winnipeg Beach" oral history project, Bill McIntosh C2124 interview.

78   Russell, *Mistehay Sakahegan*, 141

79   "Winnipeg Beach Water Carnival," *Manitoba Free Press*, 5 August 1907, 8.

80   Russell, *Mistehay Sakahegan*, 140–141.

81   "She Won Where Five Men Failed," *Winnipeg Free Press*, 20 August 1955, 10.

82   "Shlack Conquers the Lake," *Winnipeg Free Press*, 29 August 1955, 1.

83   "Winnipeg Beach," *Manitoba Free Press*, 1 July 1905, 5.

84   "The History of Winnipeg Beach" oral history project, The Boundary Creek District Development, Jack London C2119 interview, 22 May 1990, with D. Harrison and D. Carpenter, Archives of Manitoba.

85   "Winnipeg Soon to Have New Resort," *Morning Telegram*, 1 June 1901, 9, 13.

86   "Winnipeg Beach," *Manitoba Free Press*, 22 June 1912.

87   Bob Noble, "Do You Remember?" *Winnipeg Free Press-TV/Radio*, 4 August 1962, 5.

88   Robert E. Snow and David E. Wright, "Coney Island: A Case Study in Popular Culture and Technical Change," *Journal of Popular Culture* 9, 4 (1976): 966.

89   Russell B. Nye, "Eight Ways of Looking at an Amusement Park," *Journal of Popular Culture* 15, 1 (1981): 65, 66.

90   Bakhtin, *Rabelais and His World*, 10.

91   Simon, *Boardwalk of Dreams*, 29.

92   Kasson, *Amusing the Million*, 40.

93   Nye, "Eight Ways," 67.

94   Field, "A Night at the Garden(s)," 264.

95   Nye, "Eight Ways," 68, 69.

96   Dr. Paul Adams, interview with the author, 21 December 2007.

97   Lawrence Isfeld, interview with the author, 5 December 2007.

98   Raymond M. Weinstein, "Disneyland and Coney Island: Reflections on the Evolution of the Modern Amusement Park," *Journal of Popular Culture* 26, 1 (1991): 141.

99   Val Kinack, interview with the author, 16 January 2008.

100 Dafoe, "On the 'Broadwalk,'" 31.

101 Retired CN employee, interview with the author, 27 November 2007.

102 Dr. Paul Adams interview.

103 Susan, interview with the author, 11 December 2007.

104 "The History of Winnipeg Beach" oral history project, Victor Martin C2123 interview.

105 Nestor Mudry, interview with the author, 12 December 2007.

106 Cross and Walton, *Playful Crowd*, 40.

107 Palmer, *Cultures of Darkness*, 6.

108 Cross and Walton, *Playful Crowd*, 34.

109 Letter from H.A. Good, director land acquisition branch, to Hon. Sterling Lyon, minister, tourism and recreation, dated 15 May 1966, 206.11 CHOO3A, acquisition of Silverberg property, Winnipeg Beach, Archives of Manitoba.

110 Dr. Paul Adams interview.

111 Christopher Dafoe, "On the 'Broadwalk,'" 31.

112 "The History of Winnipeg Beach" oral history project, Pauline Ketch C2116 interview.

113 "The History of Winnipeg Beach" oral history project, Jack London C2119 interview.

114 Immerso, *Coney Island*, 152–153, 167.

115 Nasaw, *Going Out*, 48, 51, 61.

116 Roberts, *In Mixed Company*, 107.

117 Jack London C2119 interview.

118 Filey, *Sunnyside*, 9.

119 "The History of Winnipeg Beach" oral history project, The Boundary Creek District Development, Mildred Kelly C2114 interview, 18 July 1990, with D. Harrison and D. Carpenter, Archives of Manitoba.

120 Dr. Paul Adams interview.

121 Garth Teel interview. "The History of Winnipeg Beach" oral history project, The Boundary Creek District Development, W.J. (Lil) Teel C2135 interview, 5 September 1990, with D. Harrison and D. Carpenter, Archives of Manitoba.

122 Levine, *Coming of Age*.

123 Jessica interview.

124 Heather Manz, interview with the author, 17 December 2007.

125 "Where's My Doll?" *Winnipeg Free Press*, 25 May 1962, 14.

126 Boyer, *The Boardwalk Album*, 42.

127 Bob Noble, "Do You Remember?" *Winnipeg Free Press-TV/Radio*, 4 August 1964, 5.

128 Dorothy Lynch letter. Solicited for the Dance Hall Film Project. Badiuk, *Dance Hall Film Project*.

129 Jessica interview.

130 Val Kinack interview.

131 Nestor Mudry interview.

132 Orest interview.

133 Barney Charach interview.

134 Robert Kendall, interview with the author, 5 December 2007.

135 Dafoe, "On the 'Broadwalk,'" 31.

136 David Bell and Gill Valentine have defined this as "heterosexing" space in their *Mapping Desire: Geographies of Sexualities* (Routledge: New York, 1995), 18.

137 Kaplan, *Corner Store*, 201–202.

138 Ibid., 201, 207–208, 214–216.

139 Bell and Valentine, *Mapping Desire*, 8, 19.

140 Garth Teel interview.

141 Ibid.

142 Ibid.

143 Filey, *Sunnyside*, 80.

144 Elizabeth Comack, *Out There In Here: Masculinity, Violence and Prisoning* (Fernwood Publishing: Winnipeg, 2008) 10, 17, 18.

145 Christopher Giles, "The History of Street Gangs in Winnipeg from 1945 to 1997: A Qualitative Newspaper Analysis of Gang Activity" (master's thesis, Simon Fraser University, 2000), 50.

146 "Police Answer Two Calls for Aid in Gang Raids," *Winnipeg Free Press*, 13 January 1950, 1.

147 Giles, "Street Gangs," 52.

148 Ibid., 51, 52.

149 "Police Answer Two Calls for Aid in Gang Raids," 1.

150 Adams, *Trouble with Normal*, 72.

151 Gibson, *More Than an Island*, 227.

152 Adams, *Trouble with Normal*, 72.

153 Garth Teel interview.

154 Giles, "Street Gangs," 51, 52.

155 Garth Teel interview.

156 Dafoe, "On the 'Broadwalk,'" 31.

157 Ibid., 31.

158 Manitoba Gay/Lesbian Oral History Project, George M. Smith C1869 interview, 25 June 1990, with David Theodore, Archives of Manitoba. *Dirt*, it should be noted, was their term for gay-bashers.

159 Manitoba Gay/Lesbian Oral History Project, George M. Smith C1869 interview.

160 Bell and Valentine, *Mapping Desire*, 18.

161 "The History of Winnipeg Beach" oral history project, The Boundary Creek District Development, Kathleen Rees C2130 interview, 22 May 1990, with D. Carpenter, Archives of Manitoba.

162 "The History of Winnipeg Beach" oral history project, Mildred Kelly C2114 interview.

163 Heron, *Booze*, 282.

164 Russell, *Mistehay Sakahegan*, 124.

165 *The Report of the Manitoba Liquor Enquiry Commission* (Winnipeg, 1955), 282, 404.

166 Ibid., 434.

167 Dale Barbour, "Drinking Together: The Role of Gender in Changing Manitoba's Liquor Laws in the 1950s, in *Prairie Metropolis: New Essays on Winnipeg Social History,* ed. Esyllt Jones and Gerald Friesen (Winnipeg: University of Manitoba Press, 2009).

168 Val Kinack interview.

169 "Liquor Commission Suspends Licenses," *Manitoba Free Press,* 28 May 1928, 7.

170 Ibid.,7. "The History of Winnipeg Beach" oral history project, Mildred Kelly C2114 interview.

171 "The Government Liquor Control Act, 1928," *Manitoba Free Press,* 17 February 1927, 17.

172 "Local Notes," *Manitoba Free Press,* 11 March 1924, 2.

173 Ibid., 2.

174 "Chill Winds at Lake Resorts on Saturday," *Manitoba Free Press,* 16 June 1924, 4.

175 Nestor Mudry interview.

176 Orest interview.

177 "Chill Winds at Lake Resorts on Saturday," 4.

178 Agnes Walker letter. Solicited for the Dance Hall Film Project. Badiuk, *Dance Hall Film Project.*

179 "From Regina to Winnipeg Beach," *Manitoba Free Press,* story section, 14 July, 1925, 14.

180 "The History of Winnipeg Beach" oral history project, Doris Margolis C2121 interview, 5 December 1990, with D. Harrison and D. Carpenter, Archives of Manitoba.

181 Bailey, *From Front Porch to Back Seat,* 78.

182 Robert Kendall interview.

183 Barry Anderson, interview with the author, 10 December 2007.

184 Jessica interview.

185 Adams, *Trouble with Normal,* 43.

186 Russell, *Mistehay Sakahegan,* 125. Clark, *Musical Ghosts,* 237. Nestor Mudry interview.

187 Nestor Mudry interview.

188 Clark, *Musical Ghosts,* 237. "The History of Winnipeg Beach" oral history project, The Boundary Creek District Development, Harry Simpson C2133 interview, 24 October 1990, with D. Harrison and D. Carpenter, Archives of Manitoba.

189 Nestor Mudry interview.

190 Lawrence Isfeld interview. Orest interview.

191 Nestor Mudry interview.

192 Bailey, *From Front Porch to Back Seat,* 31.

193 Ibid., 26.

194 Cas Wouters, *Sex and Manners: Female Emancipation in the West, 1890 to 2000* (London: Sage Publications, 2004), 110.

195 Garbutt, "Fancy Free," 22.

196 Izzy Peltz, interview with the author, 15 December 2007.

197 Val Kinack interview.

198 "The History of Winnipeg Beach" oral history project, Pauline Ketch C2116 interview.

199 Peiss, *Cheap Amusements*, 89.

200 Barney Charach interview.

201 Orest interview.

202 "Winnipeg Beach," *Manitoba Free Press*, 6 April 1911, 11.

203 See Clark for a look at the wide range of clubs and dance locations that were available to people in Winnipeg during the first half of the twentieth century.

204 Nestor Mudry interview.

205 "The History of Winnipeg Beach" oral history project, Harry Simpson C2133 interview.

206 Val Werier, *The Winnipeg Tribune*, "Mixed Drinking? We've Had it for Many Years," 20 August 1955, 19. *The Report of the Manitoba Liquor Enquiry Commission*, 20.

207 Orest interview.

208 Val Kinack interview.

209 Ibid.

210 Lawrence Isfeld interview.

211 Heron, *Booze*, 270.

212 Mariana Valverde, *Diseases of the Will: Alcohol and the Dilemmas of Freedom* (Cambridge: Cambridge University Press, 1998), 158.

213 Garth Teel interview.

214 Val Kinack interview.

215 Werier, *The Report of the Manitoba Liquor Enquiry Commission*, 20.

216 Valverde, *Diseases of the Will*, 158.

217 Adams, *Trouble with Normal*, 65.

218 Garth Teel interview.

219 Val Kinack interview.

220 Peltz interview.

221 Badiuk, Agnes Walker letter.

222 Nasaw, *Going Out*, 110.

223 Palmer, *Cultures of Darkness*, 6.

224 "Winnipeg Beach," *Manitoba Free Press*, 4 July 1906, 6 and 8. Garth Teel interview.

225 Dafoe, "On the 'Broadwalk,'" 31. Lawrence Isfeld interview.

226 Tadpole, interview with the author, 8 December 2007.

227 Barry Anderson interview.

228 "The History of Winnipeg Beach" oral history project, Mildred Kelly C2114 interview.

229 "The History of Winnipeg Beach" oral history project, Pauline Ketch C2116 interview.

230 The area would be what historians refer to as a "heterosocial" zone.

CHAPTER 4

1   "Ho! For Winnipeg Beach!" *Manitoba Free Press*, 24 July 1909, 2. "Winnipeg Beach: The 'Coney Island' of the West," *Manitoba Free Press*, 6 May 1911, 9. "Youth's Fling," *Winnipeg Free Press*, 15 August 1964, 13. Raymond M. Weinstein, "Disneyland and Coney Island: Reflections on the Evolution of the Modern Amusement Park," *Journal of Popular Culture* 26, 1 (1991): 144, 145.

2   Immerso, *Coney Island*, 166.

3   Cross and Walton, *Playful Crowd*, 149. "Winnipeg Beach Amusements Close Permanently," *Winnipeg Free Press*, 8 October 1964.

4   Russell, *Mistehay Sakahegan*, 137–138.

5   Cochrane and Cochrane, *The Beach*, 8–19.

6   Freeman, *A Magical Place*, 33–35.

7   Gibson, *More Than an Island*, 247–261.

8   Nasaw, *Going Out*, 242

9   "Flames destroy Empress Hotel at Winnipeg Beach; one injured," *Winnipeg Free Press*, 28 August, 1935, 1.

10 "New Deal is Urged for Winnipeg Beach," *Winnipeg Free Press*, 22 November 1939, 19.

11 "Last Run for Famed Train?" *Winnipeg Free Press*, 8 October 1951, 13.

12 Lawrence Isfeld, interview with the author, 5 December 2007.

13 "Leaving Winnipeg Every Few minutes, Trains Carried 40,000 Travellers a Day," *CP Rail News*, CPR Archives.

14 Bowman, "The Recreational Function," 26–27.

15 Letter from H.A. Good, director land acquisition branch, to Hon. Sterling Lyon, minister, tourism and recreation, 23 May 1967,

16 "The History of Winnipeg Beach" oral history project, The Boundary Creek District Development, Jack London C2119 interview, 22 May 1990, with D. Harrison and D. Carpenter, Archives of Manitoba.

17 W.J. Wood, "A Brief History of Winnipeg Beach," 7.

18 Russell, *Mistehay Sakahegan*, 137. David Laurence Jones, *Tales of the CPR* (Calgary: Fifth House, 2002), 127.

19 "Winnipeg Beach," *Manitoba Free Press*, 15 June 1909, 10. "Trip to the Beach," *Manitoba Free Press Automobile Section*, 6 August 1910.

20 Russell, *Mistehay Sakahegan*, 137.

21 "Beaches Washing Away, Protest Lake Holidayers," *Winnipeg Tribune*, 18 July 1955, 13. "Beach Delegation Given Inspection Tour Promise," *Winnipeg Tribune*, 22 July 1955, 4. "Beach Group Asks for Annual Grants," *Winnipeg Tribune*, 25 July 1955, 13. "Ouster Bid on Beach Councillor," *Winnipeg Tribune*, 26 July 1955, 15.

22 Russell, *Mistehay Sakahegan*, 137.

23 Cross and Walton, *Playful Crowd*, 137.

24 Ibid., 160.

25 Ibid., 161.

26 Ina Drummond, interview with the author, 18 December 2007. Lawrence Isfeld interview. Garth Teel, interview with the author, 5 January 2008.

27 Orest, interview with the author, 5 December 2007.

28 Heather Manz, interview with the author, 17 December 2007.

29 Barney Charach, interview with the author, 8 December 2007. Bailey, *From Front Porch to Back Seat*, 86–87.

30 Peiss, *Cheap Amusements*, 5, 35, 72.

31 "The History of Winnipeg Beach" oral history project, The Boundary Creek District Development, Doris Margolis C2121 interview, 5 December 1990, with D. Harrison and D. Carpenter, Archives of Manitoba.

32 Cross and Walton, *Playful Crowd*, 137, 242.

33 Ibid., 243.

34 Ibid., 242.

35 Wouters, *Sex and Manners*, 50.

36 Valverde, *Diseases of the Will*, 158.

37 Adams, *Trouble with Normal*, 56.

38 "Premier Plans First Hand Look At Winnipeg Beach," *Winnipeg Free Press*, 22 July 1955, 2.

39 "65% Drink? That's Crazy Say All Students but One," *Winnipeg Free Press*, 7 September 1956, 1.

40 Dafoe, "On the 'Broadwalk,'" 31.

41 Ibid., 31.

42 Bailey, *From Front Porch to Back Seat*, 141.

43 Izzy Peltz, interview with the author, 15 December 2007.

44 "Beach Week-Enders Not Wanted – Keith," *Winnipeg Free Press*, 25 July 1955, 1.

45 "A Transient Replies," "Letters to the Editor," *Winnipeg Free Press*, 29 July 1955, 7.

46 "Winnipeg Beach Starts a New Era," 1962, Hudson's Bay Company Archives, Winnipeg Beach Vertical File.

47 Simon, *Boardwalk of Dreams*, 124.

48 Ibid., 112.

49 Ibid., 114.

50 Nasaw, *Going Out*, 248.

51 Josh Sides, *Erotic City: Sexual Revolutions and the Making of Modern San Francisco* (New York: Oxford University Press, 2009), 10.

52 Cross and Walton, *Playful Crowd*, 244.

53 Ibid., 250.

54 Ibid., 246–247.

55 "Bring the Whole Family," *Winnipeg Free Press*, 18 July 1950, 4. "Winnipeg Beach: Where there is Fun for All the Family," *Winnipeg Free Press*, 16 June 1950, 4. "Gee Mom," *Winnipeg Free Press*, 3 July 1951, 4. "Winnipeg Beach and Gimli," *Winnipeg Free Press*, 6 August 1952, 6.

56 Cross and Walton, *Playful Crowd*, 171, 172, 174.

57 Letter from H.A. Good to Hon. Sterling Lyon.

58 Cross and Walton, *Playful Crowd*, 175.

59 "Where's My Doll?," *Winnipeg Free Press*, 25 May 1962, 14.

60 Ina Drummond interview. Barry Anderson, interview with the author, 10 December 2007.

61 Orest interview.

62 Ibid.

63 Ibid.

64 Ibid.

65 Lawrence Cherniack, "And in this Corner: Beach Play Centres on Arcade, Convertibles and Motorcycles," Hudson's Bay Company Archives, Winnipeg Beach Vertical File.

66 Ibid.

67 Ibid.

68 Wouters, *Sex and Manners*, 50.

69 Russell, *Mistehay Sakahegan*, 16.

70 Roy, *Road Past Altamont*, 83.

71 "Beaches Washing Away, Protest Lake Holidayers," *Winnipeg Tribune*, 18 July 1955, 13. "Beach Delegation Given Inspection Tour Promise," *Winnipeg Tribune*, 22 July 1955, 4.

72 "Our Beaches Have Returned," *Winnipeg Tribune*, 5 July 1958, 17.

73 Lake Winnipeg Shoreline Erosion Advisory Group, "Final Report" (Province of Manitoba, September 2000), 59.

74 Ibid.

75 Garth Teel interview.

76 Heather Manz interview.

77 Russell, *Mistehay Sakahegan*, 138.

78 Chris Ladd, "Winnipeg Beach Amusements Close Permanently," *Winnipeg Free Press*, 8 October 1964, 1.

79 Letter from Lawrence Tapper to the Honourable Dufferin Roblin, 1 February 1965, Archives of Manitoba, Q026770, 206.11.

80 Interdepartmental memorandum from L.S. Mayer, administrative officer, land acquisition branch, to Mr. W.W. Danyluk, director of parks, department of tourism and recreation, Archives of Manitoba, Q026770, 206.11.

81 Russell, *Mistehay Sakahegan*, 138.

82 Interdepartmental memorandum, M.L. Beckford, senior resources analyst, to Mr. Stuart Anderson, deputy minister, 27 August 1965, Archives of Manitoba, Q026770, 206.11.

83 "Beach Area Future Still Doubtful," *Winnipeg Free Press*, 24 April 1965, 1.

84 "Winnipeg Beach," *Winnipeg Free Press*, 13 October 1964, editorial page.

85 Ibid., editorial page.

86 Christopher Dafoe, "Under the Dome," *Winnipeg Free Press*, 23 April 1965, 37.

87 Letter from Honourable G. Johnson, M.D. minster of education, to Honourable Duff Roblin, premier of Manitoba, 15 February 1965, Archives of Manitoba, Q026770, 206.11.

88 Bob Noble, "Winnipeg Beach: Memories of Yesteryear," *Winnipeg Free Press*, 20 May 1967, 8.

89 Tom Saunders, "Reclaiming Winnipeg Beach," *Winnipeg Free Press*, 16 August 1967, 31.

90 Ibid., 31.

91 Ibid., 31.

92 Filey, *Sunnyside*, 131.

93 Gibson, *More Than an Island*, 252–261.

94 Simon, *Boardwalk of Dreams*, 141–149.

95 Tina Loo, "People in the Way: Modernity, Environment, and Society on the Arrow Lakes," *BC Studies* 142/143 (2004): 164–165.

96 "Winnipeg Beach Now and Then," *Winnipeg Free Press*, June 1969 as found in Vienna Badiuk, *Dance Hall Film Project* (Winnipeg: Manitoba Culture, Heritage and Citizenship, Heritage Grants Program), 1999.

97 Cross and Walton, *Playful Crowd*, 140, 184.

98 "Winnipeg Beach Now and Then."

99 Jessica, interview with the author, 29 November 2007.

Bibliography

PRIMARY SOURCES

Oral History Sources

"The History of Winnipeg Beach" oral history project. The Boundary Creek District Development, funded by the Oral History Grants Program of Manitoba Culture, Heritage and Recreation, 1991. C2093–C2140, Archives of Manitoba and the Hudson's Bay Company Archives.

Manitoba Gay/Lesbian Oral History Project. Manitoba Gay Lesbian Archives Committee, funded by the Oral History Grants Program, Manitoba Culture, Heritage and Citizenship, 1990. C1861–C1903, Archives of Manitoba and the Hudson's Bay Company Archives.

Interviews with 18 people who travelled to or lived in Winnipeg Beach between the years of 1925 and 1965 were conducted between November 2007 and January 2008.

Newspapers

Lethbridge Herald
Minnedosa Tribune
Morning Telegram
Winnipeg Free Press (called the *Manitoba Free Press* until 1931)
Winnipeg Tribune

Government Publications

Report of the Manitoba Liquor Enquiry Commission, Winnipeg, 1955.

Archives

Canadian Pacific Archives
Archives of Manitoba
        Hudson's Bay Company Archives
University of Manitoba Archives and Special Collections
        Winnipeg Tribune Collection

SECONDARY SOURCES

Adams, Mary Louise. "Almost Anything Can Happen: A Search for Sexual Discourse in the Urban Spaces of 1940s Toronto." In "Moral Regulation," special issue of *The Canadian Journal of Sociology/Cahiers canadiens de sociologie* 19, 2 (1994): 217–232.

_____. *The Trouble with Normal: Postwar Youth and the Making of Heterosexuality.* Toronto: University of Toronto Press, 1997.

Agarwal, Sheela. "Restructuring Seaside Tourism: The Resort Lifecyle." *Annals of Tourism Research* 29, 1 (2002): 25–55.

Aiken, Don, and Chris Thain. *It Happened in Manitoba: Stories of the Red River Province.* Calgary: Fifth House, 2004.

Avila, Eric. *Popular Culture in the Age of White Flight: Fear and Fantasy in Suburban Los Angeles.* Berkeley: University of California Press, 2006.

Backhouse, Douglas C. "Aspects of a Changing Rural Landscape: A Study of Possibilities for Retirement Community Development in Winnipeg Beach." MA thesis, University of Manitoba, 1989.

Badiuk, Vienna. *Dance Hall Film Project.* Winnipeg: Manitoba Culture, Heritage and Citizenship, Heritage Grants Program, 1998.

Bailey, Beth. *From Front Porch to Back Seat.* Baltimore: The Johns Hopkins University Press, 1988.

Bakhtin, Mikhail. *Rabelais and His World.* Bloomington: Indiana University Press, 1984.

Barman, Jean. *Stanley Park's Secret: The Forgotten Families of Whoi Whoi, Kanaka Ranch and Brockton Point.* Vancouver: Harbour Publishing, 2005.

Bell, David, and Gill Valentine. *Mapping Desire: Geographies of Sexualities.* New York: Routledge, 1995.

Berger, John. *Ways of Seeing.* London: BBC and Penguin, 1972.

Binnie, Jon. "Trading Places: Consumption, Sexuality and the Production of Queer Space." In *Mapping Desire: Geographies of Sexualities,* edited by David Bell and Gill Valentine. New York: Routledge, 1995.

Blanchard, Jim. *Winnipeg 1912.* Winnipeg: University of Manitoba Press, 2005.

Boritch, Helen, and John Hagan. "A Century of Crime in Toronto: Gender, Class, and Patterns of Social Control, 1859 to 1955." *Criminology* 28, 4 (1990): 567–599.

Bowman, Joan. *The Recreational Function and Related Problems of the Winnipeg Beach-Sandy Hook Section of the Lake Winnipeg Shoreline.* MA thesis, University of Manitoba, 1966.

Boyer, Barbaranne. *The Boardwalk Album: Memories of the Beach.* Erin, ON: Boston Mills Press, 1985.

Braden, Donna R. *Leisure and Entertainment in America.* Detroit: Wayne State University Press, 1988.

Butler, Judith. *The Judith Butler Reader.* Edited by Sara Salih, with Judith Butler. Malden, MA: Blackwell Publishing, 2004.

Butler, R.W. "The Concept of a Tourism Area Lifecycle of Evolution: Implications for Management of Resources." *The Canadian Geographer* 24 (1981): 5–12.

Campbell, Robert A. "'Profit was just a circumstance': The Evolution of Government Liquor Control in British Columbia, 1920–1988." In *Drink in Canada: Historical Essays*, edited by Cheryl Krasnick Warsh, 172–192. Kingston: McGill-Queen's University Press, 1993.

_____. *Sit Down and Drink Your Beer: Regulating Vancouver's Beer Parlours, 1925–1954*. Toronto: University of Toronto Press, 2001.

Cavell, Richard. *Love, Hate, and Fear in Canada's Cold War*. Toronto: University of Toronto Press, 2004.

Chauncey, George. *Gay New York: Gender, Urban Culture, and the Making of the Gay Male World, 1890–1940*. New York: Basic Books, 1994.

Churchill, David. "Mother Goose's Map: Tabloid Geographies and Gay Male Experience in 1950s Toronto." *Journal of Urban History* 30, 6 (2004): 826–852.

Clark, Owen. *Musical Ghosts: Manitoba's Jazz and Dance Bands 1914–1966*. Winnipeg: Clark Productions, 2007.

Cochrane, Glenn, and Jean Cochrane. *The Beach: An Illustrated History from the Lake to Kingston Road*. Toronto: ECW Press, 2009.

Cohen, Lizabeth. *A Consumers' Republic: The Politics of Mass Consumption in Postwar America*. New York: Vintage Books, 2003.

Comacchio, Cynthia. "Dancing to Perdition: Adolescence and Leisure in Interwar English Canada." *Journal of Canadian Studies* 32, 3 (1997): 5–36.

Comack, Elizabeth. *Out There/In Here: Masculinity, Violence and Prisoning*. Winnipeg: Fernwood Publishing, 2008.

Cross, Gary S. "Crowds and Leisure: Thinking Comparatively across the 20th Century." *Journal of Social History* 39, 3 (2006): 631–650.

_____. *A Social History of Leisure since 1600*. Edmonton: Venture Publishing, 1990.

_____. *Worktowners at Blackpool: Mass-Observation and Popular Leisure in the 1930s*. New York: Routledge, 1990.

Cross, Gary S., and John K. Walton. *The Playful Crowd: Pleasure Places in the Twentieth Century*. New York: Columbia University Press, 2005.

Currell, Susan. *The March of Spare Time: The Promise of Leisure in the Great Depression*. Philadelphia: University of Pennsylvania Press, 2005.

Dafoe, Christopher. "On Manitoba's Inland Seas: The Lake Winnipeg/Lake Manitoba Region." In *The Lake: An Illustrated History of Manitoba's Cottage Country*, edited by Jake MacDonald. Winnipeg: Great Plains Publications, 2000.

Debord, Guy. *The Society of the Spectacle*. Detroit: Black and Red, 1995.

DeLottinville, Peter. "Joe Beef of Montreal: Working Class Culture and the Tavern, 1869–1889." *Labour/Le Travail* 8–9 (1981–1982): 9–40.

Dubinsky, Karen. *Improper Advances: Rape and Heterosexual Conflict in Ontario, 1880–1929*. Chicago: The University of Chicago Press, 1993.

_____. *The Second Greatest Disappointment: Honeymooning and Tourism at Niagara Falls*. Toronto: Between the Lines, 1999.

Dundas, Howard. *Wrinkled Arrows: Good Old Days in Winnipeg*. Winnipeg: Queenston House, 1980.

Evans, Richard J. *In Defence of History.* London: Granta Books, 2000.

Eyford, Ryan C. "Quarantined Within a New Colonial Order: The 1876–1877 Lake Winnipeg Smallpox Epidemic." *Journal of the Canadian Historical Association/ Revue de la Société historique du Canada* 17, 1 (2006): 55–78.

Field, Russell David. "A Night at the Garden(s): A History of Professional Hockey Spectatorship in the 1920s and 1930s." PhD diss., University of Toronto, 2008.

Filey, Mike. *I Remember Sunnyside: The Rise and Fall of a Magical Era.* Toronto: Dundurn Group, 1996.

Fiske, John. "Surfalism and Sandiotics: The Beach in Oz Culture." *Australian Journal of Cultural Studies* 1, 2 (1983): 120–149.

Folch-Serra, M. "Place, Voice, Space: Mikhail Bakhtin's Dialogical Landscape." *Environment and Planning D: Society and Space* 8, 3 (1990): 255–274.

Foucault, Michel. "Governmentality." In *The Foucault Effect: Studies in Governmentality,* edited by Graham Birchell, Colin Gordon, and Peter Miller, 87–104. Chicago: University of Chicago Press, 1991.

_____. "Lecture #11, 17 March 1976." In *Society Must Be Defended.* New York: Picador 1997.

_____. "Right of Death and Power over Life." In *The History of Sexuality: An Introduction.* New York: Vintage Books, 1990.

_____. "The Subject and Power." In *Power (The Essential Works of Foucault 1954–84,* vol. 3), edited by James D. Faubion. New York: The New Press, 2000.

Frager, Ruth A., and Carmela Patrias. *Discounted Labour: Women Workers in Canada, 1870–1939.* Toronto: University of Toronto Press, 2005.

Freeman, Bill. *A Magical Place: Toronto Island and Its People.* Toronto: James Lorimer and Company, 1999.

Friesen, Gerald. *The Canadian Prairies: A History.* Toronto: University of Toronto Press, 1987.

Gibson, Sally. *More Than an Island: A History of the Toronto Island.* Toronto: Irwin Publishing, 1984.

Giddens, Anthony. "Time, Space and Regionalisation." In *Social Relations and Spatial Structures,* edited by Derek Gregory and John Urry. London: Macmillan Publishers, 1985.

Giles, Christopher. "The History of Street Gangs in Winnipeg from 1945 to 1997: A Qualitative Newspaper Analysis of Gang Activity." Master's thesis, Simon Fraser University, 2000.

Gilfoyle, Timothy J. "White Cities, Linguistic Turns, and Disneylands: The New Paradigms of Urban History Author(s)." In "The Challenge of American History," special issue of *American History* 26, 1 (1998): 175–204.

Gray, James H. *Booze: The Impact of Whisky on the Prairie West.* Toronto: Macmillan of Canada, 1972.

Hamilton, Douglas L. *Sobering Dilemma: A History of Prohibition in British Columbia.* Vancouver: Ronsdale Press, 2004.

Harris, Richard. *Creeping Conformity: How Canada Became Suburban, 1900–1960.* Toronto: University of Toronto Press, 2004.

Hart, E.J. *The Selling of Canada: The CPR and the Beginnings of Canadian Tourism.* Banff, AB: Altitude Publishing, 1983.

Hayden, Dolores. *Redesigning the American Dream: The Future of Housing, Work, and Family Life.* New York: W.W. Norton, 2002.

Heron, Craig. *Booze: A Distilled History.* Toronto: Between the Lines, 2003.

_____. "The Boys and their Booze: Masculinities and Public Drinking in Working-class Hamilton, 1890–1946." *The Canadian Historical Review* 86, 3 (2005): 411–452.

Hiebert, Daniel. "Class, Ethnicity and Residential Structure: The Social Geography of Winnipeg, 1901–1921." *Journal of Historical Geography* 17, 1 (1991): 56–86.

Hill, Jeffrey. *Sport, Leisure and Culture in Twentieth-Century Britain.* Houndmills, Great Britain: Palgrave, 2002.

Hogeveen, Bryan. "'The Evils with Which We are Called to Grapple': Elite Reformers, Eugenicists, Environmental Psychologists, and the Construction of Toronto's Working-Class Boy Problem, 1860–1930." *Labour* 55 (Spring 2005): 37–68.

Hose, Ronald E. *Prohibition or Control? Canada's Experience with the Liquor Problem 1921–1927.* New York: Longmans, Green and Company, 1928.

Howell, Colin D. *Northern Sandlots: A Social History of Maritime Baseball.* Toronto: University of Toronto Press, 1995.

Illouz, Eva. *Consuming the Romantic Utopia: Love and the Cultural Contradictions of Capitalism.* Los Angeles: University of California Press, 1997.

Immerso, Michael. *Coney Island: The People's Playground.* Rutgers, NJ: Rutgers University Press, 2002.

Jasen, Patricia. *Wild Things: Nature, Culture, and Tourism in Ontario 1790–1914.* Toronto: University of Toronto Press, 1995.

Jobling, Ian, and John A. Lucas. "Troubled Waters: Fanny Durack's 1919 Swimming Tour of America amid Transnational Amateur Athletic Prudery and Bureaucracy." *OLYMPKA: The International Journal of Olympic Studies* 4 (1995): 93–112.

Jones, David Laurence. *Tales of the CPR.* Calgary: Fifth House, 2002.

Kaplan, Bess. *Corner Store.* Winnipeg: Queenston House, 1975.

Kasson, John F. *Amusing the Million: Coney Island at the Turn of the Century.* New York: Hill and Wang, 1978.

Klein, Alice, and Wayne Roberts. "Besieged Innocence: The 'Problem' and Problems of Working Women—Toronto, 1896–1914." In *Women at Work: Ontario, 1850–1930,* edited by Janice Acton, Penny Goldsmith, and Bonnie Shepard, 211–259. Toronto: Canadian Women's Education Press, 1974.

Korneski, Kurt. "Minnie J.B. Campbell, Reform and Empire." In *Prairie Metropolis: New Essays on Winnipeg Social History,* edited by Esyllt Jones and Gerald Friesen. Winnipeg: University of Manitoba Press, 2009.

Krause, Richard. *Leisure in a Changing America: Multicultural Perspectives.* New York: MacMillan College Publishing, 1994.

Latham, Angela J. "Packaging Woman: The Concurrent Rise of Beauty Pageants, Public Bathing, and Other Performances of Female 'Nudity.'" *Journal of Popular Culture* 29, 3: 149–167.

Lehr, John C., H. John Selwood, and Eileen Badiuk. "Ethnicity, Religion, and Class as Elements in the Evolution of Lake Winnipeg Resorts." *The Canadian Geographer* 35, 1 (1991): 46–58.

Levine, Allan. *Coming of Age: A History of the Jewish People of Manitoba.* Winnipeg: Jewish Heritage Centre of Western Canada and Heartland Associates, 2009.

Loewen, Royden, and Gerald Friesen. *Immigrants in Prairie Cities: Ethnic Diversity in Twentieth Century Canada.* Toronto: University of Toronto Press, 2009.

Lofgren, Orvar. *On Holiday: A History of Vacationing.* Los Angeles: University of California Press, 1999.

Loo, Tina. "People in the Way: Modernity, Environment, and Society on the Arrow Lakes," *BC Studies* 142/143 (2004): 161–196.

_____. *States of Nature: Conserving Canada's Wildlife in the Twentieth Century.* Vancouver: University of British Columbia Press, 2006.

MacDonald, Jake. *The Lake: An Illustrated History of Manitobans' Cottage Country.* Winnipeg: Great Plains Publications, 2000.

Mawani, Renisa. "Imperial Legacies and (Post)Colonial Identities: Law, Space, and the Making of Stanley Park, 1859–2001." *Law Text Culture* 7 (2003): 97–141.

Maynard, Steven. "'Horrible Temptations': Sex, Men, and Working-Class Male Youth in Urban Ontario, 1890–1935." *Canadian Historical Review* 78, 2 (1997): 191–235.

McDonald, Robert. "'Holy Retreat' or 'Practical Breathing Spot'?: Class Perceptions of Vancouver's Stanley Park, 1910–1913." *Canadian Historical Review* 65, 2 (1984): 127–153.

Mitchinson, Wendy. *Giving Birth in Canada: 1900–1950.* Toronto: University of Toronto Press, 2002.

Morgan, Sue. *The Feminist History Reader.* New York: Routledge Taylor and Francis Group, 2006.

Morton, W.L. *Manitoba: A History.* Toronto: University of Toronto Press, 1967.

Nasaw, David. *Going Out: The Rise and Fall of Public Amusements.* Cambridge: Harvard University Press, 1999.

Nye, Russell B. "Eight Ways of Looking at an Amusement Park." *Journal of Popular Culture* 15, 1 (1981): 63–75.

Palmer, Bryan. *A Culture in Conflict: Skilled Workers and Industrial Capitalism in Hamilton, Ontario, 1860–1914.* Montreal: McGill-Queen's University Press, 1979.

_____. *Cultures of Darkness: Night Travels in the Histories of Transgressions.* New York: Monthly Review Press, 2000.

Parr, Joy. *The Gender of Breadwinners: Women, Men, and Change in Two Industrial Towns, 1880–1950.* Toronto: University of Toronto Press, 1990.

Patterson, Graeme H. *History and Communications: Harold Innis, Marshall McLuhan, the Interpretation of History.* Toronto: University of Toronto Press, 1990.

Peiss, Kathy. *Cheap Amusements: Working Women and Leisure in Turn-of-the-Century New York.* Philadelphia: Temple University Press, 1986.

Pritchard, Annette, and Nigel J. Morgan. "Privileging the Male Gaze: Gendered Tourism Landscapes." *Annals of Tourism Research* 27, 4 (2000): 884–905.

Pritchard, Annette, Nigel Morgan, Irena Ateljevic, and Candice Harris. *Tourism and Gender: Embodiment, Sensuality and Experience.* Oxfordshire, United Kingdom: CABI, 2007.

Razack, Sherene H. *Race, Space, and the Law: Unmapping a White Settler Society.* Toronto: Between the Lines, 2005.

Read, Jean Tullett. "Bath-House Harry and Tales of Grand Beach." In *Through The Window of a Train: A Canadian Railway Anthology,* edited by Barbara Lange. Nepean, ON: Borealis Press, 2010.

Roberts, Julia. *In Mixed Company: Taverns and Public Life in Upper Canada.* Vancouver: University of British Columbia Press, 2009.

Rose, Suzanna, and Irene Hanson Frieze. "Young Singles' Scripts for a First Date." *Gender and Society* 3, 2 (1989): 258–268.

Roy, Gabrielle. *The Road Past Altamont.* Toronto: McClelland and Stewart, 1989.

Russell, Frances. *Mistehay Sakahegan, the Great Lake: The Beauty and the Treachery of Lake Winnipeg.* Winnipeg: Heartland, 2004.

Rutty, Christopher. "The Middle Class Plague: Epidemic Polio and the Canadian State 1936–1937." *Canadian Bulletin of Medical History* 13 (1996): 277–314.

Sanger, Carol. "Girls and the Getaway: Cars, Culture, and the Predicament of Gendered Space." *University of Pennsylvania Law Review* 144, 2 (1995): 705–756.

Sangster, Joan. *Regulating Girls and Women: Sexuality, Family, and the Law in Ontario, 1920–1960.* Don Mills, ON: Oxford University Press, 2001.

Schivelbusch, Wolfgang. *The Railway Journey: The Industrialization of Time and Space.* Berkeley: University of California Press, 1986.

Scott, Joan W., and Debra Keates. *Going Public: Feminism and the Shifting Boundaries of the Private Sphere.* Chicago: University of Illinois Press, 2004.

Shaw, Gareth, and Allan M. Williams. *Tourism and Tourism Spaces.* London: Sage Publications, 2004.

Sheller, Mimi, and John Urry. "The City and the Car." *International Journal of Urban and Regional Research* 24, 4 (2000).

Shields, Rob. "The 'System of Pleasure': Liminality and the Carnivalesque at Brighton." *Theory, Culture and Society* 7 (1990): 39–72.

Shivers, Jay S. and Lee J. deLisle. *The Story of Leisure: Context, Concepts, and Current Controversy.* Champaign, IL: Human Kinetics, 1997.

Sides, Josh. *Erotic City: Sexual Revolutions and the Making of Modern San Francisco.* New York: Oxford University Press, 2009.

Simon, Bryant. *Boardwalk of Dreams: Atlantic City and the Fate of Urban America.* New York: Oxford University Press, 2004.

Snow, Robert E., and David E. Wright. "Coney Island: A Case Study in Popular Culture and Technical Change." *Journal of Popular Culture* 9, 4 (1976): 960–975.

Strange, Carolyn. *Toronto's Girl Problem: The Perils and Pleasures of the City, 1880–1930*. Toronto: University of Toronto Press, 1995.

Tosh, John. *The Pursuit of History*. Harlow, Great Britain: Pearson Education, 2002.

Valentine, Gill. *Social Geographies: Space and Society*. Singapore: Pearson Education, 2001.

Valverde, Mariana. *The Age of Light, Soap, and Water: Moral Reform in English Canada, 1885–1925*. Toronto: McClelland and Stewart, 1991.

_____. *Diseases of the Will: Alcohol and the Dilemmas of Freedom*. Cambridge: Cambridge University Press, 1998.

_____. *Sex, Power and Pleasure*. Toronto: The Women's Press, 1985.

Walden, Keith. *Becoming Modern in Toronto: The Industrial Exhibition and the Shaping of a Late Victorian Culture*. Toronto: University of Toronto Press, 1997.

Walvin, James. *Leisure and Society 1830–1950*. London: Longman Group, 1978.

Webb, Darren, "Bakhtin at the Seaside: Utopia, Modernity and the Carnivalesque." *Theory, Culture and Society* 22, 3 (2005): 121–138.

Weinstein, Raymond M. "Disneyland and Coney Island: Reflections on the Evolution of the Modern Amusement Park." *Journal of Popular Culture* 26, 1 (1991): 131–164.

Wood, W.J. "A Brief History of Winnipeg Beach 1901–1955." Unpublished Manuscript. Hudson's Bay Company Archives, Winnipeg Beach Vertical File.

Wouters, Cas. *Sex and Manners: Female Emancipation in the West, 1890 to 2000*. London: Sage Publications, 2004.

Wright, Cynthia. "'Feminine Trifles of Vast Importance': Writing Gender into the History of Consumption." In *Gender Conflicts: New Essays in Women's History*, edited by Franca Iacovetta and Mariana Valverde, 229–260. Toronto: University of Toronto Press, 1992.

Index

Photo Credits

Frontispiece, Archives of Manitoba (AM), Winnipeg Beach 55, N17263; Page 5, AM, Canadian Pacific Railway Series 2, #20; Page 8, courtesy Fred Kelly; Page 11, AM, Hudson's Bay House Library (HBHL) collection, 1987/363-W-37/1 W28 (Royal Canadian Air Force photograph); Page 15, AM, George E. Cripps collection 18, N11751; Page 16, AM, Winnipeg Beach 32; Page 19, AM, L.B. Foote collection 1223; Page 24, AM, Thomas Burns collection 677; Page 27, AM, Winnipeg Beach 20, N11750; Pages 28 and 33, courtesy Rob McInnes; Page 34, *Morning Telegram*, 1 June 1901, 9 and 13; Page 36, *Manitoba Free Press*, 21 May 1920, 18; Page 40, University of Manitoba Archives and Special Collections (UMA), PC 18/7278/18-7278-010; Page 41, AM, Peter McAdam collection 79; Page 43, UMA, PC 18/7278/18-7278-006, N13279; Page 46, AM, Charles Hall Family collection 1; Page 52, AM, Margaret Kennedy collection 30-1; Page 55, AM, Winnipeg Beach 25, N13288; Page 57, AM, Peter McAdam collection 68; Page 59, AM, George E. Cripps collection 24; Page 63, AM, George E. Cripps collection 23, N21862; Page 68, AM, Winnipeg Beach 6, N13251; Page 71, AM, Winnipeg Beach 24, N10777; Page 76, AM, L.B. Foote collection 1219; Page 79, AM, L.B. Foote collection 1221, N2199; Page 88, AM, Winnipeg Beach 26, N13301; Page 91, AM, L.B. Foote collection 2436, N3058; Page 95, UMA, PC 18/7278/18-7278-037; Page 98, AM, Winnipeg Beach 54; Page 101, AM, L.B. Foote collection 1210, N2191; Page 104, AM, S.N.C. Joannidi collection, 141; Page 107, AM, L.B. Foote collection 1218, N2198; Page 110, AM, Winnipeg Beach 4; Page 112, AM, Winnipeg Beach 1, N13248; Page 115, AM, Winnipeg Beach 63-6; Page 120, courtesy Fred Kelly; Page 125, UMA, PC 18/7278/18-7278-013; Page 133, AM, George E. Cripps collection 21, N11748; Page 140, AM, George E. Cripps collection 19; Page 144, AM, HBHL 1987/363-W-37/2 W28 (Royal Canadian Air Force photograph); Page 147, L.B. Foote collection 1201, N20837; Page 148, AM, Frank Munton collection, 3-15-3; Page 150, AM, Winnipeg Beach 10, N13280; Page 159, AM, Winnipeg Beach 8, N13253; Page 162, AM, L.B. Foote collection 1217 1, N2197; Page 164, UMA, PC 18/7278/18-7278-031; Page 166, UMA, PC 18/7278/18-7278-052; Page 168, UMA, PC 18/7278/18-7278-057; Page 170, photo by Dale Barbour.